# Praise for *Gender Play*

"Thorne suggests that we need to understand the fluctuating significance of gender. . . . [In] taking kids and their play seriously, Thorne's penetrating and subtle analysis makes it much harder to see gender or age grades as ubiquitous or natural divides."

—*Science*

"A stunning achievement. . . . Thorne transforms our ability to see gender in social life."

—Nancy J. Chodorow, author of
*Feminism and Psychoanalytic Theory*

"Thorne sees the ritualized interactions of boys and girls as power play and makes it her central issue. She looks across the fun and games as a cycle of domination and subservience. . . . [She] re-examines the gender mystique as it develops through the grades, urging us to understand it as a social process, amenable to change."

—*The New York Times Book Review*

"Few books analyze the daily lives of children from their point of view, and even fewer still do so from a feminist perspective. . . . I recommend this book to anyone who wants more insight into the daily lives of elementary children, teachers, and schools and how they 'do gender.'"

—*Gender & Society*

"This is a beautifully observed as well as deeply reflective book. . . . Pathbreaking research is combined with vivid and enjoyable writing."

—Bob Connell, author of *Gender and Power*

"Destined to be a classic . . . a wonderful text—beautifully inflected, reflexive, responsive to diversity and differences, and grounded in careful ethnographic work."

—Laurel Richardson, author of
*The Dynamics of Sex and Gender*

T0287007

"*Gender Play* provides readers with a rich, nuanced, inside view of children's worlds in school as well as many thought-provoking discussions on complex issues in the area of childhood and gender. . . . The book raises some new and very important questions concerning the extent to which adults can successfully empower children through their research efforts as well as the extent to which solutions to current gender dilemmas lie in the hands of adults as compared to children."

—*Social Forces*

"Barrie Thorne's beautifully written and extensively researched book offers a new way to represent and interpret the strategies with which elementary school students forge notions of gender through play. . . . [Thorne's] highly engaging and reflexive analysis opens up a new way to interpret gender during elementary school."

—*American Ethnologist*

"[A] sensitive and detailed ethnographic account of two American elementary schools. . . . Thorne presents a moving rather than a static picture. [*Gender Play*] breaks new ground in both school ethnography and gender studies by emphasizing action, activity and everyday social practices in a way that allows for the integrity and agency of children."

—*Contemporary Sociology*

"*Gender Play* is a surprising book in that it traces a lot of the innovative work on 'gender socialization and development' from the early days of academic feminism. The book has an extremely strong and coherent thesis about the ways in which gender is or is not constructed through a range and variety of social processes, not crucially through formal education, but by social actors themselves, particularly children."

—*British Journal of Sociology of Education*

"Persuasive. . . . [*Gender Play*] contributes to a portrait of childhood through the description of those groups (and the settings that envelop the groups) in which our offspring spend their hours and days."

—*Journal of Contemporary Ethnography*

"Magnificent. . . . The great contribution of *Gender Play* is that while acknowledging these sharp divides between genders, this book—much more than any other with which I am familiar—fully explores the enormous range of gender behaviors that constitute the repertoire of school-age children. . . . It is a particular pleasure to read a book that is written in such a graceful, lucid manner."

—*American Anthropologist*

"Barrie Thorne's newest contribution to gender research offers a refreshing look at an old subject. Her work offers more than an interesting read to those involved in research on children's behavior. . . . [Thorne's] observations and criticisms are timely and well-founded, and her suggestions are useful."

—*Communication Education*

"Thorne's observations of and conversations with the boys and girls of the fourth and fifth grades of the two schools in the study are priceless. . . . Thorne is a master observer, and everything she reports rings true. . . . It is the richest empirical study on gender differences in schools I have yet to encounter."

—*American Journal of Education*

"Well-written. . . . Barrie Thorne's ethnographic study of children's daily life at school is a welcome contribution to the understanding of and a sensitization to the processes around the genesis of gender."

—*Gender, Place & Culture: A Journal of Feminist Geography*

# Gender Play

# Gender Play

## Girls and Boys in School
### *30th Anniversary Edition*

Barrie Thorne

*With an introduction by*
Raewyn Connell and Michael A. Messner

*and an afterword by*
C. J. Pascoe

RUTGERS UNIVERSITY PRESS

NEW BRUNSWICK, CAMDEN, AND NEWARK, NEW JERSEY

LONDON AND OXFORD

Rutgers University Press is a department of Rutgers, The State University
of New Jersey, one of the leading public research universities in the nation.
By publishing worldwide, it furthers the University's mission of dedication
to excellence in teaching, scholarship, research, and clinical care.

Rutgers University Press Classics
30th Anniversary Edition, 2024

ISBN 978-1-9788-3825-3 (paper)
ISBN 978-1-9788-3826-0 (cloth)
ISBN 978-1-9788-3827-7 (epub)

First published in cloth and paperback in the United States of America by
Rutgers University Press, 1993
First published in paperback in the United Kingdom
by Open University Press, 1993

The Library of Congress has cataloged the 1993 edition as follows:
Thorne, Barrie.
Gender play. girls and boys in school / Barrie Thorne
p. cm.
Includes bibliographical references and index.
ISBN 0-8135-1922-5 (cloth)-ISBN 0-8135-1923-3 (paper)
I Sex differences in education-United States. I. Title.
LC212.92.T46 1993
370.19'345'0973-dc:20 92-22062

References to internet websites (URLs) were accurate at the time of writing.
Neither the author nor Rutgers University Press is responsible for URLs
that may have expired or changed since the manuscript was prepared.

∞ The paper used in this publication meets the requirements of the
American National Standard for Information Sciences—Permanence
of Paper for Printed Library Materials, ANSI Z39.48-1992.

rutgersuniversitypress.org

*To Andrew and Abby,*
*who grew up with this book*

# Contents

*Acknowledgments*   ix

*Introduction*
RAEWYN CONNELL AND MICHAEL A. MESSNER   xiii

1   Children and Gender   1

2   Learning from Kids   11

3   Boys and Girls Together . . . But Mostly Apart   29

4   Gender Separation: Why and How   49

5   Creating a Sense of "Opposite Sides"   63

6   Do Girls and Boys Have Different Cultures?   89

7   Crossing the Gender Divide   111

8   Lip Gloss and "Goin' With": Becoming Teens   135

9   Lessons for Adults   157

*Afterword*
C. J. PASCOE   175

*Notes*   181

*References*   219

*Index*   235

# *Acknowledgments*

Creative work and friendship are closely intertwined, and I want to thank the many people who helped nurture this book. The late Everett C. Hughes, one of a number of remarkable teachers in the Brandeis University Sociology Department in the late 1960s, helped me discover and trust my imagination as a sociologist and an ethnographer. A group of us who were graduate students at Brandeis also became part of the early women's liberation movement. Some of these friendships have endured across many years and long distances, and I want to acknowledge the continuing support of Judith Adler, Nancy Chodorow, Donna Huse, Rachel Kahn-Hut, Marcia Millman, Margaret Rhodes, Judith Stacey, Nancy Stoller, Gaye Tuchman, and Jasminka Gojkovic Udovicki. Nancy Stoller encouraged my first steps back into elementary schools. Countless conversations with Judith Adler, Nancy Chodorow, Marcia Millman, and Judith Stacey nourished the ideas in this book; each of them read drafts of chapters and in many other ways made it all possible.

During my years of teaching sociology and women's studies at Michigan State University, I was blessed with lively companions for feminist thinking and action, including Marilyn Aronoff, Teresa Bernardez, Marilyn Frye, Ruth Hamilton, Rick Hill, Joyce Ladenson, Merry Morash, Margaret Nielsen, Lynn Paine, Kate See, Ruth Useem,

and Eileen Van Tassell. Early phases of the research were supported by
M.S.U. All-University Research Grants and by the Stanford University
Center for Research on Women, where I was a Visiting Scholar.

My understanding of children's gender relations was repeatedly
invigorated by discussions with students in my undergraduate and
graduate courses. Beverly Purrington taught me to notice the effects of
children on adult experiences. Janet Leslie helped gather some of the
data. By mutual agreement I have disguised the identities of the kids
and staff in the schools where I did fieldwork; I want to thank them for
their cooperation and goodwill. The University of Southern California
Program for the Study of Women and Men in Society and Department
of Sociology provided a supportive context for the final phase of work.

Close companions on my earlier research journey into the
field of language and gender—Nancy Henley, Cheris Kramarae, Sally
McConnell-Ginet, and Candace West—also accompanied me, by sharing ideas and commenting upon my writing, when I moved into the
study of children. My extended foray into learning about children's
everyday worlds also brought new friendships, especially with Carol
Jacklin, who kept me on the track of gender similarities and cheered
every step of the way, and Zella Luria, who generously shared her own
observations and, through wonderful conversations, sparked many
insights. My thinking about children was also enriched by ongoing dia-
logues with and comments from Candy Goodwin, Linda Hughes, and
Donna Eder.

Portions of this work have been previously published, in different form, in the following books and journals: "Girls and Boys
Together . . . But Mostly Apart: Gender Arrangements in Elementary
Schools," in *Relationships and Development*, ed. William W. Hartup and
Zick Rubin (Hillside, N.J.: Lawrence Erlbaum, 1986); with Zella Luria,
"Sexuality and Gender in Children's Daily Worlds," *Social Problems* 33
(1986): 176–190; "Re-visioning Women and Social Change: Where Are
the Children?" *Gender & Society* 1 (1987): 85–109; "Crossing the Gen-
der Divide," in *Ethnographic Approaches to Children's Worlds and Peer
Culture*, ed. Sigurd Berentzen (Trondheim: The Norwegian Centre for
Child Research, 1989); "Children and Gender: Constructions of Differ-
ence," in *Theoretical Perspectives on Sexual Difference*, ed. Deborah L.
Rhode (New Haven: Yale University Press, 1990).

Bob Connell and Carol Warren helped me imagine the bits and
pieces as a full book; they and Arlene Daniels, a mentor and unparal-
leled friend through difficult times, helped me believe in myself. Conversations with them, and with Bettina Aptheker, Lois Banner, Samoan

Barish, Pam Benton, Jane Flax, Judith Gingold, John Kitsuse, Barbara Laslett, Michael Messner, and Judith Resnik, kindled my imagination. Deena Metzger and the Wednesday-night writing group provided magical moments of creativity and community.

Warm thanks to Zella Luria, Bob Emerson, Bob Connell, and Laurel Richardson for providing helpful comments on the entire manuscript, and to the following friends and colleagues for reading and responding to various chapters: Lynn Paine, Teresa Bernardez, Carol Jacklin, Karen Sacks, Jack Katz, Joyce Canaan, Lois Banner, Michael Messner, Walter Williams, Patsy Asch, Lorraine Mayfield, Annelies Knoppers, Ellen Jordan, Nancy Lutkehaus, Jane Atkinson, Walteen Grady Truely, Ty Geltmaker, and Mary Ann Clawson. Marlie Wasserman, my editor, provided just the right combination of encouragement, prodding, and, above all, patience.

My mother, Alison Comish Thorne, herself a feminist scholar, provided continual inspiration and support, as did my father, the late David Wynne Thorne. My sisters are also my good friends and colleagues; Avril Thorne, with the sensibilities of a psychologist, and Sandra Thorne-Brown, with the insights of an innovative elementary school teacher, read and commented on many parts of the book. The supportive kindness of our brothers, Kip Thorne and Lance Thorne, gives resonance to the image of Hansel and Gretel, of sisters and brothers as a model of gender equality.

Love and thanks to Peter Lyman, who, for more than twenty years, has provided every imaginable form of emotional, intellectual, and domestic sustenance, and who, in a moment of characteristic ingenuity, thought up the book's title. Abby Thorne-Lyman and Andrew Thorne-Lyman bring sparkle to our lives and, in profound ways, have never let me forget that kids are full people.

# Introduction

RAEWYN CONNELL AND MICHAEL A. MESSNER

Barrie Thorne is widely viewed as a living treasure in feminist sociology, and her groundbreaking 1993 book *Gender Play: Girls and Boys in School* is seen by many as her crowning achievement. This thirtieth-anniversary reissue is very welcome. Its significance is amplified by a new collection of essays entitled *Gender Replay*, edited by two of Thorne's former students in celebration of her groundbreaking work (Blume Oeur and Pascoe 2023).

Thorne's work as a researcher, teacher, mentor, and activist began long before *Gender Play* appeared. She was among the generation of young scholars who made a commitment to democracy, social justice, and feminism in the 1960s and '70s. During the U.S. war in Vietnam, she worked in the antidraft movement. As a graduate student at Brandeis University, and then as a junior sociology professor at Michigan State University, she was part of the cohort of (mostly) younger women who started to build a feminist sociology, pretty much from the ground up.

This work took her through multiple fields of social science. Her early work focused on language, gendered speech, and body politics (Thorne and Henley 1975; Thorne, Kramarae, and Henley 1983). She soon became involved in debates about the family, the institution conventionally seen in static terms as the foundation of society. In her introduction to the co-edited book *Rethinking the Family* (Thorne and Yalom 1982), Thorne spelled out the feminist critique of conventional ideas and proposed a broad agenda for a better understanding of families. She was an early critic of the "sex role" paradigm (Lopata and Thorne 1978) and followed this with jolting feminist challenges to the conservative domain assumptions of the discipline of sociology as a whole (Stacey and Thorne 1985).

Thorne's first wave of publications on children and gender (Thorne 1986; Thorne and Luria 1986) thus had a wider background. They were part of an attempt to rethink social science and everyday life through feminist insights about women, children, and institutions such as families and schools. This was a collective project as well as a personal one. Barrie Thorne has been glowingly thanked in numerous scholars' acknowledgments in their books and articles. Like her work as an editor of books and journals, this is a sign of her commitment to shaping the emerging field not only through her own scholarship but also through generous feminist mentoring and teaching.

*Gender Play* is a school ethnography, a genre of social research that needs a little explanation. The term "ethnography" came from researchers who made direct studies of non-European societies in the colonized (or formerly colonized) world—the work that became known in the English-speaking world as "anthropology." A researcher would take a supply of notebooks by boat, cart, or mule to a remote community; sit watchfully in the village square, learn the language, listen to the gossip, ask many questions about gods, rituals, kinship, trade, and the state of the cattle; and then travel home to report the results in learned journals or scholarly monographs. Sociologists eventually realized that you could do all this without the mules, and classic community studies resulted in titles like *Street Corner Society* and *Family and Kinship in East London*. When education researchers realized that you could research a school in a similar way, they created the genre of school ethnography, publishing titles like *Life in Classrooms* and *Learning to Labour*. School ethnography did not usually require learning a new language, but it did imply looking at a familiar institution as if it were strange and noticing what was usually taken for granted. Thorne's fieldwork is a perfect example of that.

Children were not particularly important to mainstream social science in the 1960s and 1970s. They could be entirely ignored or treated as socially marginal. Even feminist research often did that: Thorne protested in 1987 with an article called "Re-Visioning Women and Social Change: Where Are the Children?" When children were brought into the social science picture, they were typically treated as the passive recipients of a process called "socialization"—learning norms that allowed the reproduction of the existing social order. When gender itself was understood as a matter of culturally defined "sex roles" parked on top of a biological dichotomy, this seemed to be an adequate way of thinking about children's relation to gender. They were simply sponges, soaking it up. That was an approach that Thorne's research, more than any other, was to demolish.

Feminist research projects often began with minor adjustments to the conventions of a given discipline, only gradually moving on to challenge the foundations. Through the 1970s and 1980s, there was a debate about what "feminist research" really meant—whether there was a distinctive methodology and, if so, what it was. Dorothy Smith's attempt to construct a sociology for women was perhaps the most sustained contribution to this discussion. Thorne co-edited a symposium about Smith's project (Laslett and Thorne 1992) and, a few years later, co-edited a book that explored feminist sociology via life histories of practitioners (Laslett and Thorne 1997). *Gender Play* does not emphasize questions of method, but it is helpful to know that its background was a continuing debate about feminist methodology. Some of what's distinctive in the book comes from this continued pushing of boundaries in social science.

Perhaps the first impression one gets in starting to read *Gender Play* is its vivid re-creation of everyday life in the small world of an elementary school—two schools, in fact, since the study was done in two cities. What follows is an engrossing read. The social world of the kids rises before our eyes in its intricate detail, not as biographies of individuals—though there certainly are recognizable individuals here—but as the busy collective life of classrooms and playgrounds. Gender is not just a question of individual identity in this study; it's mainly a feature of this collective life—and a busily shifting feature too, strongly emphasized in some moments, subdued in others.

Giving readers the ethnographic detail, Thorne makes good on the critique of "sex-role socialization" she had launched fifteen years earlier. These girls and boys in their everyday lives are not the passive recipients of norms for any sex role whatsoever. They are certainly connected with the gendered world of adults, in their local communities and in the wider world. But they are actively engaged with it, curious about it, energetically playing with it, sometimes affirming and sometimes subverting it, and in the older elementary school classes, beginning to rehearse for the sexualized gender of adolescence. They are engaged in a kind of social dance, and Thorne's mapping of the choreography is a delight as well as an illumination. Any discussion of *Gender Play* in a college classroom will invariably bend toward vivid (and often humorous) renderings of students' memories of their experiences on school playgrounds: surviving gendered pollution rituals (especially "cootie queens"), exhilarating in the collective eruptions of boys-chasing-girls or girls-chasing-boys, and recognizing how gendered boundaries can be rendered visible by group invasions and individual "crossers," like the boy who plays jump rope with the girls or the girl who joins the boys' football game and kicks some butt in the process. Social science can be humorous! And also sad.

A key source of the richness of *Gender Play* was Thorne's deep capacity for empathy, which she constantly extended to children. Tapping this empathy involved a conscious process of distancing herself and, to the extent it was possible, disidentifying with teachers and other adult authorities in the schools. Recognizing kids' agency in schools also came from her ability to identify with their situations and experiences. Not that this was always easy or straightforward. In *Gender Play*, Thorne needed critical reflexivity about her connection with the kids. Her own experience of having been a marginalized, nonpopular girl led her, at first, to focus too much on the high-status girls who resembled the girls she had envied when she was young. Different insights came, Thorne found, when she hung out with the marginalized girls, though she confessed too that she was sometimes repulsed by them. And Thorne accessed boys' worlds, in part, through her experience of being, at the time, the mother of a young son. Inevitably in this setting, she also viewed the kids through her own experience as a school student, having compiled "a field of As" but stung once by receiving a "C"—"the humiliation softened because it was in gym" (Thorne 1997, 104).

At one point in *Gender Play*, Thorne bemoans how scholars so often approach research on a given topic by falling into common assumptions and themes that "operate like well-worn grooves on a dirt road; when a new study is geared up, the wheels of description and analysis slide into the contrastive themes and move right along" (1993, 95–96). Her own analytic wheels jumped the well-worn grooves of gender research, and the importance of the book was soon recognized. Thirty years later, we can see its lasting importance. Google Scholar lists well over five thousand works that cite *Gender Play* in a wide range of scholarly fields, including citations in journals or books across several languages.

*Gender Play* helped to spark the growth of a new field, the sociology of childhood. Thorne's signature contribution lay in the way she positioned children as active subjects in the making of social life rather than mere objects of pressures from the adult world. Her conceptual contributions to the sociology of sex and gender were profound, moving the field away from the static individualism of sex-role theory. She showed children actively constructing and contesting gender boundaries in group settings, in classrooms, and on the playground; her concept for this process, "borderwork," has circulated in other scholars' research. The book demonstrated how to do ethnography reflexively, with a feminist sensibility. *Gender Play* has had a practical impact as well, with teachers, school principals, and parents' groups reading the book and discussing its implications for their kids' schools.

In the years after the book's publication, Thorne continued with her field research on childhood, with new emphases including ethnic complexity and international migration. Until her retirement, she continued her very active support for the field, creating networks of scholars in childhood and family studies. She served for a decade as U.S. editor for the journal *Childhood: A Global Journal of Child Research*, formed a close connection with colleagues in Norway, and wrote (more often, co-wrote with younger scholars) illuminating reports such as a well-known paper on "Transnational Childhoods" (Orellana et al. 2001).

The authors of this introduction came to know Thorne personally by teaching with her during her time at the University of Southern California. We both considered her one of the best and most interactive teachers we knew. We saw her extraordinary capacity to transform a random expression of opinions in a classroom into a collective process of exploration and to make all the participants, whatever their background or level of sophistication, feel they have something of value to add. We share, with a very wide circle, a great affection and admiration for Barrie Thorne.

*Gender Play* is a conceptual resource for scholars, a beautifully crafted ethnography, a very important statement about children's lives, and a text written with a clarity and good humor that make it accessible to many audiences. We are very pleased to introduce this republication of Thorne's splendid book.

## References

Blume Oeur, Freeden, and C. J. Pascoe. 2023. *Gender Replay: On Kids, Schools, and Feminism*. New York: New York University Press.
Laslett, Barbara, and Barrie Thorne. 1992. "Considering Dorothy Smith's Social Theory: Introduction," *Sociological Theory* 10:60–62.

————, eds. 1997. *Feminist Sociology: Life Histories of a Movement.* New Bruns-
    wick, N.J.: Rutgers University Press.

Lopata, Helena Z., and Barrie Thorne. 1978. "On the Term 'Sex Roles.'" *Signs*
    3:718–721.

Orellana, Marjorie Faulstich, Barrie Thorne, Anna Chee, and Wan Shun Eva
    Lam. 2001. "Transnational Childhoods: The Participation of Children
    in Processes of Family Migration." *Social Problems* 48 (4): 572–591.

Stacey, Judith, and Barrie Thorne. 1985. "The Missing Feminist Revolution in
    Sociology," *Social Problems* 32:301–316.

Thorne, Barrie. 1986. "Girls and Boys Together . . . but Mostly Apart: Gender
    Arrangements in Elementary Schools." In *Relationships and Develop-
    ment,* edited by W. W. Hartup and Z. Rubin, 167–184. Hillsdale, N.J.:
    Lawrence Erlbaum.

————. 1987. "Re-Visioning Women and Social Change: Where Are the Chil-
    dren?" *Gender & Society* 1 (1): 85–109.

————. 1993. *Gender Play: Girls and Boys in School.* New Brunswick, N.J.:
    Rutgers University Press.

————. 1997. "Brandeis as a Generative Institution: Critical Perspectives,
    Marginality, and Feminism." In *Feminist Sociology: Life Histories of a
    Movement,* edited by Barbara Laslett and Barrie Thorne, 103–125. New
    Brunswick, N.J.: Rutgers University Press.

Thorne, Barrie, and Nancy Henley, eds. 1975. *Language and Sex: Difference and
    Dominance.* New York: Newbury House.

Thorne, Barrie, Cheris Kramarae, and Nancy Henley, eds. 1983. *Language,
    Gender, and Society.* New York: Newbury House.

Thorne, Barrie, and Zella Luria. 1986. "Sexuality and Gender in Children's
    Daily Worlds." *Social Problems* 33:176–190.

Thorne, Barrie, and Marilyn Yalom. 1982. *Rethinking the Family: Some Feminist
    Questions.* Boston, Ma.: Northeastern University Press.

# Gender Play

# CHAPTER I

# Children and Gender

When I pass by an elementary school during recess, I pause to watch as the grassy playing fields and paved areas fill and then empty, the bursts of collective movement cued by a loud buzzer. Seen from a distance, a filled playground looks like a swirling mass, but from closer up, one can see patterned arrangements of kids and activities. The clothes of girls and boys are more similar than when I attended public elementary school in the late 1940s and early 1950s; girls now wear pants and shorts more often than dresses. But boys' and girls' activities divide in a familiar geography of gender. Many boys, and a sprinkling of girls, spread out across large grassy fields, playing games of baseball, soccer, or football. The spaces where girls predominate, playing jump rope or foursquare or standing around talking, lie closer to the school building. Girls and boys mix in games of foursquare, dodgeball, handball, kickball, and in general milling around, punctuated by episodes of chasing.

When I was growing up, separation in the activities and friendships of boys and girls was largely taken for granted as an expression of "natural," or inherent, difference. Of course, heavy social pressures were applied to those who didn't act in "natural" ways, especially boys who liked "girls'" forms of play. But the belief persisted that "boys will be boys," and presumably girls would also be girls, in some preordained way. Fed by simplistic notions of biological determinism, the belief in natural gender differences still circulates. Every few years the cover of *Time* or *Newsweek* announces that males and females are fundamentally different, and that "they are born that way." Tapping into a view of children as close to nature, the picture on the magazine cover invariably shows a young boy and girl in gender-stereotyped regalia—the boy flexes an arm muscle or handles a toy gun, while the girl, wearing a frilly dress and holding a doll, glances over with admiration.[1]

While many still see gender as the expression of natural difference, the women's movement of the 1970s and 1980s launched a powerful alternative perspective: notions of femininity and masculinity, the gender divisions one sees on school playgrounds, structures of male dominance, the idea of gender itself—*all* are social constructions.[2] Children, according to one strand of this perspective, are *socialized* into existing gender arrangements. And socializing influences, ironically well illustrated by the gender-stereotyped clothes and toys on magazine covers that make claims about biological programming, come from many directions. Parents dress infant girls in pink and boys in blue, give them gender-differentiated names and toys, and expect them to act differently. Teachers frequently give boys more classroom attention than girls. Children pick up the gender stereotypes that pervade books, songs, advertisements, television programs, and movies. And peer groups, steeped in cultural ideas about what it is to be a girl or a boy, also perpetuate gender-typed play and interaction. In short, if boys and girls are different, they are not born but *made* that way.[3]

When my husband, Peter, and I became parents, several years after I had become active in the women's movement and started to teach and do research on gender, we were alert to the forces of gender socialization. Determined to help our son and daughter break through this kind of channeling and to have more options, we stocked our household with nonsexist children's books and with records like "Free to Be You and Me." When we learned of stereotyping practices in our kids' day-care centers or schools, we politely protested and shared information about strategies for nonsexist education. Almost two decades later, we're both still committed to nonsexist parenting and education. But I've also come to see that the subject of children and gender is much more complicated than I originally thought.

Parenting returned me to the sites of childhood—the Lilliputian worlds of sandboxes, neighborhood hideouts, playgrounds, elementary school lunchrooms. I found that these sites, that the sheer presence of groups of children, evoked memories of my own childhood, of early friendships and enmities, playing jump rope and paper dolls, and riding around on a secondhand J. C. Higgins girl's bike with balloon tires. My memories of growing up as a girl are infused with poignant feelings of freedom and constraint. Those memories, and my experiences as a parent, whetted my interest in learning, more systematically, about girls' and boys' daily experiences of gender. I decided to hang out in an elementary school, keeping regular notes on my observations, especially of boys' and girls' relationships with one another.

My observations fully supported the view that gender is socially constructed. But I increasingly became dissatisfied with the frameworks of "gender socialization" and "gender development" that organize most of the literature on the social construction of gender in children's lives. For one thing, the concept of "socialization" moves mostly in one direction. Adults are said to socialize children, teachers socialize students, the more powerful socialize, and the less powerful get socialized. Power, indeed, is central to all these relationships, but children, students, the less powerful are by no means passive or without agency. As a parent and as an observer in schools, I have been impressed by the ways in which children act, resist, rework, and create; they influence adults as well as being influenced by them.[4]

Many theorists now argue that "children participate in their own socialization."[5] But that tinkering still defines children primarily as learners, as those who are socialized, who are acted upon more than acting. Beneath this view lies a double standard: social scientists grant adults the status of full social actors, but they define children as incomplete, as adults-in-the-making. The concept of "gender development," emphasizing the unfolding of inner dispositions within social environments, also suffers from what Matthew Speier calls an "adult ideological viewpoint."[6] The more time I spent in the company of children, the more I came to question that perspective. There is much to be gained by seeing children not as the next generation's adults, but as social actors in a range of institutions.

This leads to a second problem: both the "socialization" and "development" frameworks presume to know the outcome of current social practices. They assume that the forces that operate on children will produce adults who are conventionally masculine and feminine, or else "deviant" if the process slips or fails. But ultimate outcomes are uncertain and often amazingly various; children, like adults, live in present, concretely historical, and open-ended time. It distorts the vitality of children's present lives to continually refer them to a presumed distant future. Children's interactions are not preparation for life; they are life itself.[7]

Finally, the frameworks of gender socialization and development emphasize the constitution and unfolding of *individuals* as boys or girls. This emphasis has deflected other, more fully sociological, lines of inquiry.[8] In this book I begin not with individuals, although they certainly appear in the account, but with *group life*—with social relations, the organization and meanings of social situations, the collective practices through which children and adults create and recreate gender in their daily interactions. In shifting the focus from individuals to social relations, I move away from the question, Are girls and boys different? which centers much of the research on children and gender. Instead I ask: How do children actively come together to help create, and sometimes challenge, gender structures and meanings? Of course, children are strongly influenced by cultural beliefs and by parents, teachers, and other adults. But children's collective activities should weigh more fully in our overall understanding of gender and social life. One of my goals is to help bring children from the margins and into the center of sociological and feminist thought.

## The Metaphor of Play

To conceptualize the processes through which kids and adults create gender, I have drawn on a range of ideas from cross-disciplinary feminist scholarship. I have honed these ideas, and discovered others, through detailed observations of daily life in two elementary schools. As I worked to make sense of my piles of fieldnotes, I repeatedly returned to the suggestive notion of "play," first via one path of meanings, and then via another. I finally sat down with the *Compact Oxford English Dictionary* and a magnifying glass for reading the tiny print and perused the sixteen columns headed "Play." Four clusters of meaning evoke themes central to this book.

The social construction of gender is an active and ongoing process, as suggested by one sort of dictionary entry under "play": "action, activity, operation"; "actively engaged or employed." Gender categories, gender identities, gender divisions, gender-based groups, gender meanings—all are produced, actively and collaboratively, in everyday life. When kids maneuver to form same-gender groups on the playground or organize a kickball game as "boys-against-the-girls," they produce a sense of gender as dichotomy and opposition. And when girls and boys work cooperatively on a classroom project, they actively undermine a sense of gender as opposition. This emphasis on action and activity, and on everyday social practices that are sometimes contradictory, provides an antidote to the view of children as passively socialized. Gender is not something one passively "is" or "has"; in the phrasing of Candace West and Don Zimmerman, we "do gender."[9]

To an emphasis on "acting" and "doing," I would add a second strand of meaning from the *O.E.D.*: "play" as "dramatic performance." Rituals like "girls-chase-the-boys," "cooties," and bra-snapping can be understood, quite literally, as "gender play." Kids use the frame of play ("we're only playing"; "it's all in fun") as a guise for often serious, gender-related messages about sexuality and aggression. Notions of performance, or scripted action, can be used to understand shared practices that enact, and sometimes challenge, varied gender arrangements and meanings. Performances of this kind range from same-gender groups exchanging insults ("girls are dumb"; "boys are stupid") as they sit on the floor of a lunchroom, to kids constructing heterosexual couples through talk like "Bill is goin' with Cindy," to a boy crossing gender boundaries and joining a group of girls playing jump rope.

That complexity brings in a third cluster of meanings: "play" as "scope or opportunity for action," and as "brisk, fitful, or light movement," as in "a play of colors." These definitions recognize the sheer complexity of gender relations—the multiple and contradictory meanings, the crosscutting lines of difference and inequality, the fluctuating significance of gender (girls and boys are sometimes with as well as apart from one another; gender is not always at the forefront of their interactions). Those versed in current feminist theory will recognize the influences of postmodern and deconstructive ideas in the approach I develop, although I am intent on understanding discourses in the context of social practice.[10] Theorists have written that the experience of play is "grounded in the concept of possibility," and in the final chapter I argue that within the complexities, within the "play of gender," indeed lie possibilities for social change.[11]

Issues of politics and social change, which are central to feminist research, raise a fourth, and final, dimension of the metaphor of play. The word "play," when coupled with "child," connotes triviality, as in the dictionary definition: "child's play; applied to anything that involves very little trouble, or is of very little importance; a very easy or trifling matter." Here I want to call a halt to the metaphor and to sharply contradict its allusions. I am troubled when the full range of children's actions and feelings get compressed into the "play" side of our cultural dichotomy between "work" and "play"; the dichotomy falsifies the full reality of everyone's experiences.[12] Observing on school *play*grounds, I saw not only play but also serious and fateful encounters; I witnessed anger, sorrow, and boredom, as well as sport and jest. As I emphasize throughout the book, the social relations that I document entail consequential structures of *power*. The metaphor of play goes a long way in helping one grasp the social construction of gender, but at a certain point, like all metaphors, it falls short.

Children's experiences should be taken just as seriously, or lightly, as those of adults. In fact, the dichotomy between "adult" and "child," which masks enormous variation in age and capacity, itself needs close scrutiny. Like the division between "male" and "female," the division between "adult" and "child" is socially created, historically changing, filled with ambiguity and contradiction, and continually negotiated.[13] I return to this theme in later chapters when I show how age and gender constructions closely intertwine.

## An Ethnographer
## in Elementary Schools

I got to know the children and adults who inspired and now populate this book during two periods of time when I observed in elementary schools; the next chapter details my experiences as an ethnographer. During the 1976–77 school year I observed for eight months in a public elementary school in a small city on the coast of California. I gained initial access to this school, which I will call Oceanside (all names of places and people have been changed), through the teacher of a combined fourth-fifth-grade class. I regularly observed in Miss Bailey's classroom and accompanied the students into the lunchroom and onto the playground, where I roamed freely and got to know other kids as well.

In 1980, when I was living in Michigan, I did another stint of fieldwork, observing for three months in Ashton School, my pseudonym for a public elementary school on the outskirts of a large city. My entry into Ashton was facilitated by the district Title IX office. (Title IX, a piece of federal legislation passed in 1972, was designed to promote gender equity in educational opportunities.) The Title IX officer asked me to assess gender equity problems in the early grades, and we reached a formal understanding that I could also gather data for my own purposes. In addition to observing in an Ashton kindergarten and a second-grade classroom, I roamed around the lunchroom, hallways, and playground. This experience helped me broaden and gain perspective on the more focused and in-depth observations from the California school.

The demographics of the Oceanside and Ashton schools were remarkably similar. Each had around four hundred students who were mostly working-class. Around 75 percent of the students in each school were from various "white" ethnicities; between 12 and 14 percent were Chicano or Latino; around 5 percent were African-American. In the California school there were a few Filipino-American and Japanese-American students, and one child with parents from India, and in the Michigan school there were a scattering of Native American students.

As an ethnographer, I have analyzed interactions that I witnessed and recorded in the present. But the subject of children continually veers toward the future, with an almost irresistible urge to divine distant outcomes, as do students of "socialization" and "development." The topic of children also tugs back into the past, evoking memories of one's own travels through childhood. In the next chapter I discuss memory as both obstacle and resource in the process of doing fieldwork with kids.

Memories of childhood entered this work through another door as well. During my years of thinking and writing about girls' and boys' experiences in schools, I regularly taught courses on the sociology of childhood, gender, and feminist theory. When I discussed my research in class, the students often brimmed over with reminiscences about their elementary school years. Their stories intrigued me so much that I began to record them. In 1983, an undergraduate research assistant, Janet Leslie, interviewed fifteen women and ten men undergraduate students, chosen more or less at random around the campus of Michigan State University, and asked them about their recollections of fourth, fifth, and sixth grade. Information gleaned from the fields of memory should be treated with skepticism since memories are partial, malleable, and shaped by later experiences as well as by conventions for remembering. I have nonetheless included some of these recollected snippets of past time as a counterpoint to my main story, which is based on eleven months of fieldwork in two elementary schools.

I sometimes use the ethnographic present tense to give rhetorical force to social processes that I saw again and again and that probably continue today. But it should be emphasized that the fieldwork was done in 1976, 1977, and 1980, and that gender relations change over time. A decade later, and in other schools then and now, the patterns I describe may not all hold, although several current elementary school teachers who read parts of the manuscript have told me that they see the same or similar patterns today. Organizational structures like crowded environments and school routines persist, as do many practices and meanings. My analysis also brings in many other empirical studies done in schools, which gives some sense of commonality, continuity, variation, and change. Some of these studies were done in other cultures, but otherwise, this book is deeply rooted in the United States. However, I believe that my conceptual contributions, focused by the imagery of "gender play," can be extended to other times and places.

## Writing Dilemmas

Fieldwork involves extended witnessing and "sense-making"; it also takes shape, as sociological ethnographers finally have come to recognize, through the process of writing. Many of my observations concern the workings of gender categories in social life. For example, I trace the evocation of gender in the organization of everyday interactions, and the shift from boys and girls as loose aggregations to "the boys" and "the girls" as self-aware, gender-based groups. In writing about these processes, I discovered that different angles of vision lurk within seemingly simple choices of language. How, for example, should one describe a group of children? A phrase like "six girls and three boys were chasing by the tires" already assumes the relevance of gender. An alternative description of the same event—"nine fourth-graders were chasing by the tires"—emphasizes age and downplays gender. Although I found no tidy solutions, I have tried to be thoughtful about such choices. And, except when quoting others, I have, quite deliberately, disrupted the usual ordering of "boys" before "girls." Wanting both genders to be fully in view, I have loosely alternated the sequence of the words.

     The process of writing also led me to reflect upon our language for referring to children. After several months of observing at Oceanside, I realized that my fieldnotes were peppered with the words "child" and "children," but that the children themselves rarely used the term. "What do they call themselves?" I badgered myself in an entry in my fieldnotes. The answer, it turned out, is that children use the same practices as adults. They refer to one another by using given names ("Sally," "Jack") or language specific to a given context ("that guy on first base"). They rarely have occasion to use age-generic terms. But when pressed to locate themselves in an age-based way, my informants used "kids" rather than "children."

At first I resisted using their term in my formal writing; to my adult ears, "kids" sounds diminishing, with the semantic whiff of goats. But several of the group in question insisted that "children" was more of a put-down than "kids." As one sixth-grader said, "Kids is better than children; children sounds so young." Indeed, "kids" moves across the finer age divisions—"infant," "toddler," "child," "teen"—carved into the contemporary life course; some college undergraduates still call themselves "kids." The term also evokes generational solidarity, a kind of bonding in opposition to adults.

I found that when I shifted to "kids" in my writing, my stance toward the people in question felt more side-by-side than top-down. The word "children" evokes the "adult-ideological viewpoint" that I sometimes adopt, but have also tried to bracket and avoid. When, in a particular piece of analysis, I slide into an adult stance, I am more likely to write "children" instead of "kids."[14] Finally, I have avoided the term "peer group," which also sets kids apart and diminishes the full luster of their experiences. As adults, we claim "friends" and "colleagues"; why do we so often compress kids' social relations into the flattening notion of "peers?"

The topic of children and gender should be considered in close connection with social class, race, ethnicity, and sexuality and not artificially stripped from these other contexts. When I observed in the two schools, I was less sensitive to these interconnections than I am now.[15] Furthermore, since students in these particular schools were mostly working-class and white, class and race divisions were more muted than they might be in other settings. I wish I had gathered more textured detail bearing on interconnections of gender with other social divisions; for example, I wish I had spent more time observing the group of Spanish-speaking girls and boys, all recent immigrants, who played together day after day on the Oceanside playground.

The dilemma I confronted about when to use gender or age terminology also extended to race and ethnicity. On the one hand, I wanted to avoid the usual pattern of marking race only for African Americans or Chicanos, leaving whites, the dominant group, unmarked.[16] But if I included race in every description of an individual, I presumed a relevance, and even a self-definition, that may or may not have been present. I was unable to solve this dilemma, but I gave it a lot of thought along the way.

Many of us are now searching for more dynamic ways of thinking about relationships among gender, age, class, race, ethnicity, and sexuality. This book does not provide new theoretical statements about the intersection of multiple differences and inequalities, but it does come at the issue in a grounded, moment-by-moment way. I found, for example, that when participants invoke one social category as they organize an encounter, they sometimes suppress the relevance of other lines of difference. But in other situations several lines of difference may amplify or contradict one another. Furthermore, the meanings of gender are inflected by meanings associated with class, ethnicity, sexuality—and vice versa, in complex symbolic patterns. I hope that this book will show the value of ethnography, which emphasises social context, in illuminating connections of gender, and age, to other lines of difference and inequality. I hope that the contextual understanding of ethnography will also open a sense of possibility, of concrete pathways for social change.

# CHAPTER 2

# Learning from Kids

*A different reality coexisted beside my own, containing more vitality, originality, and wide-open potential than could be found in any lesson plan. How was I to enter this intriguing place, and toward what end would the children's play become my work?*

—Vivian Gussin Paley, "On Listening to What the Children Say"

When I first entered the Oceanside fourth-fifth–grade classroom as a note-taking visitor, I thought of myself as an ethnographer with an interest in gender and the social life of children. Beyond that, I had not given much reflection to what I was bringing to the research. But I slowly came to realize that within the ethnographer, many selves were at play. Responding to our shared positions as adult women and as teachers, I easily identified with Miss Bailey and the other school staff. Being around so many children also stirred my more maternal emotions and perspectives. (When I started the fieldwork, our older child was in preschool, and by the end of the year I was pregnant with a second child.) Occasionally I felt much like the fourth- and fifth-grader I used to be, and the force of this took me by surprise. This jangling chorus of selves gave me insight into the complexity of being an adult trying to learn from kids. Hearing first one, then another, of these different selves, or types of consciousness, helped shape what I discovered and how I put my ideas together.[1]

Like Westerners doing fieldwork in colonized Third World cultures, or academics studying the urban poor, when adults research children, they "study down," seeking understanding across lines of difference and inequality. When the research is within their own culture, the "studying down" comes swathed in a sense of familiarity. Despite their structural privilege, Western ethnographers who enter a radically different culture find themselves in the humbling stance of a novice. But it is hard to think of one's self as a novice when studying those who are defined as learners of one's own culture. To learn *from* children, adults have to challenge the deep assumption that they already know what children are "like," both because, as former children, adults have been there, and because, as adults, they regard children as less complete versions of themselves. When adults seek to learn about and from children, the challenge is to take the closely familiar and to render it strange.

Adrienne Rich has observed that power seems to "engender a kind of willed ignorance . . . about the inwardness of others."[2] To gain intersubjective understanding, ethnographers who "study down" often have to confront and transcend their own images of the devalued "Other."[3] Adults who study children of their own culture may encounter similar, although perhaps less conscious, barriers of consciousness. These barriers are rooted, perhaps paradoxically, in differences of power and in the fact that identifying with children may evoke the vulnerable child within each adult. The clinician Alice Miller describes deeply unconscious processes that may lead parents, who are threatened by their own sense of vulnerability, to deny their children's separate capacities for knowing and feeling.[4] Adult interest in controlling children may be driven, in part, by fear of their own sense of uncertainty and absence of control.

In my fieldwork with kids, I wanted to overcome these barriers and to approach their social worlds as ethnographers approach the worlds of adults: with open-ended curiosity, and with an assumption that kids are competent social actors who take an active role in shaping their daily experiences. I wanted to sustain an attitude of respectful discovery, to uncover and document kids' points of view and meanings.[5] To adopt that basic stance means breaking with an array of common adult assumptions: that children's daily actions are mostly trivial, worthy of notice only when they seem cute or irritating; that children need to be actively managed or controlled; that children are relatively passive recipients of adult training and socialization.

As I argued in the preceding chapter, asking how children are socialized into adult ways, or how their experiences fit into linear stages of individual development, deflects attention from their present, lived, and collective experiences. Moving back a step, one can see "socialization" and "development" as perspectives that many parents, teachers, and other adults *bring* to their interactions with children.[6] As mothers and teachers of young children, women, in particular, are charged with the work of "developing the child."[7] But children don't necessarily see themselves as "being socialized" or "developing," and their interactions with one another, and with adults, extend far beyond those models. In my fieldwork I wanted to move beyond adult-centered, individualized frameworks and learn about the daily lives of children, especially what they do together as "they mutually build social occasions and activities in each others' presence"—to quote Matthew Speier.[8]

When I started observing in the Oceanside School, I set out to learn about gender in the context of kids' interactions with one another. I began to accompany fourth- and fifth-graders in their daily round of activities by stationing myself in the back of Miss Bailey's classroom, sitting in the scaled-down chairs and standing and walking around the edges, trying to grasp different vantage points. I was clearly not a full participant; I didn't have a regular desk, and I watched and took notes, rather than doing the classroom work. As the kids lined up, I watched, and then I walked alongside, often talking with them, as they moved between the classroom, lunchroom, music room, and library. At noontime I sat and ate with the fourth- and fifth-graders at their two crowded cafeteria tables, and I left with them when they headed for noontime recess on the playground. Wanting to understand their social divisions and the varied perspectives they entailed, I alternated the company I kept, eating with different groups and moving among the various turfs and activities of the playground.

In Ashton, the Michigan school, I also followed the kids' cycle of activities, but I stuck less closely to one classroom and its students. I observed in a kindergarten and in a second-grade classroom, and I spent a lot of time in the lunchroom and on the playground mapping all the groups and trying to get an overview of the school and its organization.

Looking back on my presence in both schools, I see how much

I claimed the free-lancing privilege of an adult visitor. I could, and did, come and go, shift groups, choose and alter my daily routines. Unlike the kids, I was relatively, although not entirely, free from the control of the principal, teachers, and aides. Without a fixed, school-based routine, I also had more spatial mobility than the teachers and aides. My spatial privileges were especially obvious during severe winter days in Michigan, when the Ashton students. even if they wore skimpy clothes and had no mittens or gloves, were forced to stay outside for forty-five minutes during the noontime recess. While some of the kids stood shivering near the school, I was free, although I usually resisted the temptation, to go into the warm building.

I entered students' interactions to varying degrees. In teaching settings like classrooms and the Oceanside music room and auditorium, I felt most like an observer. In the lunchrooms where I was more visually separate from other school-based adults since teachers ate elsewhere and aides were on patrol, I joined more fully in kids' interactions by eating, conversing, and sometimes trading food with them. On the playgrounds I usually roamed and watched from the margins of ongoing activities, although I often talked with kids and sometimes joined groups of girls playing jump rope and games like "statue buyer." Whether on the margins or joining in, I was continually struck by kids' forms of physicality and by the structures of authority that separate them from adults.

## Kids' Physicality and Imagination

When I began my concerted effort to spend time with kids, I felt oversized, like a big Alice or Gulliver trying to fit into a scaled-down world. Schools are furnished for two sizes: smaller chairs, desks, and tables; and adult-sized chairs and desks, at which kids can sit often only with special permission. Staff bathrooms have big toilets and sinks, and the separate children's bathrooms have smaller toilets and sinks. I knew I had crossed more fully into kids' spaces when the sense of scale diminished, and I felt too large.

Watching kids day after day, especially on the playground, I was struck by other differences of physicality: their quick movements and high levels of energy, the rapidity with which they formed and reformed groups and activities. Public schools are unusually crowded environments, which intensifies the sense of chaos; the playgrounds were often thick with moving bodies. At first I felt like a sixteen-millimeter observer trying to grasp the speeded-up motions of a thirty-six-millimeter movie. One of the teachers told me that groups of children reminded her of bumblebees, an apt image of swarms, speed, and constant motion.

After I had observed for several months, I saw much more order in the chaos, and I developed strategies for recording rapidly shifting and episodic activity.[9] For example, when I entered the playground, I went on an initial tour, making an inventory of groups and activities. Then I focused on specific groups or individuals, sometimes following them from one activity to another, or from formation to dispersal. I tried to spend time in all the playground niches, including basketball courts, bars and jungle gyms, swings, the varied activities (foursquare, zone dodgeball, handball, jump rope, hopscotch, tetherball) that took place on the cement near the buildings, wandering groups, chasing scenes, large playing fields where, depending on the season, games of baseball, soccer, kickball, and football took place. There were also sites unique to each school: at Oceanside, "the tires," a climbing and swinging structure made of big rubber tires, and "the hill," a small rise of grass; and at Ashton, the school steps, where kids hung out and talked.

I was struck not only by kids' rapid movements but also by their continual engagement with one another's bodies—poking, pushing, tripping, grabbing a hat or scarf, pinning from behind. Since adults in our culture experience such gestures as invasions of personal space (notably, kids never poked, pushed at, or pinned me from behind), I initially interpreted these engagements as more antagonistic than, I realized over time, the kids seemed to experience or intend. Trying to sort out playful from serious intent alerted me to the nuances of kids' meanings *and* to my personal readiness to look for trouble, a readiness magnified by my outlooks as a teacher and a mother.

I came to relish kids' playful uses of their bodies, their little experiments in motion and sound, such as moving around the classroom with exaggerated hobbling or a swaggering hula, bouncing in a chair as if riding a horse, clucking like hens or crowing like roosters, returning to a desk by jerking, making engine noises, and screeching like the brakes of a car. They wrote on their bodies with pencil and pen and transformed hands into gameboards by writing "push here" across their palms. They held contests to see who could push their eyeballs farthest back and show the most white, or hold their eyes crossed for the longest time. Sometimes these performances were private, at other times, constructed with dramatic flair and a call for an audience.

These moments struck me as little oases of imagination in dryly routinized scenes. They led me to reflect on growing up as a process of reining in bodily and imaginative possibilities, a perspective shared by nineteenth-century romantic poets like Wordsworth, and by recent social critics like Edith Cobb, Vera John-Steiner, and Ernest Schachtel. These writers argue that children are more sensuous and open to the world than adults, and that adult creativity hinges on overcoming repression and gaining access to the child within.[10] This idealization of children contrasts with the idealization of adults built into many versions of the "socialization" and "development" perspectives. In assuming exaggerated dichotomies and casting value primarily in one direction, both views are limited.

## Getting around Adult Authority

My greater size; my access to special relations with the principal, teachers, and aides; and my sheer status as an adult in an institution that draws sharp generational divisions and marks them with differences in power and authority, posed complicated obstacles to learning from kids. I knew that if I were too associated with adult authority, I would have difficulty gaining access to kids' more private worlds. Nor did I want the tasks of a classroom or playground aide. The practical constraints of keeping order and imposing an agenda would, I quickly realized, run against the open-ended curiosity and witnessing that ethnography requires.

I entered the field through adult gatekeepers. A friend introduced me to Miss Bailey, the fourth-fifth–grade Oceanside teacher, and she, in turn, agreed to let me observe in her classroom, as did Mr. Welch, the school principal, who asked only that I not "disrupt" and that I report back my findings. My more formal entry into Asthon School, via the district Title IX office, seemed to make the Ashton principal a little nervous. But Mrs. Smith, the kindergarten teacher, and Mrs. Johnson, the second-grade teacher, seemed at ease when I was in their classrooms, and I had ample latitude to define my presence to the students of both schools.

In both schools I asked kids as well as staff to call me by my first name, and I called the staff by their first names when we spoke directly with one another. But when I talked with kids, and that's where I did most of my talking as well as watching, I joined them in using titles to refer to the teachers and principals. Everyone called the Ashton lunchroom aides by their first names. In my writing, I follow the kids' use of titles or first names; the actual names, of course, have all been changed.

On the playgrounds kids sometimes treated me as an adult with formal authority. Calling "Yard duty, yard duty!" or "Teach-er!" they ran up with requests for intervention—"Make Ralph give me back my ball"; "Burt threw the rope onto the roof." I responded by saying, "I'm not a yard duty," and usually by refusing to intervene, telling those who asked for help that they would have to find someone who was a yard duty, or handle the situation by themselves.

I went through the school days with a small spiral notebook in hand, jotting descriptions that I later expanded into fieldnotes. When I was at the margins of a scene, I took notes on the spot. When I was more fully involved, sitting and talking with kids at a cafeteria table or playing a game of jump rope, I held observations in my memory and recorded them later. I realized that note-taking had become my special insignia when the fourth-grader who drew my name in the holiday gift exchange in Miss Bailey's class gave me a new little spiral notebook of the kind I always carried around. As I opened the gift, the kids speculated about how many notebooks I had filled by then. They also marveled at my ability to write without looking.

This continual scribbling invited repeated inquiries about my presence and purpose. Again and again, in classrooms and lunchrooms, and on the playgrounds, kids asked me why I was taking notes. "What's that? What're you doing?" "You still takin' notes?" Sometimes they prefaced inquiry with a guess about my purpose: "You writin' a book on us?" "You spying on us?" "Is it like being a reporter?" "You're gonna have a big diary!" "You gonna be a writer?" "What are you sposed to be?" (Questions about what I was "gonna" or "sposed to be" startled me into realizing how much kids are encouraged to cast life in the future and subjunctive tenses.)

Responding to these queries, I tried to be as open and straightforward as I could. But I ran into gaps of understanding. The kids' responses clued me into the drawbacks of some of my explanations. During one of my first forays on the Oceanside playground, a boy came over and asked, "What ya writing?" "I'm interested in what you children are like," I responded; "I'm writing down what you're doing. Do you mind?" He warily edged away. "I didn't do anything," he said. Another of my early explanations—"I'm interested in the behavior of children"—also brought defensive responses. I came to see that verbs like "doing" and "behaving," which figure centrally in the language of social science, are also used by adults to sanction children. The social sciences and child-rearing are both practices geared to social control.

The kids seemed to understand more fully when I explained that I was interested in the ways that they "play" or "what it's like to be a kid." But when I elaborated, I ended up feeling irrelevant and long-winded. For example, during one Oceanside recess as I crouched, watching and scribbling, on the sidelines of a basketball game, a girl came up and asked, "What are you doing?" "A study of children and what they play." "Do you wanna be a teacher?" she asked. "I am one. I teach sociology, ever hear of that?" "No." "It's the study of people in groups." "Well, good-bye," she said, running off.

Sometimes the kids played with the dynamics of my constant written witnessing. When they asked to see my notes, I showed them, privately feeling relieved that they found my scribbles mostly indecipherable. Occasionally kids calibrated behavior and its instant representation by telling me what to write down. "Why don't you put that John goes over and sharpens his pencil," said a fifth-grader, pointing to a boy in motion. On another occasion, a boy I'll call Matt Washburn hovered by my notebook and said, "Write down: 'My best kid is Matt Washburn.'"

One girl who asked if I was "taking down names" voiced what seemed to be their major fear: that I was recording "bad" behavior and that my record would get them into trouble. I assured them again and again that I would not use their real names and that I would not report anything to the teachers, principal, or aides. But of course what I wrote was not under their control, and, like all fieldworkers, I lived with ambiguous ethics. I guarded the information from local exposure, but intended it, with identities disguised, for a much larger audience. I was the sole judge of what was or was not reported and how to alter identifying information. My fieldnotes and later writing from this project feel less guilty than the information I gathered as a participant-observer in the draft resistance movement of the late 1960s.[11] This is partly because information about kids and their doings seems much less consequential than information about adults, especially adults acting in a risky public arena. But of course that perception comes from adult consciousness, not identification with kids' sense of risk.

Although a note-taking adult cannot pass as even an older elementary school student, I tried in other ways to lessen the social distance between me and the kids.[12] I avoided positions of authority and rarely intervened in a managerial way, and I went through the days with or near the kids rather than along the paths of teachers and aides. Like others who have done participant-observation with children, I felt a little elated when kids violated rules in my presence, like swearing or openly blowing bubble gum where these acts were forbidden, or swapping stories about recent acts of shoplifting. These incidents reassured me that I had shed at least some of the trappings of adult authority and gained access to kids' more private worlds. But my experiences with adult authority had a jagged quality. Sometimes I felt relatively detached from the lines of power that divide kids and adults in schools. At other times I felt squarely on one side or the other.

I tried to avoid developing strong allegiances with the school staff and to build up loyalty to the kids, a strategy resembling that of ethnographers who want to learn about the experiences of prison inmates or hospital patients and therefore avoid obvious alliances with the wardens or medical staff. But I was tethered to adults by lines of structure and consciousness. My presence in both schools was contingent on the ongoing goodwill of the adult staff, which made me susceptible to their requests. When Miss Bailey asked me to help a student who was having trouble in math, or when Mrs. Johnson asked me to help the second-graders as they crafted dolls out of corncobs, I couldn't refuse, and I shifted with ease into the stance of an overseeing adult. Luckily, such requests were relatively rare because of my erratic schedule and because the teachers knew I was there to observe and not to help out in the classrooms.[13]

Although the teachers made few formal demands that drew me into their orbits of authority, they sometimes turned to me for a kind of adult companionship in the classrooms. While the students were seated, I usually stood and roamed the back, while the teacher often stood in front. That arrangement spatially aligned me with the teacher, and it was easy for our adult eyes to meet, literally above the heads of the kids. When something amusing or annoying happened, the teacher would sometimes catch my eye and smile or shake her head in a moment of collusive, nonverbal, and private adult commentary. During those moments, I felt a mild sense of betrayal for moving into allegiance with adult vantage points and structures of authority.

When physical injury was at stake, my intervening adult-parental-teacher sides moved to the fore. One day just before recess a physical fight broke out in Miss Bailey's fourth-fifth grade classroom, and the substitute teacher and I rushed to pull the antagonists apart. When I was observing on the Oceanside playground, a girl fell off the bars to the ground. Several other girls rushed toward her, one calling "Get the yard duty person! She can't breathe!" I ran over and asked the girl lying on the ground if she was hurt. An official "yard duty person" joined us, and she and I walked the injured girl to the office.

I could usually rely on playground aides to be on the lookout and to handle scenes of physical injury. It was harder for me to stay detached when kids hurt one another's feelings, and I sometimes tried to soothe these situations. For example, when Miss Bailey's students were drawing pictures at their desks, several girls talked about their summer plans. Jessica said she and her sisters and brother were going to Texas to see their mother. Sherry asked, "Why did your mother leave you?" Jessica replied, "She wanted to marry a guy, but they had a fight and she didn't." Almost simultaneously, Nancy spoke up, "She left because she didn't love you." Jessica blushed, and I resonated with her stung feelings. Feeling quite maternal, I tried to comfort Jessica by putting my arm around her and saying, "I'm sure it was hard for your mother to leave."

The teachers, principals, and aides generally assumed I was a colleague who would back up their rule. But I was primarily interested in the ways kids construct their own worlds, with and apart from adults. The official agenda of the schools—the lessons, the rules, the overtly approved conduct—seemed like cement sidewalk blocks, and the kids' cultural creations like grass and dandelions sprouting through the cracks. I watched eagerly for moments of sprouting and came to appreciate kids' strategies for conducting their own activities alongside and under the stated business of the hour.[14]

## The Underground Economy of Food and Objects

From my position in the back of Miss Bailey's classroom, which gives a very different perspective than the front, I could see what went on when desktops were raised, presumably on official business. Some kids had customized their desks by taping drawings or dangling objects from the inside top. In addition to official school artifacts like books, papers, rulers, pencils, and crayons, the desks contained stashes of food, toys, cosmetics, and other objects brought from market and home. These transitional objects, most of them small and pocketable, bridge different spheres of life. They also provide materials for an oppositional underlife often found in "total institutions," or settings like prisons and hospitals where a subjected population is kept under extensive control.[15] Although schools maintain far less control than prisons, students have little choice about being present, and members of a smaller, more powerful group (the staff) regulate their use of time, space, and resources. Like prison inmates or hospital patients, students develop creative ways of coping with their relative lack of power and defending themselves against the more unpleasant aspects of institutional living.

Some of the objects that kids stash and trade, like "pencil pals" (rubbery creatures designed to stick on the end of pencils), rabbit feet, special erasers and silver paper, could be found in the desks of both boys and girls. Other objects divided more by gender. Boys brought in little toy cars and trucks, magnets, and compasses; and girls stashed tubes of lip gloss, nail polish, barrettes, necklaces, little stuffed animals, and doll furniture. Patterns of trade marked circles of friendship that almost never included both girls and boys. The exception was a flat pink and yellow terri cloth pillow that Kathryn, the most popular girl in Miss Bailey's class, brought in to cushion her desk chair. Invested with the manna of Kathryn's popularity, the pillow traveled around the entire room; girls and boys sat on and tossed it around in a spirit more of honoring than teasing.

Ashton School felt like a much harsher environment than Oceanside School, in part because of the difference in weather (California was spared the cold winter of Michigan), but also because Ashton had strict rules against kids bringing objects from home. Even when it was raining, Ashton students were not allowed to carry umbrellas onto the playground, and if aides spotted any personal toys or objects, they immediately confiscated them. As a result, the school had an impoverished underground economy. (School staff might describe this differently, as eliminating distractions and maintaining order.) I saw a few sneaky sharings of food, lip gloss, and, on one occasion, a plastic whistle, but nothing like the flourishing semi-clandestine system of exchange at Oceanside School.

In subsequent chapters I return to the significance of material objects in kids' social relations, as a focus of provocation and dispute, as a medium through which alliances may be launched and disrupted, as sacraments of social inclusion and painful symbols of exclusion, and as markers of hierarchy.[16] But here I want to highlight the relatively secret and oppositional nature of these objects and their negotiation and exchange. Students are not supposed to eat, play with toy cars, or rub pink gloss on their lips in the middle of an arithmetic or social studies lesson. But I saw them do all these things, creating their own layers of activity and meaning alongside, or beneath, the layers they shared with the adult school staff.

When kids invited me to participate in their secret exchanges,

I felt pulled between my loyalty to them and my identification with and dependence on the teacher. During a social studies lesson, the fourth-fifth–grade students were supposed to be drawing pictures of early California missions. As Miss Bailey helped someone in another part of the room, I wandered to a corner where Jeremy, Don, and Bill leaned over and loudly whispered behind their raised desktops. Jeremy asked Don, "What's your middle name?" Don replied, "Top secret." Bill chimed in, "Porkchop." Don, who was taking pins from a box in his desk and sticking them through an eraser, responded, "Porkchop! I have two nicknames, Dog and Halfbrain." Jeremy reached for some pins from Don's desk and fashioned an $X$ on his pencil eraser. Bill played with an orange toy car, making "zoom" noises as he scooted it into Jeremy's open desk. Jeremy took out an almost-finished bag of potato chips, held it out to Don, and shook a few into his hands. Bill held out his hand, but Jeremy ignored the gesture. "Give me one," Bill said. "No, you're too fat; you should be on a diet." "I am on a diet," Bill said as Jeremy shook a few chips into his hands. "Give Barrie some," Bill said. Jeremy turned (I was sitting behind him) and asked, "Do you want some?" "Yes," I said and held out my hand as he shook a few chips into it. All of this forbidden activity went on behind the screen of the open desktops. Jeremy grinned, and I grinned back, feeling conspiratorial as I quietly munched the chips.

When I sociably interacted with a group of kids during work time, Miss Bailey sometimes noticed and told them to get back to work. This made me feel a trifle guilty since I realized that she suspected I was undermining rather than affirming—or even taking a neutral relationship to—classroom order. I noticed that Miss Bailey always refused when her students offered loans or gifts and the particularized, nonprofessional relationships they entail. But, seeking closer, more lateral ties, I accepted offers of potato chips, a cookie, a nickel; and I occasionally gave kids pencils and small change, which we called loans, although they were never returned. Once Miss Bailey saw me give a pencil to Matt when he asked if I had an extra one. She firmly told him to return the pencil to me and to get his own. I understood her actions; as a teacher, she tried to maintain social distance and a guise of universalistic treatment, and when I teach, I do the same thing. The kids called her "Miss Bailey," while I asked them to call me by my first name, another set of disparate practices that set me apart from the teacher.

I came to realize that within the classroom, the teacher and I were working at cross-purposes. Miss Bailey had lessons to teach, authority to maintain, the need to construct and display an orderly classroom. I was a kind of sideline booster, rooting for the moments when kids brought out their own artifacts and built their own worlds of talk and interaction.

I had an observational feast on a day when there was a substitute teacher who "couldn't keep control," in the words of a disgusted bilingual aide who came for several hours each day. The kids made lots of noise and ran boisterously about; a group of them talked loudly about who had beat up whom in the third grade, and who could now beat up whom. They brought out objects that were usually kept relatively under cover—a skateboard magazine, a rubber finger with a long nail, bags of nuts and potato chips—and openly passed them around. As the kids walked out the door for lunch, Jessie, one of the girls who had joined in the talk about fighting, got into an angry fist fight with Allen. This was the one fight where I intervened; the substitute teacher and I jointly worked to separate their flailing bodies. In the lunchroom Jessie retreated to sit with a group of girls, and talk about the fight went on for the rest of the day. After lunch a row of girls sat on the radiator and threw an eraser at several boys, who threw it back in an improvised game of catch. Another group went to the blackboard and drew hearts encircling different boy-girl paired names.

Mr. Welch, the principal, came in once and told the class to behave, but the effect was short-lived, and the substitute teacher seemed resigned to the chaos. I observed for three hours and that night typed up eleven single-spaced pages of notes, rich with descriptions of gender boundaries and antagonism, sexual idioms, interactions among boys and among girls, and crossing between same-gender groups. When I returned to the classroom two days later, Miss Bailey lamented the students' "sub behavior." Her managerial low was my highpoint of juicy witnessing.

## Tugs of Memory, and the Child Within

When I colluded with the kids in breaking rules, especially when the teacher was watching, I remembered how it felt to be caught in similar situations in my own elementary school days. In the spring just after the buzzer rang at the end of an Oceanside school day, Miss Bailey called out across the room, "Barrie, Mr. Welch wants to talk with you." Several kids picked up the ominous connotations and called around the room, "Mr. Welch wants to see Barrie!" For a moment, I felt like a child being brought to task, and the class laughed with a similar reaction. Mr. Welch, it turned out, wanted me to tell him how my research was going, an inquiry that drew my adult self back to the fore.

Tugs of memory pulled on other occasions as well, especially during the first few months of fieldwork. When I began observing, I also began a chain of remembering. There was a close familiarity with the scaled-down desks and tables, the blackboards and stylized graphics on classroom walls, the sight of worn-out red rubber kickballs and dirty jump ropes, smells of wax in the hallways and urine in the girls' bathroom, the loud buzzers that govern so many local routines, the lining up, the clatter of voices in the cafeteria, and the distinctive sing-song tones of teachers. Varied sights, smells, and sounds brought me back to the Woodruff School in Logan, Utah, in the early 1950s.

Memories of my own experiences in fourth and fifth grades scatter through my fieldnotes, especially when a specific girl (boys didn't evoke such remembering) reminded me of a vivid figure from my own childhood. Three of the girls in the Oceanside fourth-fifth–grade classroom continually evoked my memories of, and feelings about, specific girls from my past: the most popular girl; a girl who was quiet, whiny, and a loner; and a girl who was unkempt, smelled, and was treated as a pariah. When I made these associations, the names of their 1950s doubles came immediately to mind.

After a few days of observing, I had figured out that Kathryn was the most popular girl in the classroom. Her cute face, stylish curly brown hair, nice clothes, and general poise and friendliness were easy to notice, and she received a lot of deference from both girls and boys. In situations where individual privileges were granted, for example, to choose and touch bowed heads in games of "seven-up" or to hand out balls in preparation for recess, Kathryn got more than her share. Miss Bailey often chose Kathryn to run errands to the main office or to do other tasks that marked out favored students. After a few weeks at Oceanside, I realized that my fieldnotes were obsessed with documenting Kathryn's popularity. "The rich get richer," I thought to myself as I sorted out yet another occasion when Kathryn got extra attention and resources. Then I realized the envy behind my note-taking and analysis and recalled that many years ago when I was a fourth- and fifth-grader of middling social status, I had also carefully watched the popular girl, using a kind of applied sociology to figure out my place in a charged social network.

In the course of my fieldwork, I felt aversion rather than envy toward Beth, a quiet fourth grader, who continually asked me to sit by her at lunch. Initially I was glad for an invitation. But when I discovered that Beth had few friends, that sitting with her, rather than, say, next to Kathryn, brought minimal social yield, and that Beth also wanted me to stick by her on the playground, I felt, as I wrote in my fieldnotes, associating to my own elementary school past, "as if Beatrice Johnson had me trapped." When Beth requested my company, I began to respond vaguely ("maybe"; "we'll see"), much as I had in fifth grade when I felt Beatrice was trying to cling to me and I didn't want her social encumbrance.

Rita, another girl in the present who evoked strong memories from my own past childhood, was from a family with thirteen children and an overworked single-parent father (Jessica, who told the story of their mother's departure, was Rita's sister). Rita, who took care of her own grooming, had tangled hair and wore dirty, ill-fitting, and mismatched clothes; she seemed withdrawn and depressed. The first time I came close to Rita, leaning over to help her with work in the classroom, I was struck by the smell. I wrote in my fieldnotes:

> Rita's hair was quite dirty, greasy at the roots, and it smelled. There was dirt on her cheek, and her hands were smudged. She wore the same clothes she had on yesterday: a too small, short blue nylon sweater with white buttons and dirt on the back, and green cotton pants that didn't zip right. Leaning over and catching the scent of her hair, I thought of Edith Schulz, whom we all avoided in the fifth grade. I remember Edith, whose parents were immigrants from Germany, wearing a cotton sleeveless blouse and dirndl skirt in the dead of winter. The smell, the incongruous clothing—the signs, I now see, of poverty—set her apart, like Rita; both were treated like pariahs.[17]

In such moments of remembering I felt in touch with my child self. I moved from the external vantage points of an observer, an adult authority, and a "least adult" trying to understand kids' interactions in a more open and lateral way, to feeling more deeply inside their worlds. This experience occurred only when I was with girls. With boys, my strongest moments of identification came not through regression to feeling like one of them, but from more maternal feelings. Sometimes a particular boy would remind me of my son, and I would feel a wave of empathy and affection. But I generally felt more detached and less emotionally bound up with the boys.

Joel, a boy who was socially isolated and overweight, often tried to tag along with me, seeking my company and cover. After several lunchtimes spent talking with him, I made excuses to give myself more room to wander, excuses like those I offered to Beth. But I staved him off without the edge of annoyance, anchored in memories of Beatrice Johnson, that I felt with Beth. The differences in my responses to girls and to boys led me to ponder the emotional legacy of my own gender-separated elementary school years.

I felt closer to the girls not only through memories of my own past, but also because I knew more about their gender-typed interactions. I had once played games like jump rope and statue buyer, but I had never ridden a skateboard and had barely tried sports like basketball and soccer. Paradoxically, however, I sometimes felt I could see boys' interactions and activities more clearly than those of girls; I came with fresher eyes and a more detached perspective. I found it harder to articulate and analyze the social relations of girls, perhaps because of my closer identification, but also, I believe, because our categories for understanding have been developed more out of the lives of boys and men than girls and women.

Were my moments of remembering, the times when I felt like a ten-year-old girl, a source of distortion or insight? Both, I believe. The identification enhanced my sense of what it feels like to be a fourth- and fifth-grade girl in a school setting. I lived that world in another time and place, but the similarities are evocative. Memory, like observing, is a way of knowing and can be a rich resource.[18]

But memories are also fragile and mysterious, continuously reconstructed by the needs of the present and by yearnings and fears of the past. Memories can distort as well as enrich present perceptions. Beth was a different person, in another time and place, than the Beatrice that I recalled, and no doubt had mentally reworked and stereotyped, from my childhood. When my own responses, like my obsession with documenting Kathryn's popularity, were driven by emotions like envy or aversion, they clearly obscured my ability to grasp the full social situation. As Jennifer Hunt has observed, in the course of field research, unconscious processes may both enhance and interfere with empathy.[19]

As I got in touch with the effects of memory and emotion, I altered my strategies for observing. My memories evoked the standpoint of a girl in the middle of the social hierarchy, who envied those above, who was susceptible to but used strategies for avoiding the claims of someone below, and who felt contaminated by a girl on the margins. During my months in Miss Bailey's classroom I thought a lot about those experiences, and I worked to see kids' interactions from other, and varied, perspectives. Instead of obsessing over Kathryn and avoiding Beth or Rita, I tried to understand their different social positions and experiences, and those of other girls and boys. This emphasis on multiple standpoints and meanings came to inform my understanding of gender.

Before I turn to the topic of gender, I want to mention one final paradox in this particular relationship between the knower and those she sought to know. I like to think of myself as having hung out in classrooms, lunchrooms, playgrounds, relating to kids in a friendly and sometimes helpful fashion, and treating them, in my analysis and writing, with respect. But, like all fieldworkers, I was also a spectator, even a voyeur, passing through their lives and sharing few real stakes with those I studied. Several kids asked me if I was a spy, and, in a way, I was, especially when I went in search of the activities and meanings they created when not in the company of adults. Schools are physically set up to maximize the surveillance of students, with few private spaces and a staff who continually watch with eyes that mix benign pedagogical goals, occasional affection, and the wish to control. Kids sometimes resist this surveillance, and I wanted to observe and document their more autonomous collective moments. But in the very act of documenting their autonomy, I undermined it, for my gaze remained, at its core and in its ultimate knowing purpose, that of a more powerful adult.[20]

On the other hand, "adult," like "child," is too unitary a category. A growing sense of multiplicity and context brought me to question the use of dualistic frameworks not only for understanding gender, but also for understanding categories related to age. The dichotomy between "adult" and "child" is not a given of biology or nature; chronological and developmental age are complex continua, with enormous variation between and among five-, twelve-, and thirty-five-year-olds. As I discuss in Chapter 8, people often negotiate the use of labels like "child," "teen," and "adult." However, we mark and reinforce an "adult/child" dualism—we produce categories like "the adult" and "the child"— through cultural practices such as channeling young people into elementary schools where five- and eleven-year-olds are cast together in the position of students and subordinates, with adults on the other "side" (a boundary I continually encountered in my efforts to lessen social distance between me and the kids). The next chapter turns to these practices, to the evocation, marking, and muting of individual categories of identity, especially gender, age, social class, and race or ethnicity, in the organization of groups in school.

# CHAPTER 3

# Boys and Girls Together . . . But Mostly Apart

The landscape of contemporary childhood includes three major sites—families, neighborhoods, and schools. Each of these worlds contains different people, patterns of time and space, and arrangements of gender. Families and neighborhoods tend to be small, with a relatively even ratio of adults and children. In contrast, schools are crowded and bureaucratic settings in which a few adults organize and continually evaluate the activities of a large number of children.[1] Within schools, the sheer press of numbers in a relatively small space gives a public, witnessed quality to everyday life and makes keeping down noise and maintaining order a constant adult preoccupation. In their quest for order, teachers and aides continually sort students into smaller, more manageable groups (classes, reading groups, hallway lines, shifts in the lunchroom), and they structure the day around routines like lining up and taking turns. In this and the next chapter I trace the basic organizational features of schools as they bear upon, and get worked out through, the daily gender relations of kids. As individuals, we always display or "do" gender, but this dichotomous difference (no one escapes being declared female or male) may be more or less relevant, and relevant in different ways, from one social context to another.

## School Routines, Rules, and Groups

On the first day of the Ashton school year I went early so that I could be part of the opening moments in Mrs. Smith's kindergarten. The kids began to arrive, their faces etched with wariness and expectation; each held the hand of a parent (one a father, the rest mothers) and patiently stood in line waiting to meet the teacher. As each pair came up, Mrs. Smith, an energetic teacher in her late twenties, introduced herself to the parent and then kneeled down and warmly greeted the new student, pinning a name tag on the front of each dress or shirt. The teacher then said good-bye to the parent and directed the child, after comforting a few who were tearful, to a predesignated place at one of the five long tables that filled the center of the room.

Above each table, dangling by string from the ceiling, was a piece of cardboard whose color and shape matched its printed name: "Blue Circle," "Brown Triangle," "Red Diamond." Standing above the seated kids and using a loud and deliberate voice that drew the new arrivals together as a group, Mrs. Smith introduced herself and told about her pets. The kids began to talk all at once: "We're gettin' a kitty, a baby kitty"; "My mom won't let me get a kitty"; "I wonder if you're going to give me a book or a pencil to do something." Mrs. Smith broke into the verbal chaos to instruct in a kind but firm voice, "We talk one-at-a-time; you should hold up your hand if you want to talk." Hands flew up, while the chorus of spontaneous comments continued.

Raising her voice to regain their attention, Mrs. Smith asked, "Is there a big boy or girl who would volunteer to be a leader and carry the thermometer outside so we can see how hot it is?" "Me!" "Me!" urgent voices called from around the room of waving hands. "I don't call on me-me's. I'm going to pick one that doesn't say 'me.' Me-me's don't come to school," Mrs. Smith admonished. She chose Jason and asked him to go to the door and lead the line they were going to form. Tina jumped up at the same time as Jason, and Mrs. Smith told her to sit down. Raising her voice to again instruct the group, Mrs. Smith said, "When we go down the hallway, we have to stop talking. That's a rule: Be quiet in the hallway." She asked the students to repeat the rule, and they chanted together in high sing-song voices, "Be quiet in the hallway." "Now," Mrs. Smith said, "I will choose the quietest table to line up first." She paused, looked around, and then pronounced, "Blue Circle Table," moving over to prod the two boys and three girls at that table to form a single line behind Jason.

After looking around, the teacher made a second pronouncement:

"The Red Diamond Table looks ready to push in their chairs." When a short brown-haired boy jumped up and ran helter-skelter ahead of the others, Mrs. Smith admonished, "Todd, you have to walk and push in your chair." He went back to redo his actions in proper form. Mrs. Smith continued to call on tables until all thirty students, with bits of nudging and rearranging, had arrayed themselves in a single line. Admonishing them to be quiet, the teacher motioned the line to move into the hallway. Susie talked noisily, and Mrs. Smith sent her to the back of the line. "Stay in your line," Mrs. Smith called as the students moved along, "this is what you call a line; one at a time." When they passed a water fountain, several kids leaned over to drink until Mrs. Smith stated another rule: "We don't take drinks in the hall; we have a fountain in our room."

Over the next few weeks, Mrs. Smith continued to add to the young students' repertoire of school routines. They learned the named segments that divided each day: "reading time," "center time" (when they went into specialized classroom areas like "house" and "large toys"), "clean-up time," "recess." After instances of "bad behavior," the teacher sometimes threatened to take center time away, which strengthened its allure. During center time and recess the kids were relatively free to structure their own activities within bounded spaces. Mrs. Smith frequently reminded her students to take turns doing everything from sharing toys to going to the bathroom, for which she gave elaborate instructions: "You can go in when the door is open; leave the door open when you're through, but close it when you use it. Big boys and girls have doors shut in the bathroom; that's the grown-up thing to do at school."

SORTING STUDENTS INTO GROUPS

In managing almost thirty lively children within relatively small spaces, Mrs. Smith, like other teachers and aides, drew on the general power of being an adult, as well as on the more institutionalized authority of her official position. She claimed the right to regulate the students' activities, movement, posture, talking, possessions, access to water, and time and manner of eating. Such collective regulation—or "batch processing"—has a leveling effect; teachers and aides cope with the large number of students by treating them as members of groups.[2] School staff often sort students by characteristics like age, reading or math performance, or by spatial locations like "the Red Diamond Table" or "boys in the large toy area." And, when given the opportunity within classrooms, hallways, lunchrooms, and on the playground, kids also form their own groups. In the process the unique qualities of individuals (the focus of much family interaction) become subordinated to ways in which they are alike.[3]

In any mass of students there are many potential strands of "alikeness" and difference that may be used as a basis for constituting groups. Age is the most institutionalized principle of grouping; before the school year even begins, the staff assign students to first grade or fourth grade, and this sorting has a continuous effect on their activities and the company they keep. All the students in Mrs. Smith's kindergarten class were alike in being five or six years old. They differed by gender, race, ethnicity, social class, and religion, but these differences were to some degree submerged by the fact that the students, placed together because they were similar in age, confronted the same teacher, received the same work assignments, and were governed by the same rules. In both schools age-grading extended from classrooms into the cafeteria and auditorium, where each class was assigned its own space. Ashton School also had age-divided playgrounds: one for the kindergarten, first, and second grades; another for the third and fourth grades; and "the older kids' playground" for fifth- and sixth-graders. The Oceanside playground was not formally segmented by age, but younger and older students went out for recess at different times.

Within their age-homogeneous classrooms, teachers continually establish further divisions, some more or less arbitrary, like "the Red Diamond Table," and others based on differences in perceived talent or performance, like "the Bluebird Reading Group." The social categories and identities of the students—religion, social class, race and ethnicity, and gender—provide additional lines of difference that teachers and students evoke verbally and in their sorting practices, but to strikingly varied degrees.

In my observations in both schools, differences of religion figured into the organization of the school day only when several students from Jehovah's Witness families were excused from Halloween and Christmas celebrations. (I am familiar with other public schools that more routinely emphasize religious differences, for example, by allowing Mormon or Christian Covenant students to leave the school for a period of religious instruction elsewhere.)

Oceanside and Ashton teachers never explicitly invoked differences in social class, although subtleties of dress and talk marked variations in the socioeconomic backgrounds of the largely working-class students. Furthermore, class differences in these, as in other schools, were loosely related to "ability grouping" such as the composition of different reading groups.[4] In their everyday practices kids in both schools sometimes drew on and, in effect, marked class differences. For example, the Oceanside fourth- and fifth-graders avoided Rita, whose grooming and clothing displayed signs of poverty, and the emerging core of "popular girls" dressed more expensively than some of the other girls. But apart from side comments about a particular child's family or background, teachers, aides, and students never named or explicitly invoked social-class divisions when they organized groups.

In both schools the race and ethnicity of students was more emphasized than religion or social class, although in eleven months of fieldwork I observed only one classroom situation in which the staff formally sorted students along racial and ethnic lines, and that was for a practical reason. The Oceanside combined fourth-fifth–grade class included two boys, Alejandro and Miguel, who had recently immigrated from Mexico and who spoke little English. These two boys sat at the boundary that divided boys from girls in the U-shaped arrangement of desks, and during part of each school day, they moved to a table at the side of the room to work with a Spanish-speaking aide. Two other boys in that classroom, Allen and Freddy, spoke both Spanish and English, and several times the teacher asked one of them to translate for Miguel or Alejandro. Otherwise, Allen and Freddy had little contact with the recent immigrants, and the staff never set apart all Chicanos/Latinos as a distinctive group. Three other students were visibly of race and ethnic backgrounds different from the white or Euro-American majority: Jessie, from an African-American family; Rosie, whose parents came from the Philippines; and Neera, whose parents were from India. While adults did not formally draw on race or ethnicity in dealing with these students, ethnic and racial meanings, as I illustrate in later chapters, emerged in some encounters.

In the lunchrooms and on the playgrounds of both schools, African-American kids and kids whose main language was Spanish occasionally separated themselves into smaller, ethnically homogeneous groups. These groupings, such as five or six African-American older boys who often ate lunch together and then played basketball on the Ashton playground, were usually homogeneous by gender and, loosely, by age. Like other researchers, I found that students generally separate first by gender and then, if at all, by race or ethnicity.[5]

One regular play group on the Oceanside playground was a notable exception: seven to ten primarily Spanish-speaking girls and boys, including Alejandro and Miguel, regularly got together in a large game of dodgeball. The group, which probably coalesced because of the comfort of speaking the same language in an alien milieu, mixed kids of different ages as well as genders.

Apart from age, of all the social categories of the students, gender was the most formally, and informally, highlighted in the course of each school day. Gender is a highly visible source of individual and social identity, clearly marked by dress and by language; everyone is either a female or a male. In contrast, categories of race, ethnicity, religion, and social class tend to be more ambiguous and complex. Furthermore, recent public policy has set more proscriptions against officially marking race and religion (in the law, both are regarded as "suspect categories"), compared with gender (where, in a tangle of inconsistency, the law both does and does not mark difference).[6]

## "BOYS AND GIRLS": THE VERBAL MARKING OF GENDER
In both schools when the public address system crackled an announcement into a classroom or the cafeteria, the voice always opened with, "Boys and girls . . ." (the word "boys" invariably came first). Teachers and aides often used gender to mark out groups of students, usually for purposes of social control. For example, while the second-graders at Ashton School worked at their desks, the teacher, Mrs. Johnson, often walked around the room, verbally reining in the disruptive and inattentive: "There's three girls need to get busy. . . . You two boys ought to be busy." Other teachers also peppered their classroom language with gendered terms of address ("You boys be quiet"; "Girls, sit down"; "Ladies, this isn't a tea party"), implying that gender defined both behavior and social ties.

Why are gender terms so appealing as terms of address? Occasionally, the staffs of both schools used words like "people" or "students" to call for general attention. But they much more often used "boys and girls," perhaps because, as one of the principals reflected, "it feels more specific." Indeed, gender categories provide a striking blend of the specific *and* the all-encompassing. Since everyone is assigned to either one or the other gender category, the paired terms, "boys and girls," drop an inclusive net over a group of any size. (Note that "boys and girls" is used as the generic; "boy," unlike the word "man," has never been claimed as a generic, perhaps because children of both genders are subordinated to adults, and boys have less power over girls compared with men over women.[7]) "Boys and girls" may also be an appealing term of address because the words are marked for age, making it clear that children, not adults, are the focus of a comment. The language comes in handy since the structural separation of adults and children is so fundamental to schools.[8] Finally, terms like "the Blue Circle Table" and "fourth-graders" have fleeting connections with individual identities; the words "girls" and "boys" sink more deeply into a person's sense of self.

Spencer Cahill has also noted the centrality of gender categories in the "languages of social identification" used by and toward children. Observing in a preschool, he found that the adult staff used "baby" as a sanctioning term, contrasted with "big girl" and "big boy," which they employed as more positive forms of address. Cahill argues that children pick up the association of gender labels with the praiseworthy state of maturity and begin to claim "big girl" and "big boy" identities to distinguish themselves from "babies."[9]

Use of "big boy" and "big girl" as terms of praise continues in the early years of elementary school. On the first day of kindergarten Mrs. Smith asked for a "big boy or girl" to volunteer to carry the thermometer outside, and she later described the proper bathroom comportment of "big boys and girls." By fourth grade the terms "big girl" and "big boy" have largely disappeared, but teachers continue to equate mature behavior with grown-up gendered identities by using more formal and ironic terms of address, like "ladies and gentlemen." By frequently using gender labels when they interact with kids, adults make being a girl or a boy central to self-definition, and to the ongoing life of schools.

Gender dichotomies ("girl/boy" as basic social categories and as individual identities) provide a continuously available line of difference that can be drawn on at any time in the ongoing life of schools. The manner of drawing, however, varies a great deal. In some situations, gender is highlighted; at other times, it is downplayed. As Gregory Bateson once commented, in the ongoing complexity of social life, a given difference does not always *make* a difference.[10] Individuals enter situations as girls or boys, displaying gender through details like names, dress, and adornment. But gender may or may not be central to the organization and symbolism of an encounter. In some situations (I provide many examples in Chapter 5), participants mark and ritualize gender boundaries. In other situations, gender may be far less relevant. Note that this line of analysis separates aspects of gender that are always present (individuals never leave aside their membership in the category "girl" or "boy") from those that are more fluctuating (the marking or muting of gender in the organization and symbolism of different social situations).

As my fieldwork progressed, I came to ask: How, when, and why does gender make a difference—or *not* make a difference in everyday interaction in schools? And when gender does make a difference, what sort of difference is it? When they create groups, adults or kids may invoke or ignore gender, thereby separating boys from girls, or drawing them together. I began to think of the patterning as a kind of dance, a choreography of separation and integration, laden with complex and even contradictory meanings. Images of photography also came to mind. I initially thought in snapshot frames, noting patterns setting by setting; then I began to shift to a mental moving camera, tracing the processes by which boys and girls mixed together and pulled apart.

## The Choreography of Gender
## Separation and Integration

A series of snapshots taken in varied school settings would reveal extensive spatial separation between girls and boys. This phenomenon, which has been widely observed by researchers in schools, is often called "sex segregation among children," a term evoking images of legally enforced separation, like purdah in some Islamic societies. But school authorities separate boys and girls only occasionally. Furthermore, girls and boys sometimes interact with one another in relaxed and extended ways, not only in schools but also in families, neighborhoods, churches, and other settings. Gender separation—the word "segregation" suggests too total a pattern—is a variable and complicated process, an intricate choreography aptly summarized by Erving Goffman's phrase "with-then-apart."[11]

Boys and girls separate (or are separated) periodically, with their own spaces, rituals, and groups, but they also come together to become, in crucial ways, part of the same world. In the following verbal snapshots of classrooms, hallways, cafeterias, and school playgrounds, it is crucial to note that although the occasions of gender separation may seem more dramatic, the mixed-gender encounters are also theoretically and practically important. Note also that groups may be formed by teachers, aides, or by kids themselves, and that criteria of group formation may or may not be explicitly mentioned or even in conscious awareness.

### THE "WITH-THEN-APART" OF CLASSROOMS
In organizing classroom seating, teachers use a variety of plans, some downplaying and others emphasizing the significance of gender.

When Mrs. Smith, the kindergarten teacher at Ashton School, assigned seats, she deliberately placed girls and boys at each table, and they interacted a great deal in the formal and informal life of the classroom. Mrs. Johnson, the second-grade teacher at the same school, also assigned seats, but she organized her classroom into pairs of desks aligned in rows. With the layout came a language—"William's row" . . . "Monica's row" . . . "Amy's row"—for the five desks lined up behind William, Monica, Amy, and the other three students seated at the front. The overall pattern mixed girls and boys, and they participated together in much of the classroom whispering and byplay.

I asked Mrs. Johnson, who was nearing retirement after many years of teaching, what she had in mind when she assigned classroom seats. She responded with weary familiarity: "Everybody is sitting somewhere for a reason—hearing, sight, height. No two in the same reading group sit together, so I make sure they do their own work in their workbook. Or they sit in a particular place because they don't get along, or get along too well, with someone else." Differences of hearing, sight, height, and reading performance cut across the dichotomous division between boys and girls; sorting the students according to these criteria led to largely gender-integrated seating. However, the last of Mrs. Johnson's criteria, the degree to which two children get along, embeds a gender skew. Since friends are usually of the same gender, splitting up close friends tends to mix girls and boys.

Instead of assigning seats, Miss Bailey, the teacher of the combined fourth-fifth grade in Oceanside School, let the students choose their own desks in a U-shaped arrangement open at the front of the room. Over the course of the school year there were three occasions of general choosing. Each time, the students' choices resulted in an almost total cleavage: boys on the left and girls on the right, with the exception of one girl, Jessie, who frequently crossed gender boundaries and who twice chose a desk with the boys and once with the girls (such "crossing" between same-gender groups, with Jessie as a key example, is the topic of Chapter 7). The teacher and students routinely spoke of "a boys' side" and "a girls' side" in the classroom.[12]

Miss Bailey made clear that she saw the arrangement as an indulgence, and when the class was unusually noisy, she threatened to change the seating and "not have a boys' side and a girls' side." "You have chosen that," she said on one such occasion, "you're sitting this way because you chose to do it at the first of the year. I may have to sit you in another way." The class groaned as she spoke, expressing ritualized preference for gender-separated seating. Miss Bailey didn't carry out her threat, and when she reseated individual students in the name of classroom order, she did so within each side. Miss Bailey framed the overall gender separation as a matter of student choice and as a privilege she had granted them, but she also built on and ratified the gender divide by pitting the girls against the boys in classroom spelling and math contests. (I return to this ritualized separation in Chapter 5.)

Physical separation of girls and boys in regular classroom seating affects formal and informal give-and-take among students. One day Miss Bailey wrote sentences on the board and said she would go around the room and give each student a chance to find an error in spelling, grammar, or pronunciation. "We'll start with Beth," she said, gesturing to the right front of the U-shaped layout of the desks. Recognizing that to go around the room meant she would call on all the girls first, Miss Bailey added, "that leaves the hard part for the boys." Picking up the theme of gender opposition, several boys called out, "We're smart!" The divided seating pattern also channeled informal byplay, such as whispering, casual visiting, and collusive exchanges, among boys and among girls, whereas in classrooms with mixed-gender seating, those kinds of interaction more often took place between girls and boys.

When Miss Bailey divided the class into smaller work groups, gender receded in formal organizational importance. On these occasions, the teacher relied on sorting principles like skill at reading or spelling, whether or not someone had finished an earlier task, counting off ("one-two-one-two"), or letting students choose from alternative activities such as practicing for a play or collectively making a map out of papier-mâché. Sometimes Miss Bailey asked the fourth- and fifth-graders to meet separately and work on math or spelling. These varied organizational principles drew girls and boys out of separate halves of the classroom and into groups of varied gender composition standing at the blackboard or sitting on the floor in front or at round tables at the side of the room. When they found places in these smaller groups, girls often scrambled to sit next to girls, and boys to sit next to boys. But if the interaction had a central focus such as taking turns reading aloud or working together to build a contour map, boys and girls participated together in the verbal give-and-take.

Although I did not do systematic counting, I noticed that during formal classroom instruction, for example, when Miss Bailey invited discussion during social studies lessons, boys, taken as a whole, talked more than girls. This pattern fits with an extensive body of research finding that in classroom interaction from the elementary through college levels, male students tend to talk more than female students.[13] It should be emphasized that these are statistical and not absolute differences, and that researchers have found much variation from classroom to classroom in the degree to which boys are more visible than girls, and the degree to which individual teachers treat boys and girls differently. We need further research (my data are too sparse for these purposes) exploring possible relationships between seating practices, and patterns of talk and interaction in classrooms.

LIFE ON THE LINE

When Mrs. Smith announced to her kindergarten class, "This is what you call a line . . . one at a time," she introduced a social form basic to the handling of congestion and delay in schools. In Ashton School, where classrooms opened onto an indoor hallway, kids rarely moved from the classroom unless they were in carefully regulated lines. The separate lines meandering through the hallways reminded me of caterpillars, or of planes on a runway slowly moving along in readiness to take off. In the layout of the Oceanside School each of the classrooms opened to the outside, an arrangement facilitated by the warm California climate. Although this lessened the problem of noise and thereby relaxed the amount of adult control, the Oceanside teachers still organized students into loose lines when they headed to and from the library and the playground and when they went to the lunchroom.

Gender threaded through the routines of lining up, waiting and moving in a queue, and dispersing in a new place. In Oceanside School it was customary for girls and boys to line up separately, a pattern whose roots in the history of elementary schooling are still evident on old school buildings with separate entrances engraved with the words "Girls" and "Boys."[14] Several adults who have told me their memories of elementary school recall boys and girls lining up separately to go to different bathrooms. One woman remembered waiting in the girls' line several feet away from a row of boys and feeling an urgent need to urinate; she held her legs tightly together and hoped no one—especially the boys—would notice. This experience of bodily shame gave an emotional charge to gender-divided lines.

Like the schools of these adult memories, Oceanside had separate girls' and boys' bathrooms shared by many classrooms. But unlike the remembered schools, Oceanside had no collective expeditions to the bathrooms. Instead individual students asked permission to leave the classrooms and go to either the boys' or girls' bathroom, both of which, like the classrooms, opened to the outside. In Ashton School, as in many contemporary school buildings, each classroom had its own bathroom, used one-at-a-time by both girls and boys. This architectural shift has eliminated separate and centralized boys' and girls' facilities and hence the need to walk down the hall to take turns going to the toilet.

In Oceanside School the custom of separate girls' and boys' lines was taken for granted and rarely commented on. One of the fourth graders told me that they learned to form separate boys' and girls' lines in kindergarten and had done it ever since. A first-grade teacher said that on the first day of school she came out to find the boys and the girls already standing in two different lines. When I asked why girls and boys formed separate lines, the teachers said it was the children's doing. With the ironic detachment that adults often adopt toward children's customs, Miss Bailey told me that she thought the gender-separated lines were "funny." A student teacher who joined the classroom for part of the year rhetorically asked the kids why they had a girls' line and a boys' line. "How come? Will a federal marshal come and get you if you don't?" There was no reply.

Miss Bailey didn't deliberately establish separate lines for boys and girls; she just told the students to line up. It took both attention and effort for the kids to continually create and recreate gender-separated queues. In organizing expeditions out of the classroom, Miss Bailey usually called on students by stages, designating individuals or smaller groups ("everyone at that side table"; "those practicing spelling over in the corner") to move into line as a reward for being quiet. Once they got to the classroom door—unless it was lunchtime, when boys and girls mixed in two lines designated "hot lunch" and "cold lunch"—the students routinely separated by gender. The first boy to reach the door always stood to the left; the first girl stood to the right, and the rest moved into the appropriate queue.

The kids maintained separate boys' and girls' lines through gestures and speech. One day when the class was in the library, Miss Bailey announced, "Line up to go to assembly." Judy and Rosie hurried near the door, marking the start of one line on the right; Freddy and Tony moved to the left of the door. Other girls lined up behind Rosie, who became a sort of traffic director, gesturing a boy who was moving in behind her that he should shift to the other line. Once when the recess bell had rung and they began to line up for the return to class, a boy came over and stood at the end of a row of girls. This evoked widespread teasing—"John's in the girls' line"; "Look at that girl over there"—that quickly sent him to the row of boys. Off-bounds to those of the other gender, the separate lines sometimes became places of sanctuary, as during the close of one recess when Dennis grabbed a ball from Tracy, and she chased after him. He squeezed into line between two boys, chanting "Boys' line, boys' line," an incantation that indeed kept her away and secured his possession of the ball.

Several years before I arrived at Ashton School, the staff had moved from dual to single lines. This may have been partly a result of Title IX, the 1972 federal legislation mandating that girls and boys should have equal access to all school activities. One teacher told me she used to organize separate boys' and girls' lines, but someone told her that "wasn't the thing to do these days," so she followed her colleagues in shifting to single lines. Although individual girls and boys often stood in front of and behind one another in the single lines, they also had strategies for maneuvering within formal constraints and separating into same-gender clusters.

The front of the line is a desired and contested zone. As a reward, the teachers often let a specific child—the "line leader" or "goodest one," as a kindergartner explained—go first. After that initial selection there is often pushing and shoving for a place near the front. Because of the press to be near the front, kids usually protest attempted cuts in that zone. Farther back, individuals or smaller groups can sometimes tuck in a friend or two; it takes protest to make a cut a cut, and the deed is less likely to be challenged in back than in front. The back of the line is sometimes defined as the least desired space, even a place of punishment as suggested by the much-repeated rule: "If you cut, you have to go to the back of the line."

Although generally a devalued space, the back of the line has its uses. During the process of lining up, socially marginal kids often wait to join the line near the end, thereby avoiding the pushing and maneuvering at the front. Since the end is less tightly surveyed by teachers, aides, and other students, groups of friends may go to the back of the line so they can stand and talk together without having to be vigilant about holding their places. Occasionally when a student leaves a place in line and moves to the end, it appears to be out of a sense of being in the wrong gender territory. For example, in Ashton School after they finished eating lunch, students routinely lined up in the cafeteria waiting for a lunchtime aide to escort them to the playground. In one sequence of actions a girl moved into line behind three boys, then a boy got in line behind her. When she noticed this, a look of discomfort crossed her face, and she shifted farther back in the emerging line, joining three other girls.

Life on the line is time spent waiting. (Educational researchers have found that the time students spend waiting takes up as much as a third of each school day.[15]) The process of waiting in line was especially protracted in the Ashton School lunchroom, where lines formed slowly, the time drawn out by the varied speed of the eaters and by waiting for a lunchtime aide to finish wiping tables before she could lead the lines through the hallways and out to the playground. Bored by the delay, the waiting kids created their own forms of entertainment. They often clustered into same-gender groups, sometimes marking their solidarity with shared motions: girls sat on the floor facing one another and played clapping games (I never saw boys do this); a boy jogged shoulders with the next boy in line, starting a chain reaction that stopped when a girl was next. Separate clusters of kids, usually of different genders, marked boundaries between them by leaving a gap of space and/or through physical hassling. In one emerging lunchroom lineup of Ashton third-graders, there was a row of seven boys at the front, then several feet of empty space, then three girls, a few feet of space, then three boys. A girl reached around and leaned across the space to poke the boy behind her; he then pinned down her arms from behind, letting her go after she protested. When everyone had finally finished eating and joined the line, the aide signaled that they could go. There was a lot of pushing as smaller groups eased into the shared motion of one moving line.

THE GENDER GEOGRAPHY OF LUNCHROOM TABLES

Seating in school lunchrooms falls between the more fixed spaces of classroom desks and the arrangements kids improvise each time they sit on the floor of the classroom or the auditorium; an Oceanside teacher once referred to "their strange conglomeration way of sitting," describing the clusters, primarily of either girls or boys, arrayed on the floor. Eating together is a prime emblem of solidarity, and each day at lunchtime there is a fresh scramble as kids deliberately choose where, and with whom, to eat. The scrambling takes place within limits set by adults and defined by age-grading. In both schools, each classroom, in effect an age-grade, had two designated cafeteria tables, placed end to end from the wall.

Table seating takes shape through a predictable process: the first arrivals (who have cold lunches, a reason some children say they prefer to bring lunch from home) stake out territory by sitting and spreading out their possessions, usually at the far ends of each table. The tables fill through invitations, squeezing in, or individuals or groups going to an empty space. The groups who maneuver to eat together are usually friends and mostly of the same gender. The result is a pattern of separated clusters; many of the tables have a mix of girls and boys, but they are divided into smaller same-gender groupings. On the other hand, late-arriving individuals, who have less choice of where to sit, move into leftover spaces and tend to integrate the seating.

The collective table talk often includes both boys and girls, as do some daily rituals, like one that accompanied the opening of plastic bags of cutlery in both schools. As kids pulled out their plastic forks, they looked for and announced the small numbers stamped on the bottom: "I'm twenty-four, how old are you?" "I must have flunked; I'm in the fourth grade and I'm forty-five." "Ninety-three." "You're stupid; you were really held back in school."

Even when boys and girls are seated at the same table, their same-gender clustering may be accompanied by a sense of being on separate turfs. This became apparent when there were temporary changes in the physical ecology at Oceanside School. The combined fourth-fifth–grade class usually had two tables, but one day when the kids arrived for lunch, one of the tables was temporarily designated for another class. The kids began to crowd around the remaining table. Sherry, who had a cold lunch and arrived first, chose her usual seat by the wall; girls usually filled up that end. Scott and Jeremy sat down across from her, while three girls with hot lunches chose seats at the other end of the table. Scott looked around and asked, "Where are all the boys? Where are all the boys?" Four boys arrived and sat across from Scott and Jeremy and next to Sherry, who began to crouch in her corner. In a small anxious voice she asked them, "What are you doing on the girls' side?" "There isn't room," one of the newly arrived boys explained.

Occasionally those who are already seated look around, take the lay of the developing table, and change places, sometimes with a gender-marking pronouncement. In the Ashton School lunchroom when the two second-grade tables were filling, a high-status boy walked by the inside table, which had a scattering of both boys and girls. He said loudly, "Oooo, too many girls," and headed for a seat at the other, nearly empty table. The boys at the inside table picked up their trays and moved to join him. After they left, no other boy sat at that table, which the pronouncement had made effectively taboo. So in the end, girls and boys ate at separate tables that day, although this was not usually the case.

I recorded many inventories of seating in the two lunchroom

shifts in Ashton School. There was a great deal of variation from classroom to classroom and day to day, but completely separate boys' and girls' tables were much more frequent in fifth and sixth than in the younger grades. The sixth-graders talked matter-of-factly about "the girls' table" and "the boys' table," spaces so ritualized that they could be deliberately disrupted. A group of sixth-grade girls told me about a day when they plotted ahead, hurried into the lunchroom, and grabbed the boys' table, which was always the one next to the wall. When the boys arrived, they protested, but the girls held out, and on that day, which the girls remembered with humor, the girls and the boys switched territories.

### PLAYGROUND DIVISIONS OF SPACE AND ACTIVITY

In classrooms, hallways, and lunchrooms boys and girls do the same core activities: working on math or spelling, moving from one area to another, or eating a meal. Same-gender groups might add their own, sometimes collusive agendas, such as a group of girls passing around a tube of lip gloss during a grammar lesson or a group of boys discussing sports or setting up arm wrestling during lunch. But there is no pronounced division of activity by gender.[16] In contrast, on the playground, an area where adults exert minimal control and kids are relatively free to choose their own activities and companions, there is extensive separation by gender. Activities, spaces, and equipment are heavily gender-typed; playgrounds, in short, have a more fixed geography of gender.

My inventories of activities and groups on the playground showed similar patterns in both schools. Boys controlled the large fixed spaces designated for team sports: baseball diamonds, grassy fields used for football or soccer, and basketball courts. In Oceanside School there was also a skateboard area where boys played, with an occasional girl joining in. The fixed spaces where girls predominated—bars and jungle gyms and painted cement areas for playing foursquare, jump rope, and hopscotch—were closer to the building and much smaller, taking up perhaps a tenth of the territory that boys controlled.[17] In addition, more movable activities—episodes of chasing, groups of younger children playing various kinds of "pretend," and groups milling around and talking—often, although by no means always, divided by gender. Girls and boys most often played together in games of kickball, foursquare, dodgeball, handball, and chasing or tag.

Kids and playground aides pretty much take these gender-divided patterns for granted; indeed, there is a long history in the United States of girls and boys engaging in different types of play, although the favored activities have changed with time.[18] The Ashton School aides openly regarded the space close to the building as girls' territory and the playing fields "out there" as boys' territory. They sometimes shooed away children of the other gender from what they saw as inappropriate turf, especially boys who ventured near the girls' area and seemed to have teasing in mind.

In both schools the transition from the classroom or the lunchroom to the playground began when a teacher or aide allocated equipment. Girls rarely made a bid for footballs, softballs, or basketballs, and boys rarely asked for jump ropes (an Ashton aide once refused a boy's request for a jump rope, saying with a tone of accusation, "You only want it to give rope burns"). Both boys and girls asked for the rubber balls used for kickball, handball, and foursquare. An individual with equipment could gain relatively easy access to designated play space such as a basketball or foursquare court. To indicate that they wanted to join a given activity, kids without equipment went to the routinized space, for example, getting in line to play handball or milling around the court with other would-be basketball players. Then, in games where numbers were limited or sides were essential, negotiations began. Boys rarely sought access to a game of jump rope or hopscotch, or girls to a game of softball, football, soccer, or basketball, although there were important exceptions (which I discuss in Chapter 7).

Kids sometimes excluded others by claiming they already had too many players, or simply by saying "you can't play." Sometimes they used gender as an excuse, drawing on beliefs connecting boys to some activities and girls to others.[19] Day after day on the Ashton playground I noticed that Evan, a first-grade boy, sat on the stairs and avidly watched girls play jump rope, his head and eyes turning around in synchrony with the rope. Once when a group of girls were deciding who would jump and who would "twirl" (the less desirable position), Evan recognized a means of access to the game and offered, "I'll swing it." Julie responded, "No way, you don't know how to do it, to swing it. You gotta be a girl." He left without protest. Although kids sometimes ignored pronouncements about what boys or girls could or could not do, I never heard them directly challenge such claims.

## Other Research on Gender Separation among Children

My observations of extensive separation in the activities and social relations of boys and girls echo a recurring finding in the research literature.

In fact, in nearly every study of school situations where kids from age three through junior high are given the opportunity to choose companions of the same age, girls have shown a strong preference to be with girls, and boys with boys. (Because as much as 90 percent of research on children's peer groups has been done in schools, the finding of gender separation among children dominates the literature.[20] Studies of children's social relations in neighborhoods and a study in a children's museum have found much more mixing of girls and boys than is typical in schools.)

To grasp the magnitude of the gender divide, a number of researchers have counted the relative proportions of mixed and same-gender groups in various school settings. For example, Zella Luria and Eleanor Herzog did inventories of the playground groups of fourth- and fifth-graders in two elementary schools in Massachusetts. They found that in a private, upper-middle-class school, 63 percent of the groups were same-gender, compared with 80 percent same-gender groups in a middle-class public school of about the same size and racial composition. In another study on the East Coast, Marlaine Lockheed and Abigail Harris found that in twenty-nine fourth- and fifth-grade classrooms where students constituted their own work groups, 86 percent were same-gender.[21]

In short, there is ample evidence of extensive separation between girls and boys within contemporary coeducational schools. Numerical counts, moreover, may underestimate the degree of separation. Luria and Herzog note that their method of counting all playground clusters regardless of activity may overrate the extent and "quality" of cross-gender activity. For example, in the public school in their study, half of the 20 percent of play groups mixed by gender were integrated by one girl and hence were token situations.[22] The method of simply counting all-boy, all-girl, and boy-girl groups also neglects meanings. For example, by these researchers' counting methods, girls-chase-the-boys, a favorite game on both the Ashton and Oceanside playgrounds, would be chalked up as a mixed-gender group or interaction. However, as I show in Chapter 5, the organization of this activity dramatizes gender boundaries and maintains a sense of separation between the girls and the boys as distinctive groups.

Information not only about the quantity of gender separation, but also about the quality and meaning (e.g., the degree of felt intimacy or social distance) of kids' social relations can be found in their perceptions of friendship. Researchers who have asked kids of different ages to name their best friends have found that in at least 75 percent of the cases, boys name only boys and girls name only girls.[23] Socio-metric studies that go beyond "best" friendships to ask about and map broader self-reported patterns of affiliation and avoidance have also documented a deep division by gender. For example, in a study of four fourth-, fifth-, and sixth-grade classrooms, Maureen Hallinan found that all the cliques that the students identified were either of girls or of boys; not one crossed the line of gender.[24] Although she observed, and the students reported, some cross-gender friendships, they were not integrated into the larger, more public and visible groupings or cliques.

In short, although girls and boys *are* together and often inter-act in classrooms, lunchrooms, and on the playground, these contacts less often deepen into friendship or stable alliances, while same-gender interactions are more likely to solidify into more lasting or acknowl-edged bonds. Much of the daily contact between girls and boys, as Janet Schofield comments, resembles that of "familiar strangers" who are in repeated physical proximity and recognize one another but have little real knowledge of what one another are like.[25] Some of the stu-dents in the middle school where Schofield observed felt that the gulf between boys and girls was so deep that it was fruitless to try to form cross-gender friendships, which they saw as different from romantic liaisons.

Whether painted with narrative or by numbers, the prevalence of gender separation, especially on school playgrounds and in pat-terns of children's friendship, is quite striking. But separation between boys and girls is far from total, and the "with" occasions should be sketched into view. In the next chapter I move in and around an obvi-ous question: When given a choice, why do girls and boys so often separate from one another? The answers, I suggest, should be far more complex and contextual than the approaches currently offered by devel-opmental psychologists.

# CHAPTER 4

# Gender Separation:
# Why and How

The extensive research on "sex segregation among children" points to what social scientists call a "robust" finding: study after study concludes that when boys and girls have a choice of companions, they more often separate than integrate.[1] But in schools like Oceanside and Ashton gender separation is rarely total; even when 80 percent of playground groups are either all-girl or all-boy, 20 percent of the groups contain both girls and boys. Furthermore, playgrounds are typically more gender-separated than other school settings. Emphasizing only the prevalence of "segregation" does little to illuminate an underlying question: What makes girls and boys more likely to separate *or* to choose to be together? Comparing kids' gender relations in different contexts—in schools and in neighborhoods, and across varied school settings such as classrooms, playgrounds, and lunchrooms—can help answer that question.

On the whole, schools like Ashton and Oceanside appear to foster more separation between girls and boys than is characteristic of kids' interactions in many neighborhoods. Since I couldn't go home with the kids I got to know in school, I wasn't able to observe them in their other social worlds. But some students talked about their activities and companions outside school, and these reports sometimes, although by no means always, showed a striking contrast. For example, on the Oceanside playground I never saw Sherry, a fifth-grader, play in the organized sports where boys predominated. But she told me that she often played soccer with boys in her neighborhood, including with Eddie, a neighbor who was also in Miss Bailey's classroom.

Asked about their memories of being ages nine to twelve, a number of college women recalled playing baseball, soccer, or games like "capture-the-flag" with groups of boys and girls in their neighborhoods. When asked what they played when they were at school, the same women would often reply, "Oh, at school I played only with girls." Or, "at school I didn't play any of those games; I stood around with the girls." One man recalled that when he was in fourth grade he regularly played with a girl in his neighborhood, but when he was in school, he rarely played with girls.

There may be more cross-gender affiliation than is apparent in the public life of schools. When I stood on the Ashton playground talking with Melanie, a sixth-grader, I learned of a girl-boy friendship that went underground in school. After Jack walked by without even glancing at her, Melanie whispered to me, "He's one of my best friends." "But you didn't even nod or say hello to each other," I said. "Oh," she replied, "we're friends in our neighborhood and at church, but at school we pretend not to know each other so we won't get teased." In preschools cross-gender friendships are more public, but the risk of heterosexual teasing increases across the years of elementary school, limiting public displays of affiliation between boys and girls.[2] Note that fear of teasing may skew self-reports of who is friends with whom, leading social scientists to exaggerate the amount of gender separation.[3]

There is some systematic evidence that groups formed in neighborhoods tend to be more mixed by gender and by age than children's groups at school. Shari Ellis, Barbara Rogoff, and Cindy Cromer observed children (ages one to twelve, a total of 198 girls and 238 boys) at home and out-of-doors on summer afternoons in a middle-income, largely white neighborhood of Salt Lake City. They found that the children were as likely to be with cross-age as with near-age companions, and that of all the groups, 33 percent were same-gender and 28 percent were mixed-gender (the remaining groups included adults). Among children older than seven or eight, same-gender companionship was more common, but there was still a lot of mixing. The researchers found that gender separation and age separation went together; children in same-gender groups were more likely to be with near-age than with cross-age companions. And mixed-gender groups were also likely to be mixed in age.[4]

Why is gender separation more extensive in schools than in many neighborhoods? Organizationally, schools like Oceanside and Ashton push in contradictory directions: in some ways they lessen, but in other ways they enhance the likelihood of gender separation among students. Boys and girls have been drawn together by a long history of coeducational public schooling in the United States.[5] And teachers hold an ideal of treating students "fairly," which usually means either the same or as distinctive individuals. Both of these stances may lessen the importance of gender. As Mrs. Johnson, the Ashton second-grade teacher said to me, "It's not whether it's a boy or a girl; I have to watch out that everyone gets a fair share."[6]

Of course, the ideal of fair treatment does not always match actual practice; within the last two decades, many researchers have uncovered "hidden curricula" of race, class, and gender in both the content and processes of schooling.[7] Social biases (of which school staff may or may not be consciously aware) may infuse various practices of schooling, such as: stereotypes in books, graphics, and the content of classroom talk; expectations that help shape processes of academic tracking; differential attention given to boys compared with girls, or white compared with African-American or Chicano students. Far from muting preexisting forms of stratification, schools may help reproduce class, racial, and gender inequalities that are fundamental to the larger society.[8]

The practices of school staff are complex and often contradictory, sometimes reinforcing and sometimes undermining social divisions and larger patterns of inequality. The organizational features of schools also work in both ways; in some respects, as I have already enumerated, they diminish, but in other ways they enhance the likelihood of separation between girls and boys. Several basic features of schools that distinguish them from neighborhoods—their *formal age-grading*, their *crowded and public* nature, and the continual presence of *power and evaluation*—enter into the dynamics of gender separation and integration. I will now draw these strands of analysis together, sketching the overall choreography of "with" and "apart" that emerges across different school settings.

## Gender Separation Is Related to Age

Age enters into patterns of gender separation and mixing in several ways. Many researchers have found that as children grow older, they tend to separate more and more by gender, with the amount of gender separation peaking in early adolescence.[9] This change with age may be rooted in processes of individual development, major shifts of setting (e.g., entering school), and in culturally organized transitions (e.g., adopting the symbols and prescribed desires of "teen culture"). These factors obviously interact, but they also point to disjunctures that undermine a widespread assumption that gender separation is somehow "natural" or an "imperative" of development.

Age has another facet that helps illuminate boys' and girls' patterns of being apart and together. Although age as a primary principle of sorting has the effect of mixing girls and boys, the genders are more likely to separate from one another in same-age than in mixed-age contexts. In their observations in Salt Lake City neighborhoods, Ellis and her colleagues found a striking correlation between same-age and same-gender play. Drawing on observations in six cultures, and a review of other studies, Beatrice Whiting and Carolyn Edwards conclude that "there are some suggestions that sex segregation emerges especially in peer groups rather than mixed-age groups."[10]

Why do age separation and gender separation enhance each other? As already discussed, the forces of bureaucratization that play upon and use age divisions also, at some points, pick up on gender divisions. In addition, if children are of roughly the same age, they may be more likely to share interests and behavioral styles and to search for even greater homogeneity, separating by gender.[11] Furthermore, girls and boys who are closer in age are more likely to be seen as potential romantic partners, and hence as vulnerable to the heterosexual teasing that pushes the genders apart. Whatever the reasons, where age separation is present, gender separation is more likely to occur. By institutionalizing age divisions, schools both draw girls and boys together *and* structurally enhance the conditions for gender separation.

## Gender Separation Is More Likely in Crowded Settings

Schools are more densely populated than neighborhoods, providing more potential companions of the same gender and age. If students or staff want to form groups composed only of fourth-grade girls or second-grade boys, the means—sufficient numbers of the "right" categories—are available.[12] Neighborhoods contain fewer potential companions; without as much choice, kids are more likely to interact with someone of another age or a different gender. Several women told me that when they were girls, they learned how to play baseball or ice hockey in their neighborhoods because another player was needed to carry off a game; either they volunteered, or boys cajoled them to join.

Crowds provide not only many potential companions but also potential witnesses; schools are much more public environments than are neighborhoods. And the witnessing—the continual surveillance by teachers, aides, and other students, many of whom are near strangers—is often loaded with evaluation. Teasing, a prevalent form of criticism among kids, has powerful emotional and behavioral consequences for gender relations.

TEASING

I frequently observed kids, and occasionally adults, tease a boy or girl who chose to be with an individual or group of the other gender. For example, when several Ashton girls noticed that a boy was sitting in the midst of a group of girls at a third-grade cafeteria table, they loudly exclaimed, "Bobby's a girl!" If a girl and a boy chose to work on spelling or to play together, they risked being teased for "liking," "having a crush on," or "goin' with" each other. Heterosexual idioms might seem to unite the genders, but when used in teasing contexts, these idioms create risks that drive girls and boys apart.

A telling episode of heterosexual teasing emerged when I conversed with a group of third-grade girls over lunch in the Ashton cafeteria. When Susan asked me what I was doing, I replied that I was observing the things kids do and play. Nicole volunteered, "I like running, boys chase all the girls. See Tim over there? Judy chases him all around the school; she likes him." Judy, sitting across the table, quickly responded. "I hate him. I like him for a friend." "Tim loves Judy," Nicole taunted in a loud, sing-song voice. Judy looked embarrassed.

The language for heterosexual relationships consists of a very few, often repeated, and sticky words; the charge that a particular girl "likes" a particular boy (or vice versa) may be hurled like an insult. Teasing always has a target, evoking feelings of discomfort and humiliation, especially if there are witnesses. Furthermore, teasing often calls for a response. Judy grappled for a way to deny the accusation, first with an absolute negation ("I hate him") and then a qualification ("I like him for a friend"). Since the teasing took place in a crowded setting, the presence of an audience enhanced the sting, and if she wanted to avoid further teasing, Judy had to avoid interacting with Tim.

Teasing makes cross-gender interaction risky, increases social distance between girls and boys, and has the effect of marking and policing gender boundaries. The risk of being teased may dissuade kids from publicly choosing to be with someone of the other gender. Hence, the phenomenon of underground friendships; if Melanie and Jack displayed their friendship at school, they became vulnerable to teasing. As Amy, a sixth-grader, told me with a sigh, "It's hard for girls and boys to stay friends." "Why?" I asked. "I guess because boys are afraid other boys will call them sissy or say that they have a crush on a girl." These are heavy risks indeed, and I return to them in Chapters 7 and 8.

PUBLIC SITUATIONS OF CHOOSING

When groups are constructed through acts of *witnessed choice*, a situation ripe for teasing, boys and girls tend to avoid one another. But if groups are constituted by some other means, such as simply getting into line, girls and boys are more likely to be together.

In my initial playground roaming, I began to wonder why girls and boys most often played together in kickball, handball, and dodgeball. The answer, I finally decided, lay not in the commonality of rubber balls on cement, but rather in rules for gaining access to these compared with other activities. One can join a game of handball (the most gender-, race-, and age-integrated of all the activities on the Oceanside playground) simply by going to the end of one of the lines on either side of the backboard. When one of the paired players misses the ball, he or she goes to the end of the line, and the person at the front moves into play. Analogously, to join a dodgeball game, one finds a place in the circle of players who throw a rubber ball and try to hit, and thus declare "out," those in a smaller group in the center. Both games can be joined through individual initiative (one doesn't have to ask or negotiate permission to enter), and they are relatively open-ended (one has only to squeeze into a circle or get in line to be part of the game).

In contrast, baseball, soccer, and basketball involve elaborate choosing of teams and hence being witnessed and possibly teased for choosing a player of the other gender. One does not choose up teams to play jump rope or hopscotch, but the number of players is limited, and negotiation is usually required to join a given game. Kickball does involve forming teams (who, in a format like baseball, take turns kicking a big rubber ball and running around bases), so my ease-of-entry explanation does not hold. However, like handball and dodgeball, kickball is relatively easy to play.[13] Games that accommodate varied levels of skill may also be more gender-integrated. Dodgeball, handball, and kickball may have withstood becoming labeled as either "boys'" or "girls'" games because of these features.

## Adult Presence Tends to Undermine Gender Separation

In addition to age-grading and crowds, the power of the adult staff, who continually manage and constrain the actions of a large group of subordinated children, is another basic organizational feature of schools. In contrast, in neighborhoods kids are relatively freer from adult control. Using their power, teachers and aides engage in contradictory practices; on some occasions they sustain, and on other occasions they challenge, the separation of girls and boys. Miss Bailey let her fourth-fifth–grade students choose their classroom seats and then legitimated the almost total division between boys and girls by joining in talk about a boys' side and a girls' side and by organizing boys against the girls for math and spelling contests. But when she organized reading groups, she used her authority to draw girls and boys together, thereby lessening the salience of gender.

As I look at the practices of the Oceanside and Ashton staff, across settings and day-by-day, it was clear that adults more often mixed than separated girls and boys. In their daily practices teachers and aides juggle multiple concerns that cut across lines of gender, for example, teaching a fixed curriculum to an entire classroom while coping with differences in academic preparation and maintaining some semblance of order. Whether a student is a boy or girl recedes in organizational importance when adults organize groups on the basis of age (e.g., separating fourth- from fifth-graders), counting off ("one-two-one-two"), type of lunch (hot or cold), language performance, reading or math ability, or by the multiple criteria (height, hearing, academic skills) that Mrs. Johnson, the second-grade teacher, used in allocating seats in her classroom. Adults exert much more control over classrooms than over playgrounds, a major reason why girls and boys mix more in the former than in the latter setting.[14]

Furthermore, because school staff generally want to treat students fairly and make sure that everyone gets opportunities, they sometimes question kids' patterns of exclusion. To keep the interaction more open, teachers and aides may intervene ("let her play") or establish rules ("the blocks are there for everyone to play with")—practices that lessen the amount of gender separation. As noted earlier, Luria and Herzog studied gender integration on the playgrounds of two schools and found that 63 percent of the groups in one school were same-gender as opposed to 80 percent in the other. The school with more gender integration had rules, jointly developed by teachers and students, for admitting new players to ongoing games. There was also a rule that no one could be refused access to a game unless there were too many players. The school with more gender separation did not have these rules.[15]

Even in the absence of adult-imposed rules or efforts to intervene, the sheer presence of an adult (who might intervene, and who might also be seen as drawing a group together) may open a wedge into a same-gender group. When I or another adult sat down at a lunchroom table where only girls or only boys were present, or when one of us adults moved into an all-boy or all-girl group clustered on the floor in the auditorium, kids of the other gender were more likely to move into the group as well. Adult presence legitimates the possibility of entering a turf controlled by the other gender; the adult becomes the focus of the group, which lessens the risk of teasing.

In addition to reducing the threat of teasing, the presence of adults alters the dynamics of power. Girls and boys, who share the subordinated position of being children, sometimes draw together to resist or maneuver around adult authority. One day a much disliked Oceanside teacher who was on yard duty punished Don, a fourth-grader, for something he didn't do. He was very upset, and other kids who were playing in the vicinity and witnessed or heard about the incident began to talk angrily about the injustice. Girls and boys talked about the situation together, and they joined as a group to argue with the teacher.

## Why Are Kids So Intent on Separating by Gender?

The characteristics of different settings—the physical ecology, numbers and types of participants, array of activities, structuring of power—help explain variations in the degree to which girls and boys interact with or separate from one another. But why are boys and girls, at least in middle childhood, so intent on avoiding one another in the first place? When they have a choice of companions, why do boys so often choose boys and girls choose girls? What makes gender so enormously relevant in kids' patterns of friendship? Experts in child development have pursued this question by theorizing about *individual motivations* in relation to gender.

Three major explanations have been set forth to explain why children may prefer to be with others of the same gender, and/or want to avoid those of the other gender: (1) shared interests or "behavioral compatibility"; (2) psychoanalytic processes: (3) the cognitive dynamics of gender labeling and identity. I will briefly discuss each of these lines of argument and then return to the importance of social relations, collective practices, and context—considerations that move beyond, although they may also help shape, individual motivation.

## SHARED INTERESTS OR "BEHAVIORAL COMPATIBILITY"

It has often been assumed that through a combination of biological factors and cultural learning, girls and boys develop different types of temperament, styles of play, and/or sets of interests. Because of such sex/gender differences, it has been argued, boys find it more rewarding to interact and play with boys, and girls to interact and play with girls. There are striking examples of this pattern; in preschools and kindergartens, girls more often gravitate to housekeeping corners and doll-play, and boys to the area with large blocks and toy cars and trucks. But note that this sort of commonsense example may well presuppose what it sets out to explain; if girls and boys, starting at relatively young ages, are given different toys and exposed to gender stereotypes, forces have already been set in motion that would result in loosely differentiated interests and perhaps even separate gender subcultures. (In Chapter 6 I return to this theme.)

Commonsense examples aside, as Eleanor Maccoby and Carol Jacklin show in a careful review of research, there is *not* overwhelming support for the "behavioral comparability" explanation for gender separation among young children.[16] Even where statistical gender differences have been found (findings of "no difference" are extremely frequent, though underreported), they never fall into a dichotomous pattern. In other words, it is never the case that every boy differs from every girl. For example, in preschools and kindergartens some boys never or rarely play with large blocks and toy vehicles, and some girls do. On *average*, boys have a somewhat higher activity level than girls, but the ranges between the most and least active boy, and the most and least active girl, are much greater than the statistical difference between all the girls compared with all the boys.[17] One should be wary of what has been called "the tyranny of averages," a misleading practice of referring to average differences as if they are absolute.

Maccoby and Jacklin, who followed three cohorts of girls and boys from birth into elementary school, found that when the children were four and a half years old, there was no correlation between a given boy's activity level and his degree of preference for same-sex playmates. Among girls, those with higher activity levels tended to prefer to play with other girls rather than with boys, who, on average, also had higher activity levels. Among first-graders, Maccoby and Jacklin found no gender differences in activity level, although there was extensive gender separation in the children's choice of playground companions. The researchers found no support for the expectation that children would seek out playmates with similar activity levels—one piece of evidence (they cite others as well) negating the claim that behavioral compatibility accounts for choice of playmates.

Maccoby and Jacklin conclude that gender segregation is more a "group phenomenon" than the result of characteristics of individual children. They then speculate about the "origins," "foundation," or *initial* impetus for separation between girls and boys. Several researchers doing observations and experiments with children of preschool age have found that at an age as young as three, girls can influence other girls but have difficulty influencing boys, whereas boys tend to be successful in influencing both girls and boys. Maccoby and Jacklin speculate that this pattern of male dominance in mixed-gender interaction may lead girls to avoid boys and turn their attention to girls, whom they can influence with greater ease. In short, girls, at least initially, may separate from boys in order to avoid being dominated. Maccoby and Jacklin acknowledge that it is less clear why boys should avoid interacting with girls, although there is ample evidence that they often do.

Although this explanation is gaining speed in the literature, I find it less than satisfactory. While several studies of young children have found this pattern, the literature on children of different, including preschool, ages reveals great complexity, not unrelenting dominance of boys over girls. Maccoby and Jacklin seem to be looking for origins, for a precipitating cause with lasting effects. But there is no evidence linking these preschool interactions to later dynamics among children. Even if this were the "origin" (and I'm generally suspicious of "origins tales," which are more rapidly trotted out in matters of gender—and children—than in other areas of social life[18]), it would account neither for the maintenance of, nor for complicated changes and variations in, children's patterns of gender separation and integration over time and in varied places. Furthermore, this origins scenario only pushes the "why" question back a step, implying that there is an ultimate cause—some primal, perhaps presocial kind of dominance of boys over girls. This "cause," of course, remains unexplained.[19]

FEMINIST PSYCHOANALYTIC THEORIES

Working in a different tradition, feminist psychoanalytic theorists like Nancy Chodorow and Myra Dinnerstein have argued that boys are motivated to separate from and to devalue "things feminine" in order to gain separation from their mothers.[20] Because mothers do the bulk of primary parenting, both boys and girls initially identify with and are strongly attached to a woman. Girls have special difficulty separating from their mothers, partly because they are of the same gender. In contrast, boys develop a separate sense of self founded on acute awareness of being a different gender than the mother; this motivates boys to deny female attachment and to devalue girls and women. By bonding with other boys and derogating girls, boys mark separation and seek to consolidate their somewhat shaky gender identities.

Reviewing explanations of gender separation among children, Miriam Johnson puts together the Maccoby and Jacklin emphasis on girls avoiding male dominance, with the psychoanalytic focus on boys shoring up a sense of masculinity by distancing themselves from things feminine, including girls. Johnson concludes that "childhood gender segregation may help to minimize gender insecurities for boys and allows girls to grow and develop outside the confines of male dominance."[21]

This is a thought-provoking synthesis, although it leaps across epistemological gaps, since the evidence acceptable to experimentalists like Maccoby and Jacklin differs from the clinical evidence favored in psychoanalytic arenas. Furthermore, both lines of theorizing may already assume what they set out to explain: the presence and persistence of male dominance and of separation between boys and girls. Nor can these theories explain why girls and boys would ever voluntarily choose to be together, which they clearly sometimes do. Whetted on difference, the theories are not fully satisfactory unless they can also account for patterns of no difference; the occasions when girls and boys are together are as much a component of gender relations as the occasions when girls and boys are apart.

GENDER CLASSIFICATION

The cognitive awareness of being a girl or a boy is clearly a prerequisite for creating separate girls' and boys' groups. Two interrelated dimensions of gender—the culturally constructed dichotomous gender categories (male/female, girl/boy, man/woman) and core gender identity, or the deep sense of self as either male or female—are the only gender differences that are fully binary. All biological phenomena—including chromosomes, hormones, reproductive physiology, and secondary sex differences like facial hair and breasts—come in a complex range rather than in tidy, isomorphic polarities. Nor, as this book should make amply clear, do organizational and symbolic gender sort into neat dichotomies.

A number of scholars have argued that the sheer knowledge that one is a girl or a boy, an awareness that consolidates around age two, and the child's growing ability to use and apply gender categories in relation to others may set processes of gender separation into motion.[22] Differences of age and of gender are concrete and visible and socially marked from a young age. Each girl comes to realize that she shares a category with others labeled "girl," and each boy realizes he shares a category with others labeled "boy." That awareness, these theorists suggest, in itself may lead girls to want to be with girls, and boys with boys. Being with those of "one's own kind," and avoiding those of "the other kind," confirms "girlness" or "boyness" and fills a need for self-discovery.[23] In short, when boys associate with boys, and girls with girls, they have found a powerful way of "doing gender," of announcing and sustaining separate gender identities.[24] Once same-gender groups are formed, other processes come into play, such as the dynamics of group loyalty, stereotyping of the other group, and the teasing of individuals who try to violate patterns of separation. (One wonders how this theory can account for the motivations of children when they willingly, even eagerly associate with those of the other gender.)

Combining psychoanalytic and cognitive assumptions, Talcott Parsons briefly sought to account for the sex segregation of "latency period peer groups." Parsons took from Freud an assumption that middle childhood is a period of "latency" between the more overtly sexual periods of early childhood and of adolescence. The channeling of interest and attachment to those of about the same age and of the same gender has a dual significance, Parsons argued. "On the one hand, it reinforces the individual's self-categorization by sex by creating a solidarity transcending the family between persons of the same sex. On the other hand, for the first time the individual becomes a member of a group which both transcends the family and in which he [sic] is not in the strongly institutionalized position of being a member of the *inferior* generation class. It is the first major step toward defining himself [sic] as clearly *independent* of the authority and help of the parental generation."[25] Adolescents, Parsons theorized, engage in an erotically loaded shift away from their same-gender peers and toward individuals of the other gender (Parsons assumed heterosexuality).

This line of theorizing has a good deal of merit but is, I believe, too steeped in the status quo. Parsons, and psychologists of child development like Maccoby and Jacklin, assume that any present piece of behavior—in this case, prevalent separation of girls and boys in children's relationships—exists because it is somehow "functional." If this is the case, then how does social change happen? What about contradictions and tensions in existing arrangements? How does one account for children who affiliate across lines of gender? What about the fact that gender separation is far from absolute, that sometimes girls and boys *do* choose to interact with one another?

## "How" May Be a Better Question Than "Why"

After forays into the terrain of ultimate explanation, I return feeling only partially satisfied. These responses to "why" seem too much on the trail of the ultimate, positing *one key to* or *the basic cause of* complex phenomena. Even when the accounts are combined, as both Johnson and Parsons try to do, they center on individual motivations and neglect the importance of social context, collective dynamics, and shared practices. Present social circumstances are often more telling than individual motives that are assumed to precede and to cause them. As I have repeatedly noted, each of these frameworks has been evoked to explain why girls and boys choose to be apart; none can account for the occasions when girls and boys choose to be together. *These frameworks cannot grasp the fluctuating significance of gender in the ongoing scenes of social life.*

To understand the choreography of gender separation and integration among children (and among adults), we need to understand the dynamics of different social institutions and situations, a core theme of this book. Explorations of *how* gender separation and integration take place, of ongoing process rather than presumed origins, can go a long way toward satisfying persistent curiosity about *why* gender separation exists.[26] The next chapter further pursues "how" questions by examining the processes by which girls and boys mark and undermine group boundaries. It turns from the organization of gender, the emphasis thus far, to pay closer attention to symbols and meanings.

# Creating a Sense of "Opposite Sides"

*It's like girls and boys are on different sides.*
                                    —Heather, age eleven, discussing
                                        her experiences at school

When I first began to wander the Oceanside School playground, with gender on my mind, I came upon a noisy group at the edge of a grassy playing field. A tall, brown-haired girl leaned toward two shorter boys and yelled, "You creeps! You creeps!" Then she laughingly pretended to hide behind a much shorter girl at her side. As one of the boys moved toward them, he asked, "What did you call me?" "Creep!" the tall girl, Lenore, repeated emphatically as she turned and slowly began to run. The boy, Ronnie, loped after her for about fifteen feet and grabbed her ponytail, while she shrieked. Lenore then spun around, shook loose, and reversed the direction of the chase, setting out after Ronnie. In the meantime, Sherry chased after Brad with her arms extended. As they ran, Brad called, "Help, a girl's chasin' me!" When Sherry approached him, she swung her right leg into the air and made an exaggerated karate kick. Then they reversed directions, and Brad started running after Sherry.

I could tell from the laughter and stylized motions that this was a form of play, and I immediately recognized the genre from my own childhood schoolyard days: boys-chase-the-girls/girls-chase-the-boys. This kind of encounter, when "the girls" and "the boys" become defined as separate and opposing groups, drew me like a magnet; it seemed like the core of their gender relations. I gradually came to see that the occasions when boys and girls interact in relaxed and non-gender-marked ways are *also* significant, although, and this bears thought, it is more difficult to analyze and write about the relaxed situations within the rubric of "gender." Gender is often equated solely with dichotomous difference, but, as Chapters 3 and 4 have emphasized, gender waxes and wanes in the organization and symbolism of group life, and that flux needs close attention.

Tracing the circumstances in which girls and boys separate or mix, Chapters 3 and 4 emphasized *social organization*. This chapter, which attends more closely to *meaning*, examines boys' and girls' experiences of varied situations of "together" and "apart." It explores the ways in which boys and girls interact to create, and at other points to dismantle, group gender boundaries, or a sense of "the boys" and "the girls" as separate and opposing sides. It also probes the magnetism of gender-marked events for observers, for participants, and in the realms of memory.

## Borderwork

Walking across a school playground from the paved areas where kids play jump rope and hopscotch to the grassy playing field and games of soccer and baseball, one moves from groups of girls to groups of boys. The spatial separation of boys and girls constitutes a kind of boundary, perhaps felt most strongly by individuals who want to join an activity controlled by the other gender. When girls and boys are together in a relaxed and integrated way, playing a game of handball or eating and talking together at a table in the lunchroom, the sense of gender as boundary often dissolves. But sometimes girls and boys come together in ways that emphasize their opposition; boundaries may be created through contact as well as avoidance.

The term "borderwork" helps conceptualize interaction across—yet interaction based on and even strengthening—gender boundaries. This notion comes from Fredrik Barth's analysis of social relations that are maintained across ethnic boundaries (e.g., between the Saami, or Lapps, and Norwegians) without diminishing the participants' sense of cultural difference and of dichotomized ethnic status.[1] Barth focuses on more macro, ecological arrangements, whereas I emphasize face-to-face behavior. But the insight is similar: *although contact sometimes undermines and reduces an active sense of difference, groups may also interact with one another in ways that strengthen their borders.* One can gain insight into the maintenance of ethnic (and gender) groups by examining the boundary that defines them rather than by looking at what Barth calls "the cultural stuff that it encloses."[2]

When gender boundaries are activated, the loose aggregation "boys and girls" consolidates into "the boys" and "the girls" as separate and reified groups. In the process, categories of identity that on other occasions have minimal relevance for interaction become the basis of separate collectivities. Other social definitions get squeezed out by heightened awareness of gender as a dichotomy and of "the girls" and "the boys" as opposite and even antagonistic sides. Several times I watched this process of transformation, which felt like a heating up of the encounter because of the heightened sense of opposition and conflict.

On a paved area of the Oceanside playground a game of team handball took shape (team handball resembles doubles tennis, with clenched fists used to serve and return a rubber ball). Kevin arrived with the ball, and, seeing potential action, Tony walked over with interest on his face. Rita and Neera already stood on the other side of the yellow painted line that designated the center of a playing court. Neera called out, "Okay, me and Rita against you two," as Kevin and Tony moved into position. The game began in earnest with serves and returns punctuated by game-related talk—challenges between the opposing teams ("You're out!" "No, exactly on the line") and supportive comments between team members ("Sorry, Kevin," Tony said, when he missed a shot; "That's okay," Kevin replied). The game proceeded for about five minutes, and then the ball went out of bounds. Neera ran after it, and Tony ran after her, as if to begin a chase. As he ran, Rita shouted with annoyance, "C'mon, let's play." Tony and Neera returned to their positions, and the game continued.

Then Tony slammed the ball, hard, at Rita's feet. She became angry at the shift from the ongoing, more cooperative mode of play, and she flashed her middle finger at the other team, calling to Sheila to join their side. The game continued in a serious vein until John ran over and joined Kevin and Tony, who cheered; then Bill arrived, and there was more cheering. Kevin called out, "C'mon, Ben," to draw in another passing boy; then Kevin added up the numbers on each side, looked across the yellow line, and triumphantly announced, "We got five and you got three." The game continued, more noisy than before, with the boys yelling "wee haw" each time they made a shot. The girls—and that's how they now seemed, since the sides were increasingly defined in terms of gender—called out "Bratty boys! Sissy boys!" When the ball flew out of bounds, the game dissolved, as Tony and Kevin began to chase after Sheila. Annoyed by all these changes, Rita had already stomped off.

In this sequence, an earnest game, with no commentary on the fact that boys and girls happened to be on different sides, gradually transformed into a charged sense of girls-against-the-boys/boys-against-the-girls. Initially, one definition of the situation prevailed: a game of team handball, with each side trying to best the other. Rita, who wanted to play a serious game, objected to the first hint of other possibilities, which emerged when Tony chased Neera. The frame of a team handball game continued but was altered and eventually overwhelmed when the kids began to evoke gender boundaries. These boundaries brought in other possibilities—piling on players to outnumber the other gender, yelling gender-based insults, shifting from handball to cross-gender chasing—which finally broke up the game.

Gender boundaries have a shifting presence, but when evoked, they are accompanied by stylized forms of action, a sense of performance, mixed and ambiguous meanings (the situations often teeter between play and aggression, and heterosexual meanings lurk within other definitions), and by an array of intense emotions—excitement, playful elation, anger, desire, shame, and fear. I will elaborate these themes in the context of several different kinds of borderwork: contests; cross-gender rituals of chasing and pollution; and invasions. These stylized moments evoke recurring themes that are deeply rooted in our cultural conceptions of gender, and they suppress awareness of patterns that contradict and qualify them.

CONTESTS

Girls and boys are sometimes pitted against each other in classroom competitions and playground games. Since gender is a relatively unambiguous and visible category of individual identity that divides the population roughly in half, it is a convenient basis for sorting out two teams. When girls and boys are on separate teams, gender may go unremarked as a grounds of opposition, as in the beginning of the team handball game; but more often gender, marked by talk and other actions, becomes central to the symbolism of the encounter. In the Oceanside fourth-fifth–grade classroom, where regular seating was almost totally divided by gender, the students talked about a boys' side and a girls' side. Drawing on and reinforcing the kids' self-separation, Miss Bailey sometimes organized the girls and the boys into opposing teams for spelling and math competitions.

Early in October, Miss Bailey introduced a math game. She would write addition and subtraction problems on the board, and a member of each team would race to be the first to write the correct answer. She designated the teams with two score-keeping columns on the blackboard: "Beastly Boys" . . . "Gossipy Girls." Several boys yelled, "Noisy girls! Gruesome girls!" and some of the girls laughed in response. Shaping themselves into a team, the girls sat in a row on top of their desks; sometimes they moved their hips and shoulders from side to side in a shared rhythm and whispered "pass it on." The boys stood along the wall, with several reclining against their desks. When members of either group came back victorious from the front of the room, they passed by their team members and did a "giving five" handslap ritual with each in turn.

By organizing boys and girls into separate teams and by giving them names with (humorously) derogatory gender meanings, Miss Bailey set up a situation that invited gender antagonism. Disparaging the other team/gender and elevating one's own became a running joke. A few weeks later, when the teacher once again initiated the math game, Tracy ran to the board, grabbed the chalk, and wrote two column heads: "Boys" . . . "Great Girls." Then Bill ran up, erased the "Great," and substituted "Horrible."

When teachers organize gender-divided classroom contests, students pick up on and elaborate the oppositional and antagonistic meanings. When free to set up their own activities, kids also sometimes organize girls-against-the-boys games, especially of kickball. Compared with games where each side has a mix of girls and boys, these gender-divided games are highly unstable, which may, of course, be the intention and much of the fun. As in the team handball example, the participants usually end up tugging the thread of gender and sexual meanings and thereby unraveling the ongoing game.

For example, on the fifth-sixth–grade side of the Ashton playground, I came upon a kickball game with all boys in the field and all girls up to kick; about a fourth of the players on each side were Black and the rest were white, but the emphasis on gender seemed to submerge potential racial themes. As the game proceeded, it was punctuated by episodes of cross-gender chasing. When one of these episodes involved a boy chasing a girl who had the rubber ball, the game changed into an extended version of "keepaway," with girls and boys on opposite sides, and a lot of chasing, pushing, screaming, and grabbing.

CHASING

Cross-gender chasing dramatically affirms boundaries between boys and girls. The basic elements of chase and elude, capture and rescue are found in various kinds of tag with formal rules, as well as in more casual episodes of chasing that punctuate life on playgrounds.[3] These episodes begin with a provocation, such as taunts ("You creep!"; "You can't get me!"), bodily pokes, or the grabbing of a hat or other possession. A provocation may be ignored, protested ("Leave me alone!"), or responded to by chasing. Chaser and chased may then alternate roles. Christine Finnan, who also observed schoolyard chasing sequences, notes that chases vary in the ratio of chasers to chased (e.g., one chasing one, or five chasing two), the form of provocation (a taunt or a poke); the outcome (an episode may end when the chased outdistances the chaser, with a brief touch, wrestling to the ground, or the recapturing of a hat or a ball); and in use of space (there may or may not be safety zones).[4] Kids sometimes weave chasing with elaborate shared fantasies, as when a group of Ashton first- and second-grade boys played "jail," with "cops" chasing after "robbers," or when several third-grade girls designated a "kissing dungeon" beneath the playground slide and chased after boys to try to throw them in. When they captured a boy and put him in the dungeon under the slide, two girls would guard him while other boys pushed through the guards to help the captured boy escape.

Chasing has a gendered structure. Boys frequently chase one another, an activity that often ends in wrestling and mock fights. When girls chase girls, they are usually less physically aggressive; for example, they less often wrestle one another to the ground or try to bodily overpower the person being chased. Unless organized as a formal game like "freeze tag," same-gender chasing goes unnamed and usually undiscussed. But children set apart cross-gender chasing with special names. Students at both Oceanside and Ashton most often talked about "girls-chase-the-boys" and "boys-chase-the-girls"; the names are largely interchangeable, although boys tend to use the former and girls the latter, each claiming a kind of innocence. At Oceanside I also heard both boys and girls refer to "catch-and-kiss," and at Ashton, older boys talked about "kiss-or-kill," younger girls invited one another to "catch boys," and younger girls and boys described the game of "kissin'." In addition to these terms, I have heard reports from other U.S. schools of "the chase," "chasers," "chase-and-kiss," "kiss-chase," and "kissers-and-chasers." The names vary by region and school but always contain both gender and sexual meanings.[5]

Most informal within-gender chasing does not live on in talk unless something unusual happens, like an injury. But cross-gender chasing, especially when it takes the form of extended sequences with more than a few participants, is often surrounded by lively discussion. Several parents have told me about their kindergarten or first-grade children coming home from school to excitedly, or sometimes disgustedly, describe "girls-chase-the-boys" (my children also did this when they entered elementary school). Verbal retellings and assessments take place not only at home but also on the playground. For example, three Ashton fourth-grade girls, who claimed time-out from boys-chase-the-girls by running to a declared safety zone, excitedly talked about the ongoing game: "That guy is mean, he hits everybody"; "I kicked him in the butt."

In girls-chase-the-boys, girls and boys become, by definition, separate teams. Gender terms blatantly override individual identities, especially in references to the other team ("Help, a girl's chasin' me!"; "C'mon Sarah, let's get that boy"; "Tony, help save me from the girls"). Individuals may call for help from, or offer help to, others of their gender. And in acts of treason, they may grab someone from their team and turn them over to the other side. For example, in an elaborate chasing scene among a group of Ashton third-graders, Ryan grabbed Billy from behind, wrestling him to the ground. "Hey girls, get 'im," Ryan called.

Boys more often mix episodes of cross-gender with same-gender chasing, a pattern strikingly evident in the large chasing scenes or melees that recurred on the segment of the Ashton playground designated for third- and fourth-graders. Of the three age-divided playground areas, this was the most bereft of fixed equipment; it had only a handball court and, as a boy angrily observed to me, "two stinkin' monkey bars." Movable play equipment was also in scarce supply; the balls were often lodged on the school roof, and for a time the playground aides refused to hand out jump ropes because they said the kids just wanted to use them to "strangle and give ropeburns." With little to do, many of the students spent recesses and the lunch hour milling and chasing around on the grassy field. Boys ran after, tackled, and wrestled one another on the ground, sometimes so fiercely that injuries occurred. Girls also chased girls, although less frequently and with far less bodily engagement than among boys. Cross-gender chases, in every sort of numeric combination, were also less physically rough than chasing among boys; girls were quick to complain, and the adult aides intervened more quickly when a boy and a girl wrestled on the ground. Cross-gender chasing was full of verbal hostility, from both sides, and it was marked by stalking postures and girls' screams and retreats to spots of safety and talk.

In cross-gender and same-gender chasing, girls often create safety zones, a designated space that they can enter to become exempt from the fray. After a period of respite, often spent discussing what has just happened, they return to the game. The safety zone is sometimes a moving area around an adult; more than once, as I stood watching, my bubble of personal space housed several girls. Or the zone may be more fixed, like the pretend steel house that the first- and second-grade Ashton girls designated next to the school building. In the Oceanside layout the door to the girls' restroom faced one end of the playground, and girls often ran into it for safety. I could hear squeals from within as boys tried to open the door and peek in. During one of these scenarios eight girls emerged from the restroom with dripping clumps of wet paper towels, which they threw at the three boys who had been peeking in, and then another burst of chasing ensued.

***Variations by Age.*** Although the basic patterns of cross-gender chasing are remarkably persistent across all age levels, I noticed some variations by age. Several times I saw younger children go through a process of induction, as in the early fall at Ashton when a second-grade boy taught a kindergarten girl how to chase. He slowly ran backward, beckoning her to pursue him, as he called, "Help, a girl's after me." She picked up the loping movement and paced herself behind him, as he looked back to make sure she was following. Then he slowly veered around and said, "Now I'll chase you."

Chasing often mixes with fantasy scenarios in the play of younger kids. An Ashton first-grade boy who said he was a "sea monster" made growling noises and curled his fingers like claws at the end of his outstretched arms as he stalked groups of girls. "There's a sea monster, c'mon, we gotta save our other friend, you know, Denise," Bonnie said to the three other girls beside her on the sidewalk. They ran from "the sea monster" to grab Denise's hand and then move into the safety of their "steel house." By the fourth and fifth grades, chasers have perfected the exaggerated movements and sounds—stalking, screams, karate kicks—that accompany scenes of chasing among older girls and boys, and that help frame them as play.

Sexual meanings, highlighted by names like "chase-and-kiss" and "kissers-and-chasers," infuse cross-gender chasing at every age. The threat of kissing, most often girls threatening to kiss boys, is a ritualized form of provocation, especially among younger kids. When Shana, a third-grader, brought a tube of lipstick from home, she and her friends embellished games of kissin' by painting their lips dark red and threatening to smear the boys with kisses. This caused an uproar on the playground, and both boys and girls animatedly talked about it afterward. "The kiss gives you cooties," a boy explained to me.

I only once saw kisses used as a weapon in within-gender relations, when Justin, a second-grade boy, puckered his lips and told another boy that he would kiss him if he didn't leave him alone; the threat worked, and the other boy left. I never saw a girl use a kiss to threaten another girl, although young girls sometimes kissed one another with affection.

At both schools overt threats of kissing were more prevalent among younger kids, but they sometimes appeared in the play of fourth-, fifth-, and sixth-graders. At Oceanside I watched Lisa and Jill pull along Jonathan, a fourth-grade boy, by his hands, while a group of girls sitting on the jungle gym called out, "Kiss him, kiss him." Grabbing at his hair, Lisa said to Jill, "Wanna kiss Jonathan?" Jonathan wrenched himself away, and the girls chased after him. "Jill's gonna kiss your hair," Lisa yelled.

Sexual meanings may extend beyond kisses to other parts of the body. Margaret Blume, who observed on the Oceanside playground several years after I did, recorded a variant of chasing that the third- and fourth-graders called "scoring high with the girls."[6] When Margaret talked with a group who had been playing the game, a girl named Becky exclaimed, "They're trying to pinch our butts!" "Do you pinch them back?" Margaret asked. "No, I scratch; I hit them." A boy bragged, "I got fifty [pinches] now." "I guess we're popular," Becky said to Lois, as they both giggled.

Among fifth- and sixth-graders, cross-gender chasing involves more elaborate patterns of touch and touch avoidance than among younger kids. As I watched the stylized motions of grabbing at girls in ways that avoided their fronts, it seemed to me that older chasers often took account of girls' "developing" (or soon-to-be-developing) bodies, especially the growing visibility of their breasts. Principals, teachers, and aides generally ignored cross-gender chasing among younger kids, unless it got physically rough. Sometimes adults found it amusing, as when a first-grade teacher came up to me on the playground and, teasing the little girls who were standing next to her, told me, "Write down that first-grade girls kiss the boys." But if a fourth-, fifth-, or sixth-grade girl and boy ended a chase by wrestling on the ground (an infrequent occurrence; that sort of physical pummeling between boys and girls diminished with age), playground aides were quick to intervene, even when it was clear the tussle was being enacted in a mode of play. The Ashton principal told the sixth graders that they were not to play "pom-pom tackle," a complicated chasing game, because it entailed "inappropriate touch" between boys and girls.

*Troupes.* At every age some kids gravitate to boys-chase-the-girls, while others, both girls and boys, avoid it. Individuals may gain a reputation for their interest in cross-gender chasing, like a second-grade girl who was teased for being a "kisser." But younger boys and girls mix bursts of chasing with other activities, rather than making it the focus of all their playground time. This continues to be true for older boys; for example, Bill, a fifth-grader whom an Oceanside aide said was "crush-prone," often played chasing games with girls, but he engaged in other playground activities as well. In both schools, however, a handful of fifth- and sixth-grade girls organized themselves into troupes who roamed the playground in search of "action"—primarily chasing—with boys. (Once the word "troupe" occurred to me, it stuck because it so aptly grasps the imagery of the wandering and performing female groups.)

At the center of a troupe are usually one or more "well-developed" (in both schools, the favored adult word for big-breasted and tall) girls, such as Lenore, who led the Oceanside chase scene described at the beginning of this chapter. The other girls (troupe numbers range from two to six), who may or may not be "developed," follow the lead of those at the center. Other groups of girls who stick together on the playground, like the ones I came to think of as "the jump rope girls," engage mostly with one another and the activity at hand. In contrast, the members of a wandering troupe spend their time in an open-ended search for ritual contact with boys. Troupes cover a lot of territory; they stride across the playground, looking around, wearing their breasts like badges, and drawing boys into bouts of chasing.

In both schools there were interracial troupes of girls. For example, two white girls and three Black girls, all of them fifth- and sixth-graders, constituted the largest and most visible troupe on the Ashton playground. One of the white girls and two of the Black girls were tall and had breasts and full hips. The other two girls were shorter and flat-chested. They walked along together, sometimes five in a row, sometimes snapping their fingers in shared rhythms or doing dance steps. Their stylized motions evoked the culture of African-American dance and movement, which, of course, is a major influence on U.S. teen culture.

One day, when this troupe came near three white boys, one of the Black girls leaned over and said tauntingly, "It's not nice to talk about Mother Nature." The boys ran, and she chased them for a short distance and then returned to the striding troupe. Then one of the white girls stuck out her foot, threatening to trip two white boys who stood at the fringes. She broke into a run, as one of the boys chased after her. Another white girl said, "I won't let him touch you," and ran after him. He grabbed at her hands; she kicked her leg out, got him down, and sat on him. He pushed her off and walked away, while the rest of the girls stood watching and laughing. The girls reconstituted their row and walked along until they came to the grassy field where a small group of fifth- and sixth-grade boys were playing football. One of the girls ran over, caught the football, and tossed it to another member of the troupe. The boys, who were much shorter than the three tallest girls, rushed to get the ball, but the girls kept it away from them. In a gesture unusual for boys this age, they went to complain to an aide, "Us boys can't play football without the girls gettin' in"; "The girls are gettin' in the way." The aide told the girls to leave the boys alone.

These girls were highly visible because of their size and mobility, their coordinated movements and display, and their unusual actions. Only twice did I see a group of girls—both times this troupe—deliberately disrupt the ongoing play of boys; it is usually boys who invade the activities of girls. This group claimed space and asserted themselves with a style that mixed sexuality with claims to power. Some other playground participants seemed to regard this group with ambivalence. A sixth-grade girl pointed to the group and said to me, with an edge of resentment, "They're so proud, they think they're so smart; they go marching around."

## "COOTIES" AND OTHER POLLUTION RITUALS

Episodes of chasing sometimes entwine with rituals of pollution, as in "cooties" or "cootie tag" where specific individuals or groups are treated as contaminating or carrying "germs." Cooties, of course, are invisible; they make their initial appearance through announcements like "Rochelle has cooties!"[7] Kids have rituals for transferring cooties (usually touching someone else, often after a chase, and shouting

"You've got cooties!"), for immunization (writing "CV"—for "cootie vaccination"—on their arms, or shaping their fingers to push out a pretend immunizing "cootie spray"), and for eliminating cooties (saying "no gives" or using "cootie catchers" made of folded paper).[8] While girls and boys may transfer cooties to one another, and girls may give cooties to girls, boys do not generally give cooties to other boys.[9] Girls, in short, are central to the game.

Either girls or boys may be defined as having cooties, but girls give cooties to boys more often than vice versa. In Michigan, one version of cooties was called "girl stain"; the fourth-graders in a school on the East Coast used the phrase "girl touch."[10] And in a further shift from acts to imputing the moral character of actors, individuals may be designated as "cootie queens" or "cootie girls."[11] Cootie queens or cootie girls (I have never heard or read about "cootie kings" or "cootie boys") are female pariahs, the ultimate school untouchables, seen as contaminating not only by virtue of gender, but also through some added stigma such as being overweight or poor.[12] And according to one report, in a racially mixed playground in Fresno, California, "Mexican" (Chicano/Latino) but not Anglo children gave cooties; thus inequalities of race, as well as of gender and social class, may be expressed through pollution games.[13] In situations like this, different sources of oppression may compound one another.

I did not learn of any cootie queens at Ashton or Oceanside, but in the daily life of schools *individual* boys and girls may be stigmatized and treated as contaminating. For example, a third-grade Ashton girl refused to sit by a particular boy, whom other boys routinely pushed away from the thick of all-male seating, because he was "stinky" and "peed in his bed." A teacher in another school told me that her fifth-grade students said to newcomers, "Don't touch Phillip's desk; he picks his nose and makes booger balls." Phillip had problems with motor coordination, which, the teacher thought, contributed to his marginalization.

But there is also a notable gender asymmetry, evident in the skewed patterning of cooties; *girls as a group are treated as an ultimate source of contamination*, while boys *as* boys—although maybe not, as Chicanos or individuals with a physical disability—are exempt. Boys sometimes mark hierarchies among themselves by using "girl" as a label for low-status boys and by pushing subordinated boys next to the contaminating space of girls. In Miss Bailey's fourth-fifth–grade class other boys routinely forced or maneuvered the lowest-status boys (Miguel and Alejandro, the recent immigrants from Mexico, and Joel, who was overweight and afraid of sports) into sitting "by the girls," a space treated as contaminating. In this context, boys drew on gender meanings to convey racial subordination. In contrast, when there was gender-divided seating in the classroom, lunchroom, music room, or auditorium, which girls sat at the boundary between groups of girls and groups of boys had no apparent relationship to social status.

Boys sometimes treat objects associated with girls as polluting; once again, the reverse does not occur. Bradley, a college student, told me about a classroom incident he remembered from third grade. Some girls gave Valentine's Day cards with pictures of Strawberry Shortcake, a feminine-stereotyped image, to everyone in the class, including boys. Erik dumped all his Strawberry Shortcake valentines into Bradley's box; Bradley one-upped the insult by adding his own Strawberry Shortcake valentines to the pile and sneaking them back into Erik's box.

Recoiling from physical proximity with another person and their belongings because they are perceived as contaminating is a powerful statement of social distance and claimed superiority. Pollution beliefs and practices draw on the emotion-laden feeling of repugnance that accompanies unwanted touch or smell. Kids often act out pollution beliefs in a spirit of playful teasing, but the whimsical frame of "play" slides in and out of the serious, and some games of cooties clearly cause emotional pain. When pollution rituals appear, even in play, they frequently express and enact larger patterns of inequality, by gender, by social class and race, and by bodily characteristics like weight and motor coordination. When several of these characteristics are found in the same person, the result may be extreme rituals of shaming, as in the case of cootie queens. Aware of the cruelty and pain bound up in games of pollution, teachers and aides often try to intervene, especially when a given individual becomes the repeated target.

What is the significance of "girl stain," of the fact that girls, but not boys, become cast as an ultimate polluting group? Beliefs in female pollution, usually related to menstruation and reproductive sexuality, can be found in many cultures but not, at least from the reports I've been able to find, among prepubertal children. Cooties, which is primarily played by first-, second-, and third-graders (or kids ages six to nine), is therefore unusual. These pollution rituals suggest that in contemporary U.S. culture even young girls are treated as symbolically contaminating in a way that boys, as a group, are not. This may be because in our culture even at a young age, girls are sexualized more than boys, and female sexuality, especially when "out of place" or actively associated with children, connotes danger and endangerment. Furthermore, even before birth girls are, on the whole, less valued than boys; it is still the case, for example, that prospective parents more often wish for a son than a daughter. Pollution rituals connect with themes of separation and power, to which I will return later in the chapter.

INVASIONS

In contests and in chasing, groups of girls and groups of boys confront one another as separate "sides," which makes for a kind of symmetry as does the alternation of chasing and being chased. But rituals of pollution tip the symmetry, defining girls as more contaminating. Invasions, a final type of borderwork, also take asymmetric form; boys invade girls' groups and activities much more often than the reverse. When asked about what they do on the playground, boys list "teasing the girls" as a named activity, but girls do not talk so routinely about "teasing boys."[14] As in other kinds of borderwork, gendered language ("Let's spy on the girls"; "Those boys are messing up our jump rope game") accompanies invasions, as do stylized interactions that highlight a sense of gender as an antagonistic social division.

On the playgrounds of both schools I repeatedly saw boys, individually or in groups, deliberately disrupt the activities of groups of girls. Boys ruin ongoing games of jump rope by dashing under the twirling rope and disrupting the flow of the jumpers or by sticking a foot into the rope and stopping its momentum. On the Ashton playground seven fourth-grade girls engaged in an intense game of foursquare; it was a warm October day, and the girls had piled their coats on the cement next to the painted court. Two boys, mischief enlivening their faces, came to the edge of the court. One swung his arm into the game's bouncing space; in annoyed response, one of the female players pushed back at him. He ran off for a few feet, while the other boy circled in to take a swipe, trying to knock the ball out of play. Meanwhile, the first boy kneeled behind the pile of coats and leaned around to watch the girls. One of the girls yelled angrily, "Get out. My glasses are in one of those, and I don't want 'em busted." A playground aide called the boys over and told them to "leave the girls alone," and the boys ran off.

Some boys more or less specialize in invading girls, coming back again and again to disrupt; the majority of boys are not drawn to the activity.[15] Even if only a few boys do most of the invading, disruptions are so frequent that girls develop ritualized responses. Girls verbally protest ("Leave us alone!"; "Stop it, Keith!"), and they chase boys away. The disruption of a girls' game may provoke a cross-gender chasing sequence, but if girls are annoyed, they chase in order to drive the boy out of their space, a purpose far removed from playful shifting between the roles of chaser and chased. Girls may guard their play with informal lookouts who try to head off trouble; they are often wary about letting boys into their activities. And they sometimes complain to playground aides.

COMPLAINING TO ADULTS

There is an empirical as well as stereotypical association of younger kids, and of girls of all ages, with complaining to adults about the behavior of other kids.[16] The word "tattling" is often used for this behavior, which conveys the telling of tales, of secrets, and thus the betrayal of one's kind. The negative connotation builds in a judgment I want to query. Sometimes the less powerful, or those not trained to be physically aggressive, have little recourse except to complain to adults.[17]

As Mrs. Smith's kindergarten students entered the culture of schooling, they continually assessed the reach of adult authority, including whether and when to "tell" on one another. Boys and girls peppered their daily talk with threats like "I'm gonna' tell the teacher" and "I'm tellin'." Mrs. Smith tried to set limits by simply ignoring the requests for intervention and by repeatedly telling the students that she wanted "none of that tattling stuff." The amount diminished over time, but "tattling" continued even when the teacher refused to intervene.

Students develop codes about when it is appropriate to complain to an adult about the misconduct of peers, with boys placing and accepting firmer limitations than girls.[18] The boys' code is illustrated by a brewing conflict on the Ashton playground. A third-grade boy wearing a dark-green shirt angrily leaned toward a girl who was holding the arm of a boy in a blue jacket and said, "He hit me in the gut; he's dead." The girl let go of the second boy's arm and said, "He's yours." The boy in the green shirt continued, "I already beat his butt," as he and the other boy, both with hostile facial expressions, squared off to fight. As they pushed toward each other, a much taller boy came up behind and said calmly, "Break it up." The two pushed some more as the tall boy inserted himself between them. The boy in the blue jacket stomped away, calling over his shoulder, "I'm tellin'." "Only tattletales tell," the boy in the green shirt taunted after him. The boy who had threatened to tattle continued to walk off the playing field but didn't approach an adult.

Girls also chastize one another for being tattletales, but they do so far less often than boys. And when boys invade their play, girls are quick to complain to the playground aides, who sometimes intervene, especially when physical harm (like breaking a pair of glasses) or active sexuality (such as an older girl and boy wrestling on the ground) seem to be at stake. Sometimes, however, the aides ignore or challenge girls' complaints. A third-grade girl came up to a playground aide and complained, "Robert's hurtin' me." The aide dismissed the charge, saying, "You've been chasing him; go on."

Aides recognize that boys invade girls' ongoing play much more than the reverse, and they frequently witness these scenes since most of the girls' games (jump rope, foursquare) take place in the cement area by the building, where the aides usually stand. (This vantage point, as well as the fact that they are all women, may lead aides to see the playground world more from the vantage point of girls than of boys.) Anticipating trouble, Ashton aides often shooed away boys from areas where girls were playing, even when the boys hadn't done anything to provoke. This strategy may have warded off immediate conflicts, but it enhanced gender separation on the playground.

Aides do not anticipate trouble from girls who seek to join groups of boys, with the exception of girls intent on provoking a chase sequence. Indeed, if they seek access to a boys' game, girls usually play with boys in earnest rather than breaking up the game. The scenario of girls complaining and of aides then intervening may limit boys' aggression, but it also supports boys' views of girls as weaker and as tattletales.[19] Girls have less access than boys to physical aggression, which gives some of them little recourse except to turn to adults. But power derived from adults does not transfer to settings where those adults are not present or will not intervene.


## Is Borderwork "All in Play"?

I once asked Jeremy, one of the Oceanside fifth-graders, why girls and boys in Miss Bailey's class formed separate lines. "So they won't fight so much," he promptly replied. A variety of terms—"fighting," "teasing," "hassling," "bothering"—have been used to suggest the heightened emotions and the playful and real conflict that characterize borderwork.[20] Are the various incidents I have described really "fighting?" Or are they mostly "play?" When a girl repeatedly yells "You creep!" at a boy, is she insulting him or just fooling around? When a boy and a girl chase each other and wrestle on the ground, are they fighting, or expressing real sexual desire, or is it "all in fun?" Of course it all depends on context, and meanings are often mixed. Ambiguity is a feature of all types of borderwork and contributes to their volatility.

The anthropologist Gregory Bateson once observed that "play" does not name actions but the "frame" for actions.[21] An incident may at first glance look like a fight, but if the participants smile, restrain their physical force, use certain tones of voice, and engage in exaggerated movements, they can cue that it is a "play fight" and therefore not to be taken seriously. The cues, or metacommunication (that is, the communication *about* communication), signal the message "this is play." The "play" frame, like the related frame of "humor," brackets an encounter, setting it apart from ongoing, more "serious" life. Situations of play and humor have a loosened relationship to consequences; if pressed to take responsibility for their actions, participants can say, "we're only playing" or "this is just a joke."[22] The frames of play and humor "lighten up" a situation, moving it toward the more voluntary and spontaneous, and emphasizing process rather than product.[23]

All forms of borderwork partake, to varying degrees, in the frame or mode of "play." Some types of borderwork, like boys against the girls in kickball or in classroom math competitions, are organized as games, a rule-governed type of play. Episodes of chasing and cooties are more informal; participants signal the play frame by using scripted talk ("Help! A girl's chasin' me!"), laughter, stylized movements, and exaggerated kicks in the air. And when they disrupt a game of jump rope, boys often wear playful expressions and bend over with laughter when the jumper gets tangled in the rope.

"Play" is a fragile definition; participants have to continually signal the boundary that distinguishes play from not-play, and play and humor easily slide in and out of other, more "serious" meanings. This ambiguity creates tension, since one is never sure in what direction it will swing; a tease may move from playful to irritating to malicious and back again. Multiple layers of meaning also provide maneuvering room to try out one message with the option of falling back on another, safer meaning; the ambiguity lessens potential risks and leaves room for denial. Aggression and sex are the dangerous desires in school, as elsewhere in the world, and these are the messages that often lurk within the lightened frames of play and humor that surround episodes of borderwork. (As Chapters 6 and 7 elaborate, girls and boys tangle with issues of sexuality and aggression in same-gender as well as cross-gender relations.).

I have already touched on varied kinds of aggression, ranging from verbal insults to outright physical coercion, that thread through incidents of borderwork. When girls and boys confront one another as rival groups, their boundaries defined by gender, the situation invites verbal insults, like those that accompanied the math game in Miss Bailey's class. Sometimes kids voice insults in anger, as when Rita, Neera, and Sheila yelled, "Bratty boys! Sissy boys!" in the heated-up game of team handball. At other times, the rivalry may be more playful and almost ritualized, as when three girls, sitting in one of the waiting lines that crisscrossed the Ashton lunchroom floor, chanted in cheery unison, "Girls are smart, boys are bogue" ("bogue" means "stupid and uncool"). The boys across from them smiled and, quickly fishing for a retort, came up with "Boys are better, girls are dumb."

Kids often carry out episodes of playground chasing in a whimsically scripted way, providing many cues that "this is play." But in both same-gender and cross-gender chasing, provocations that violate bodies, possessions, and selves may not be intended or perceived as very playful, and they may spur an angry pursuit. In the course of my fieldwork one of the few times I heard overtly racist insults was during episodes of cross-gender chasing; "Na, na, colored boy," a white third-grade girl at Ashton School yelled at an African-American boy, who then chased her. At Oceanside Lenore, a fifth-grade white girl, repeatedly yelled "Mexican monkey" as she chased with a Chicano boy. Chasing sequences may contain physical as well as verbal aggression, with the chased being pummeled to the ground, tripped, and sat upon. This kind of "play fighting" sometimes shades into "real fighting," especially among boys, whose chasing tends to be quite physical. In cross-gender chasing, when girls complain to aides that the boys are getting too rough, or on the rarer occasions when boys complain, the frame of play breaks down and the issue of aggression comes to the fore.

In the charges and countercharges that attend some episodes of tattling, one party may define the situation as a serious violation, while the other party insists that they were "just playing." This pattern recurs in the wake of playground invasions; boys, far more often the invaders, often claim a play frame, but girls, more often the targets of invasion, refuse to accept that definition. The asymmetry increases with age; many fourth- and fifth-grade girls see male invasions as a playground nuisance that simply makes them angry. This pattern resembles the structuring of sexual harassment. The harasser, nearly always male, often claims that verbal and physical intrusions into the target's personal space are "all in fun," while the target, usually female, sees it as unwanted and even coercive attention. Hierarchies help determine whose version of reality will prevail.[24]

Kids and adults often use the word "teasing" to describe episodes of chasing and invasion; "teasing" suggests targeted humor, with an angry or aggressive edge. This mix again provides multiple possibilities for action and interpretation. Teasing may express affection and solidarity, but, as Freud persuasively demonstrated, humor may also be a guise for hostility. The ambiguity titillates, and the possibly serious import of humor may be raised for negotiation.[25]

SEXUAL AND ROMANTIC THEMES

The ambiguities of borderwork allow the signaling of sexual or romantic, as well as aggressive, meanings, and the two often mix together. If a girl repeatedly chases a particular boy, or vice versa, it may be taken as a sign of "liking." Participants are fully aware of this potential interpretation, as shown during one vivid incident when a participant suddenly, teasingly named that tune. On the Ashton playground, Ken, a third-grader, growled and stalked after two of his classmates, Sharon and Jenny, who ran to the proclaimed safety of "the cage," as they called the area by the bars. Lisa came over and taunted, "Ken can't get me," and Ken chased her while she screamed. Then Ken circled back to the area of the bars and, his arms outflung, ran after Sharon and Jenny. The pursuit ended when Ken grabbed Jenny, and they ended up face-to-face with his arms around her. Jenny suddenly, teasingly said, "What you huggin' me for?" "I'm not," he replied in a slightly stunned voice, while she flashed a triumphant smile. Ken quickly let go.

Running after someone, pinning their arms from the front or behind, or verbally insulting them may all be intended and/or interpreted as positive signs of attention. A woman college student remembered "antagonizing guys" in fifth grade; "you chased them, yelled at them, and called them shocking names, but you really liked the guy." Invasions may also, ambiguously, convey positive interest, as noted by Susan Allen Toth in her memoirs of growing up in Ames, Iowa, in the 1950s. She describes summers in the community swimming pool when she was on the cusp of puberty:

> Tommy or Bob or Lon glided under water toward us, often in twos or threes, as though they needed support. We girls pretended not to notice them coming until they

spouted to the top, with loud shouts, and pounced on us to dunk us. . . . Being shoved under water was recognized as a sign that a boy had noticed you. He had at least taken the trouble to push you down. We certainly never complained, though I sometimes swallowed water and came up coughing. At other times the boys would ignore us and engage in their own elaborate games, diving for pennies or playing tag. We girls clung to the side, hanging onto the gutters, and watched.[26]

Other researchers have pondered the mix of aggression and liking that infuses boundaries between boys and girls. In her research in a desegregated junior high, Janet Schofield observed a lot of physical "bothering" and "pushing" not only between girls and boys, but also between Blacks and whites. But she argues that these forms of hassling differ in fundamental ways: "Whereas relations with gender outgroups are fundamentally influenced by the knowledge of future positive ties, relations between blacks and whites are fundamentally shaped by the history and present existence of racial separation, hostility and discrimination in our society."[27]

Schofield's argument about the history and structure of race relations, and racism, in the United States is well taken. But this interpretation tends to naturalize gender relations instead of observing that they are *also* shaped by history and by patterns of separation, hostility, and discrimination. Adult cross-gender relations cannot be chalked up simply as "future positive ties"; not everyone is heterosexual, and the "liking" relations of adults, as well as of fifth-graders and junior high students, mix caring and antagonism, pleasure and hostility. These patterns should not be taken for granted; gender relations, like race relations, are always changing, and, as I argue in Chapter 9, they can be deliberately altered.

ISSUES OF POWER

Power is another consequential structure that moves in and out of the leavening frame of "play." Much borderwork is symmetrical—girls and boys both avoid one another, exchange insults, square off as separate sides in games of math or kickball, or alternate roles in games of chasing. But telling asymmetries skew the marking of gender difference toward patterns of male dominance among children as well as, although generally less than, among adults.

Space, an especially valuable resource in the crowded environment of schools, is the locus of one basic asymmetry between girls and boys. On school playgrounds boys control as much as ten times more space than girls, when one adds up the area of large playing fields (plus basketball courts and, at Oceanside, skateball courts) and compares it with the much smaller areas (for jump rope, hopscotch, foursquare, and doing tricks on the bars) where girls predominate.[28] In addition to taking up more space, boys more often see girls and their activities as interruptible; boys invade and disrupt all-female games and scenes of play much more often than vice versa. This pattern, coupled with the much larger turf under boys' control, led Zella Luria, another playground observer, to comment that playgrounds are basically male turf; even girls' smaller enclaves are subject to invasion.[29]

Boys' control of space can be seen as a pattern of claimed entitlement, perhaps linked to patterns well documented among adults in the same culture. For example, there is ample evidence, reviewed and analyzed by Nancy Henley, that adult men take up more personal and public space than adult women. Furthermore, men more often interrupt or violate the space, as well as talk, of women.[30]

Beliefs about female pollution also express and help maintain separation between the genders, and female subordination, in the social relations of U.S. elementary school children as well as in cultures of the Mediterranean and of highland New Guinea.[31] But, as anthropologists have recently argued, pollution beliefs have multiple and even contradictory dimensions.[32] In some contexts women, and girls, may use belief in female contamination to further their own ends and even as a source of power. Male susceptibility to female pollution can be experienced as a source of vulnerability; if a girl is designated as having cooties or threatens to plant a dangerous kiss, it is the boy who has to run.[33] In complex dialectics of power, boys treat girls' spaces, activities, and sheer physical presence as contaminating, but girls sometimes craft their perceived dangerous qualities into a kind of weapon. Several of the third-grade boys who talked about the "lipstick girls who gave cooties" seemed not only excited but also a little fearful. Furthermore, on some occasions girls and boys who *share* other features in the crisscross mix of social identities—who, for example, are Anglos (rather than Chicanos) or who are not cootie queens—unite in treating some "Other" as polluting. In these contexts, "sides" shift, and being a girl or boy becomes less important than *not* being the school pariah or a member of a racially marginalized group. Gender dominance is only one strand of an intricate mesh of power relationships.

The dynamics of power in children's social relationships are extremely complex, and in many ways, in the words of a playground aide, "girls give as well as get." Girls sometimes turn pollution into a weapon; they challenge and derogate boys; they guard their own play and respond angrily to invasions; they stave off provocations by ignoring them; they complain to adults. But in several notable ways, girls act from a one-down position, a pattern both enacted and dramatized in the processes of borderwork.

## Why Is Borderwork So Memorable?

The imagery of "border" may wrongly suggest an unyielding fence that divides social relations into two parts. The image should rather be one of many short fences that are quickly built and as quickly dismantled. Gender boundaries are episodic and ambiguous, and *the notion of "borderwork" should be coupled with a parallel term—such as "neutralization"—for processes through which girls and boys (and adults who enter into their social relations) neutralize or undermine a sense of gender as division and opposition.*[34] The situations (e.g., less crowded in space, with fewer potential witnesses and participants) and practices (e.g., teachers or children organizing encounters along lines other than gender) that draw girls and boys together are a first step. But these "with" situations can go in varied directions: when girls and boys are together, gender may be marked and boundaries evoked, the theme of this chapter, or gender may become muted in salience.

At the beginning of the chapter I described a team handball game in which gender meanings heated up. Heated events also cool down. After the team handball game transmuted into a brief scene of chasing, the recess bell rang and the participants went back to their shared classroom. Ten minutes later the same girls and boys interacted in reading groups where gender was of minimal significance. Gender boundaries may also be dismantled on the playground, as when boys and girls left their mostly gender-divided activities while defending Don against mistreatment by a teacher who was on "yard duty." In that incident, girls and boys found another source of solidarity—being in the same class and chafing under the authority of the adult "yard duty"—and gender divisions receded in importance.

Here I must stress *levels of analysis*. As *individuals*, we are (with a few ambiguous exceptions, such as transsexuals) each assigned to a fixed gender category, and by age three we develop relatively firm individual identities as either girls or boys. Over the course of our lives we continually enact and construct individual gender (being a male, being a female, with multiple styles of masculinity and femininity) through talk, dress, movement, activities.[35] But when the level of analysis shifts from the individual to *groups and situations*, gender becomes more fluid. A boy may always be a "boy," and that fact will enter into all of his experiences. But in some interactions he may be much more aware of that strand of his identity than in others, just as his ethnicity or age may be more relevant in some situations than in others. Multiple identities may also compound one another; sometimes it is highly salient that one is an African-American boy.

The salience of gender may vary from one situation to another, and gender and other social divisions (age, ethnicity, social class) may, depending on the context, "abrade, inflame, amplify, twist, dampen, and complicate each other" (in the phrasing of R. W. Connell and his colleagues).[36] Given these complexities, why are the occasions of gender borderwork so compelling? Why do episodes of girls-chase-the-boys and boys-against-the girls *seem* like the heart of what "gender" is all about? Why do kids regard those situations as especially newsworthy and turn them into stories that they tell afterward and bring home from school? And why do adults, when invited to muse back upon gender relations in their elementary school years, so often spontaneously recall "girls-chase-the-boys," "teasing girls," and "cooties," but less often mention occasions when boys and girls were together in less gender-marked ways? (The latter kinds of occasions may be recalled under other rubrics, like "when we did classroom projects.")

The occasions of borderwork may carry extra perceptual weight because they are marked by conflict, intense emotions, and the expression of forbidden desires. These group activities may also rivet attention because they are created by kids themselves, and because they are ritualized, not as high ceremony, but by virtue of being stylized, repeated, and enacted with a sense of performance.[37] I have described the scripted quality of contests, chasing, invasions, and tattling. This ritual dimension, as Mary Douglas has written, "aides us in selecting experiences for concentrated attention" and "enlivens the memory."[38] Cross-gender chasing has a name ("chase-and-kiss"), a scripted format (the repertoire of provocations and forms of response), and takes shape through stylized motions and talk. The ritual form focuses attention and evokes dominant beliefs about the "nature" of boys and girls and relationships between them.

Erving Goffman coined the term "genderism" to refer to moments in social life, such as borderwork situations, that evoke stereotypic beliefs. During these ritually foregrounded encounters, men and women "play out the differential human nature claimed for them."[39] Many social environments don't lend themselves to this bifurcated and stylized display, and they may even undermine the stereotypes. But when men engage in horseplay (pushing, shoving) and mock contests like Indian wrestling, they dramatize themes of physical strength and violence that are central to hegemonic constructions of masculinity.[40] And in various kinds of cross-gender play, as when a man chases after and pins down a woman, pretends to throw her off a cliff, or threatens her with a snake, the man again claims physical dominance and encourages the woman to "provide a full-voiced rendition [shrinking back, hiding her eyes, screaming] of the plight to which her sex is presumably prone."[41] In short, men and women—and girls and boys—sometimes become caricatures of themselves, enacting and perpetuating stereotypes.

Games of girls-against-the-boys, scenes of cross-gender chasing and invasion, and episodes of heterosexual teasing evoke stereotyped images of gender relations. Deeply rooted in the dominant culture and ideology of our society, these images infuse the ways adults talk about girls and boys and relations between them; the content of movies, television, advertising, and children's books; and even the wisdom of experts, including social scientists. This hegemonic view of gender—acted out, reinforced, and evoked through the various forms of borderwork—has two key components:

*1. Emphasis on gender as an oppositional dualism.* Terms like "the opposite sex" and "the war between the sexes" come readily to mind when one watches a group of boys invade a jump rope game and the girls angrily respond, or a group of girls and a group of boys hurling insults at one another across a lunchroom. In all forms of borderwork boys and girls are defined as rival teams with a socially distant, wary, and even hostile relationship; heterosexual meanings add to the sense of polarization. Hierarchy tilts the theme of opposition, with boys asserting spatial, physical, and evaluative dominance over girls.

*2. Exaggeration of gender difference and disregard for the presence of crosscutting variation and sources of commonality.* Social psychologists have identified a continuum that ranges from what Henri Tajfel calls the "interpersonal extreme," when interaction is largely determined by *individual* characteristics, to the "intergroup extreme," when interaction is largely determined by the *group membership* or social categories of participants.[42] Borderwork lies at the intergroup extreme. When girls and boys are defined as opposite sides caught up in rivalry and competition, group stereotyping and antagonism flourish. Members of "the other side" become "that boy" or "that girl." Individual identities get submerged, and participants hurl gender insults ("sissy boys," "dumb girls"), talk about the other gender as "yuck," and make stereotyped assertions ("girls are crybabies"; "boys are frogs; I don't like boys").

Extensive gender separation and organizing mixed-gender encounters as girls-against-the-boys set off contrastive thinking and feed an assumption of gender as dichotomous and antagonistic difference. These social practices seem to express core truths: that boys and girls are separate and fundamentally different, as individuals and as groups. Other social practices that challenge this portrayal—drawing boys and girls together in relaxed and extended ways, emphasizing individual identities or social categories that cut across gender, acknowledging variation in the activities and interests of girls and boys—carry less perceptual weight. As do efforts by kids and adults to challenge existing gender arrangements (the focus of Chapters 7 and 9). *But the occasions where gender is less relevant, or contested, are also part of the construction of gender relations.*

I want to conclude by raising another interpretive possibility. The frames of "play" and "ritual" set the various forms of borderwork a bit apart from ongoing "ordinary" life. As previously argued, this may enhance the perceptual weight of borderwork situations in the eyes of both participants and observers, highlighting a gender-as-antagonistic-dualism portrayal of social relations. But the framing of ritualized play may also give leeway for participants to gain perspective on dominant cultural images. Play and ritual can comment on and challenge, as well as sustain, a given ordering of reality.[43]

The anthropologist Clifford Geertz interprets the Balinese cockfight, a central ritual and form of gaming in that culture, not as a direct expression of the hierarchy of Balinese social structure but rather as a "metasocial commentary upon the whole matter of assorting human beings into fixed hierarchical ranks and then organizing the major part of collective existence around that assortment." The cockfight has an interpretive function; it is a "Balinese reading of Balinese experience, a story they tell themselves about themselves."[44]

Geertz's interpretation came to my mind when I watched and later heard an aide describe a game the Oceanside students played on the school lunchroom floor. The floor was made up of large alternating squares of white and green linoleum, rather like a checkerboard. One day during the chaotic transition from lunch to noontime recess,

Don (the same boy whose protest against unjust punishment was actively supported by a united group of girls and boys later in the year) jumped, with much gestural and verbal fanfare, from one green square to another. Pointing to a white square, Don loudly announced, "That's girls' territory. Stay on the green square or you'll change into a girl. Yuck!"

It occurred to me that Don was playing with gender dualisms, with a basic structure of two oppositely arranged parts, whose boundaries are charged with risk. From one vantage point the square-jumping game, as a kind of magical playing with borderwork, may express and dramatically reaffirm structures basic to, although far from exhaustive of, the gender relations of the school. In the dichotomous world of either green or white, boy or girl, one misstep could spell transformative disaster. But from another vantage point, Don called up that structure to detached view, playing with, commenting on, and even, perhaps, mocking its assumptions.

# CHAPTER 6

# Do Girls and Boys Have Different Cultures?

*. . . a play of differences that is always on the move, and can neither be reduced to gender differences nor considered apart from them.*

— Edward Snow, "The Play of Sexes
in Bruegel's *Children's Games*"

A familiar story line runs through the literature on gender and the social relations of children. The story opens by emphasizing patterns of mutual avoidance between boys and girls and then asserts that this daily separation results in, and is perpetuated by, deep and dichotomous gender differences. Groups of girls and groups of boys have contrasting ways of bonding and expressing antagonism and conflict; they act upon different values and pursue divergent goals; in many ways they live in separate worlds The story often concludes by drawing lessons for adults.[1] For example, in one popularized version, Deborah Tannen argues that because they grew up in the gender-separated worlds of childhood, adult men and women are locked into patterns of miscommunication, with women repeatedly seeking intimacy, while men are preoccupied with marking status.[2]

Reading the social science literature and sorting through my own observations, I have circled around and around this influential portrayal. The separate-and-different-worlds story is seductive. It gives full weight to the fact that girls and boys often *do* separate in daily interactions, especially when they create more lasting groups and friendships. The marking of boundaries between groups of boys and groups of girls, as analyzed in the previous chapter, further drives the genders apart and creates spaces in which they can build and teach different cultures. And when I, like other observers, have compared the dynamics of groups of girls with those of groups of boys, I have been struck by apparent differences.

Furthermore, boys and girls—the "native informants"—sometimes use different rhetorics to describe their same-gender relationships: boys talk about "buddies," "teams," and "being tough," whereas girls more often use a language of "best friends" and "being nice." And when girls and boys come together, they occasionally comment on experiences of gender difference. When a troupe of Ashton sixth-grade girls grabbed a football from the ongoing play of a group of boys, the aide tried to reason with the warring parties by asking the boys, "Why can't the girls play football with you?" The boys hotly replied, "They don't do it our way. They can't tackle; when we tackle 'em, they cry." A similar episode emerged on the Oceanside playground when a group of girls vied with a group of boys for use of a foursquare court. The yard duty tried to resolve the dispute by suggesting that the girls and boys join into one game. This time the girls protested, saying, "They don't play our way." One of the girls later explained, "The boys slam the ball, and we don't."

In short, much of what has been observed about girls and boys, especially in the relationships they create apart from the surveillance of adults, can be fitted into the model of "different worlds or cultures." But as I've tried to line up that model with my own empirical observations and with the research literature, I have found so many exceptions and qualifications, so many incidents that spill beyond and fuzzy up the edges, and so many conceptual ambiguities, that I have come to question the model's basic assumptions.

In previous chapters I have aired one major objection to the model of "different cultures": it implies that girls and boys are always apart and gives no theoretical attention to the moments of "with" and comfortable sharing. Girls and boys interact in many families, as well as in neighborhoods, churches, and schools, but the different-cultures model basically ignores these experiences. In this chapter I add other criticisms of the different-cultures approach: it embeds the experiences of dominants and marginalizes many other groups and individuals; and it collapses "a play of differences that is always on the move" (in

Edward Snow's compelling phrase) into static and exaggerated dualisms. The different-cultures framework gains much of its appeal from stereotypes and ideologies that should be queried rather than built on and perpetuated as social fact. It is, I have concluded, simply inadequate as an account of actual experience and is, in many ways, a conceptual dead end.

But before I unravel and then create a more complex account, I knit a fuller portrayal of the "different cultures of boys and girls," drawing on the extensive literature that is organized along those lines. I use my own data in the initial knitting *and* in the unraveling and reknitting in order to demonstrate that the same realities can be seen in varied ways and to argue that the complex reknitting is the more insightful version. I frame the initial portrayal in the tone of factual assertion found in the literature; my doubting voice comes later. The generalizations center on ages nine to twelve, although parts of the portrayal are echoed in studies ranging from preschool through high school.

## Contrasting the Different Cultures of Boys and Girls

After emphasizing patterns of avoidance and separation between boys and girls, the different-cultures portrayal shifts to a series of contrasts. The structure and dynamics of boys' groups are usually described first, organized around a series of key characteristics—large, public, hierarchical, competitive—that are then contrasted with the features of all-girls' groups—smaller, more private and cooperative, and focused on relationships and intimacy. The strategy of contrast is often built into the design of research, for example, sociolinguists separately tape the interactions of groups of boys and groups of girls and then look for differences. Working from the contrastive model in the initial analysis of my fieldnotes, I also went searching for group gender difference. I highlighted the incidents that fit the prevailing generalizations about, and cultural images of, boy-boy versus girl-girl interactions. But, as I later discuss, I also found many incidents that contradicted the model, which, along with various theoretical concerns, gradually led me to question the dualistic approach.

### THE BOYS' WORLD

Contrasts between the world of boys and the world of girls usually begin with themes of location and size. Boys more often play outdoors, and, as discussed in the previous chapter, their activities take up much more space than those of girls.[3] As Janet Lever has argued in much-cited articles comparing the play of fifth-grade boys and girls, boys' groups tend to be larger. They form "flocks," "gangs," "teams," or groups of "buddies," while girls organize themselves into smaller, more intimate groups and friendship pairs.[4]

Many researchers have reported that boys engage in more rough- and-tumble play and physical fighting than do girls.[5] As I noted in my earlier description of the chasing melees on the Ashton playground, boys more often grabbed one another from behind, pinned down one another's arms, pushed and shoved, wrestled one another to the ground, and continually pressed the ambiguous line between "play" and "real" fighting. When girls chased other girls, they pushed and pinned from behind, but they rarely shoved one another down or ended up wrestling, and their physical encounters never resulted in physical injury.

In separate observational studies, Raphaella Best, Janet Schofield, and Andy Sluckin found that boys' talk, as well as their actions, frequently revolve around themes of physical strength and force.[6] On the first day of Mrs. Smith's kindergarten class when Karl loudly announced, "I'm tough," a chorus of boys (but no girls) joined in: "I'm tough too"; "Me too"; "Me too"; "My daddy says I'm tough." In the Ashton cafeteria I listened to a group of fourth-grade boys talk excitedly about a game they called "tackle": "You push 'em down, or you trip 'em." "When they're running real fast, that's when you trip 'em; I jump on 'em." "We play anything that's fun and rough, don't we, Tom?"

Standing near the "boys' side" of the fourth-fifth–grade classroom in Oceanside, I more often heard verbal threats than when I stood near the "girls' side." The threats—"Shut up Kevin, or I'll bust your head"; "I'm gonna punch you"—were sometimes issued in annoyance or anger, and sometimes in a spirit of play. Groups of boys in both schools talked at length about who had and could "beat up" whom. And when arguments erupted into serious physical fights, crowds gathered on the playground, and talk stretched out the events for hours.

It is often asserted that boys' social relations tend to be overtly hierarchical and competitive. They repeatedly negotiate and mark rank through insults, direct commands, challenges, and threats.[7] John, the highest-status boy in Miss Bailey's classroom, successfully directed the actions of the other boys (and one girl) in the bonded group of seven or eight that seemed to anchor "the boys' world." John, who was the tallest boy in the class and one of the best athletes in the school, deftly handled challenges to his authority. Dennis, who was not very good at sports or at academics, was at the other end of the pecking order. John and the rest of the group called Dennis "Dumbo" and insulted him in other ways; in a kind of ritual submission, Dennis more or less accepted the insults.

Not only do boys compete in sports; they also, as Best has observed, turn other activities into contests.[8] On the Oceanside playground I watched four boys from Miss Bailey's classroom start to climb up the "dirt pile" at the edge of the glassy playing field. As they climbed and compared the gripping power of their shoes, Matt suggested that they have "a falling contest; see who can fall the farthest," which they proceeded to do, negotiating and arguing about the rules as they climbed and slid. On the wintry Ashton playground I watched a similar episode: a group of boys competed to see who could slide the farthest on a patch of ice. Contests sometimes take the form of bragging, as in a classroom interaction on the "boys' side" of Miss Bailey's classroom. Bill began, "I got a science lab." Matt retorted, "I got a zoom 750 microscope." Bill replied, "So what, I got a telescope." Freddie chimed in, "I got an 880 microscope." Matt, "There isn't such a thing. My dad has a 750." This kind of technical talk was also more typical of boys' than of girls' conversations.

Lever has argued that the larger size of boy's groups, and their preoccupation with competition and with relative position, may be related to their involvement in organized sports, both as a favored activity, and as a metaphor for their social relations (boys sometimes talk about their cliques as "teams" with a "captain"). She contrasts the complex structure of team sports (many separate and independent positions; a large number of explicit rules) with the simpler, turn-taking structure of "girls' games" like hopscotch and jump rope.[9] I also noted that more Oceanside and Ashton boys than girls were caught up in team sports, both on the playground and in later conversations, when they retold their sports encounters, play by play.

Boys like to make and argue about rules, and they also collectively break them more often than girls do. Combining our data from Massachusetts, Michigan, and California, Zella Luria and I noted that boys more often publicly violated rules, for example, against saying "dirty words" on the playground. Their larger numbers give a degree of anonymity and support for transgression that is lacking in girls' friendship pairs. Boys bond through the risk of rule-breaking and through aggressing against other boys (called "girls," "fags," or "sissies") who are perceived to be weaker. Boys also bond by aggressing against girls, as in the playground invasions described in the previous chapter.[10]

THE GIRLS' WORLD

The different-cultures literature contrasts the larger, hierarchical groups of boys with the smaller groups that girls typically form—pairs of "best friends" linked in shifting coalitions.[11] These pairs are not "marriages"; the pattern is more one of dyads moving into triads, since girls often participate in two or more pairs at one time, resulting in quite complex social networks. Girls often talk about who is "best friends with," "likes," or is "being mean to" whom. Relationships sometimes break off, and girls hedge bets by structuring networks of potential friends. Girls often carry out the activity of constructing and breaking dyads and maneuvering alliances through talk with third parties.[12] In her vivid memoirs, Toth recalls the intense but unstable friendships, the staking of rival claims, and the "triangles of tension" among her and her close friends.[13]

This pattern of shifting alliances, wrapped in skeins of talk, was especially evident among three of the girls in Miss Bailey's class. Jessie frequently said that Kathryn, the most popular girl, was her "best friend." Kathryn didn't proclaim the friendship as often; she also played and talked a lot with Judy. After watching Kathryn talk to Judy during a transition period in the classroom, Jessie went over, took Kathryn aside, and said in an accusing tone, "You talk to Judy more than me." Kathryn responded defensively, "I talk to you as much as I talk to Judy."

In gestures of intimacy that one rarely sees among boys, girls stroke or comb their friends' hair.[14] They notice and comment on one another's physical appearance such as haircuts or clothes, and they borrow and wear one another's sweatshirts or sweaters. (In contrast, touch among boys is rarely relaxed and affectionate; they express solidarity through the ritual handslap of "giving five," friendly teasing, and through the guise of mock violence—pushing, poking, grabbing from behind—whose context affirms good feelings.)

Among girls, best friends monitor one another's emotions.[15] They share secrets and become mutually vulnerable through self-disclosure, with an implicit demand that the expression of one's inadequacy will induce the friend to disclose a related inadequacy. In contrast, when a boy discloses a weakness to other boys, it is far more likely to be exposed to others through joking and a kind of collective shaming. Boys tend to be more self-protective than girls.

On school playgrounds, as Lever and others have documented, girls are less likely than boys to play team sports. They more often engage in small-scale, turn-taking, cooperative kinds of play, and by fifth and sixth grades many of them spend recess standing around and talking.[16] When they jump rope or play on the bars, girls take turns performing and watching others perform in stylized movements that may involve considerable skill. On both playgrounds I saw girls work out group choreographies, counting and jumping rope in unison, or swinging around the bars. In other synchronized body rituals, clusters of fifth- and sixth-grade girls practice cheerleading routines or dance steps.

Thus, the different-cultures literature concludes, boys stress position and hierarchy, whereas girls emphasize the construction of intimacy and connection. Girls affirm solidarity and commonality, expressing what has been called an "egalitarian ethos." In a study of conversations among children in an urban African-American neighborhood, Marjorie Harness Goodwin found that when they were engaged in shared tasks, groups of boys more often used direct commands ("go get the pliers") that marked hierarchy, while groups of girls more often used language like "let's" and "we gotta" that generated action in a collaborative way. The girls also criticized girls who acted conceited, or seemed to place themselves above the others.[17] Donna Eder has described the "cycle of popularity" among junior high girls, whom other girls seek to befriend, but also resent because they stand out from the others.[18]

Although they talk about being "nice," girls are far from goody two-shoes; beneath that rhetoric and overt concern with group harmony often lies considerable tension and conflict.[19] But the conflict is not expressed as directly as among boys. Goodwin found that girls more often talked about the offenses of other girls in their absence, as I noticed during an extended argument between Jessie and Kathryn. When their friendship was in a rocky period, they each told third parties that the other was "mean," and Jessie called Kathryn names like "flywoman" behind her back but rarely to her face. The protracted dispute, much of it carried out through reports to and by third parties, illustrates the indirect forms more characteristic of conflict among girls than among boys.[20]

## Problems with the Different-Cultures Approach

The central themes of the different-cultures portrayal—large versus small, public versus private, hierarchy versus connection—operate like well-worn grooves on a dirt road; when a new study is geared up, the wheels of description and analysis slide into the contrastive themes and move right along. This path may be compelling because it evokes experience; adults have seen groups of boys insulting and challenging one another and girls negotiating who is "best friends" with whom. These patterns may also resonate with childhood memories. I, for one, remember a time in the fourth grade when Kitty, my best friend, and I had a falling out. Feeling like an outcast, I took a pencil and paper and mapped the alliances then in place among the girls. My diagram indicated that Marlene was also without a best friend and hence the logical girl with whom to pair up. My problem was that I didn't like Marlene very much and couldn't force my feelings to abide by the logic.

But does the evocative power of these themes come solely from the force of reality, or in part from deep-seated cultural beliefs about "the nature" of girls compared with boys? Because the portrayal skirts around stereotypes (e.g., boys are tough, girls are nice), and because the contrastive grooves by no means cover all the pathways of experience, we should view the different-cultures approach with a degree of skepticism.

I will now give voice to the questions, to the array of "but what about . . . ?"s that kept popping up as I tried to fit my own observations into the dualistic framework. When I searched through my fieldnotes to see how they related to patterns put forward in the literature, I found that much of the supportive evidence came from my observations of the most popular kids in Miss Bailey's classroom. This tips off one central problem with the separate-and-different-worlds literature: not everyone has had an equal hand in painting the picture of what boys and girls are "like." Furthermore, because it is based on dichotomies, the different-cultures approach exaggerates gender difference and neglects within-gender variation, including crosscutting sources of division and commonality like social class and ethnicity. These facts seriously undermine the tidy set of contrasts that build up the different-cultures view, and they raise the challenge of how to grasp complex patterns of difference, and commonality, without perpetuating stereotypes.

WHOSE EXPERIENCES ARE REPRESENTED?
In an early phase of my project, when I largely accepted the different-cultures framework, I went through my fieldnotes on Miss Bailey's fourth-fifth–grade class and tried to compare the dynamics of boys' groups with those of girls. During this search I felt like an explorer shining a flashlight on selected parts of a dark cave. Guided by prior

expectations (e.g., that boys would move in larger, more hierarchical, and girls in smaller, more intimate groups), I could indeed light up those patterns in my fieldnotes. But the light mostly hovered around the "popular kids"—the group of six or seven boys (and one girl) who deferred to John as their leader, and, to a lesser degree, the dyads and triads that maneuvered around Kathryn, the most popular girl in the class. I am not alone; *a skew toward the most visible and dominant—and a silencing and marginalization of the others—can be found in much of the research on gender relations among children and youth.*

John's group was visible in part because it was the largest and most stable clique in the classroom, including John, Nick, Kevin, Allen, Tony, Jessie, Freddy, and Dennis at the margins or on the bottom, depending on one's perspective. Members of the group shared food, maneuvered to sit together, and called one another "buddies"; they routinely played team sports (soccer, baseball, and basketball, depending on the season) and talked about their games in the interstices of the school day. (Here lies a striking "but what about?" The group that seemed to anchor the boys' world included a girl, Jessie. As I detail in the next chapter, she acted out what has been called "boys' culture" more dramatically than did many other boys in the classroom, and she was also part of a shifting alliance among girls. Not irrelevantly, she was the only African-American student in the classroom).

John's group not only was large but also included the most popular boys in the classroom. Kathryn shared this source of visibility since she was by far the most popular girl. The lives of the popular often become public drama, and Kathryn's breakups and renewed affiliations with Jessie and Judy drew attention and even participation, as gossips and messengers, from the rest of the class. As I discussed in Chapter 2, Kathryn also got more than her share of attention in my fieldnotes; socially constructed contours of visibility skew ethnographic reports.

*The "Big Man Bias" in Research on Boys.* What about the other boys? Apart from John's group, they did not hang out in large, bonded "gangs," "flocks," or "teams," as the literature claims boys do. Matt, Roger, Eddie, and Don were sociable and regularly played team sports, so they could be seen in large groups heading to and from the soccer or baseball fields. But they were not part of a stable clique. Others were loners, including Joel, who was overweight, afraid of sports, and brought extra food and fancy toys from home to gain momentary attention; Neil, who was shy and physically uncoordinated; and Bert, who was slow on the uptake and at the bottom of the class in academic performance. Miguel and Alejandro, the recent immigrants from Mexico, hung out on the playground with a group of Spanish-speaking boys and girls who played zone dodgeball day after day. Their mixed-gender experiences are, of course, totally obscured by the different-cultures approach, which assumes virtually total separation between boys and girls.

The relationships of four of the boys—Jeremy, Scott, Bill, and Don—fit the "dyad into triad" description better than relationships among any girls in the classroom, except for Kathryn, Jessie, and Judy.[21] Jeremy, who had a creative imagination, spun fantasy worlds with one other boy at a time—acting as detectives tracking footprints on the playground, or as Starsky and Hutch, the television police buddies. Jeremy and his partner of the moment would also share treasured objects; for example, Jeremy brought in a compass and put it in his desk. He loudly told Scott (thereby announcing it was off-bounds to everyone else), "You can take my compass, but don't let nobody touch it."

The identity of Jeremy's adventuring partner shifted between Scott and Bill via a "break up" process often claimed to be typical of girls. The boy on the outs would sometimes sulk and talk about the other two behind their backs. When Scott was excluded, he would activate a long-standing affiliation with Don; when Bill was on the outs, he went solo. Over the course of the school year I saw each of the shifting pairs—Jeremy and Bill; Jeremy and Scott; Scott and Don—celebrate themselves as "best buddies." Once Jeremy and Scott toasted each other ("Here's to you and me!") with milk cartons at lunch. The overall pattern fit the shifting alliances claimed to typify girls' social relations, but *boys* were the protagonists.

In short, when I mold my data into shapes provided by the literature characterizing boys' social relations (in this case, the claim that boys are organized into large, hierarchical groups), I have to ignore or distort the experiences of more than half the boys in Miss Bailey's classroom. And I am not alone. The literature on "the boys' world" suffers from a "Big Man bias" akin to the skew found in anthropological research that equates male elites with men in general.[22] In many observational studies of children in preschools and early elementary school, large, bonded groups of boys who are physically assertive, engage in "tough talk," and actively devalue girls anchor descriptions of "the boys' world" and themes of masculinity. Other kinds of boys may be mentioned, but not as the core of the gender story.[23]

By fourth grade, as in Miss Bailey's classroom, the Big Men are defined not only by physical self-assertion and group bonds, but also by their athletic skill. In the United States, ethnographers typically detail the social relations of older boys from the vantage point of a clique of popular athletes: "Don's group" in Robert Everhart's study of a junior high; "the athletic group" in Philip Cusick's ethnography of a high school; in a participant-observation study of Little League baseball teams, Gary Alan Fine chose the "leaders" as his chief informants.[24] I detect a kind of yearning in these books; when they went back to scenes from their earlier lives, the authors couldn't resist hanging out at the top. Cusick writes about his efforts to shake off male "isolates": "I was there to do a study not to be a friend to those who had no friends."[25]

British sociologists and anthropologists have done pioneering ethnographic research in schools and on "youth culture" more generally. This literature also has a systematic bias, but because Marxist assumptions guide the British researchers, the "Big Men" who get attention are the ones—again bonded in larger groups—who are working-class, flamboyantly masculine, and resisting dominant class structures. *Learning to Labour*, an ethnography done in a vocational high school in England, is the classic of this genre. The author, Paul Willis, focuses on "the lads," a group who created an oppositional culture of aggression and joking tied to the working-class masculine subculture of factory workers. The lads' subculture, different from that of more conforming boys (whom the lads called the "ear 'oles"), ironically helped reproduce their eventual position in the working class. We have yet to see an ethnography written from the experiences of more "conformist" working-class boys like the "ear 'oles."[26]

Bonded groups of boys who uphold stereotyped masculine values may grab the attention of ethnographers for a variety of reasons. Acting in groups increases the power of individuals, and the boys' groups that are most often studied exert added influence through the charisma of being popular or because they disrupt classroom order. Ruth Goodenough observed that in kindergartens one group of this kind can "set the tone" for the other boys and draw them into contempt for girls.[27] Bonded and disruptive male groups cause trouble for teachers; Vivian Paley, a kindergarten teacher, has reflected on her ambivalence toward a male "superhero clique," and Ellen Jordan has discussed the problems that bonded aggressive groups of boys raise for teachers in preschools in Australia. The eyes of school researchers are often linked to the eyes of teachers.[28]

Finally, large bonded groups of boys may get more than their share of attention because their talk and actions fit prevailing images of masculinity. And here the literature moves in a circle, carting in cultural assumptions about the nature of masculinity (bonded, hierarchical, competitive, "tough"), then highlighting behavior that fits those parameters and obscuring the varied styles and range of interactions among boys as a whole. For example, in his study of Little Leaguers, Fine observed a lot of variation from team to team, but when he writes specifically about "preadolescent male behavior," he emphasizes the themes of aggression and sexuality found, by his own statement, more often among the Sharpstones (the focus of his discussion of masculinity) than other teams. Fine's data seem far more complex than his generalizing claims about masculinity.[29]

In *Making the Difference*, a pathbreaking ethnography of class and gender relations among secondary school students in Australia, R. W. Connell and his colleagues argue that there are multiple masculinities, some hegemonic and others submerged or marginalized; the patterns are contradictory and continually negotiated. The authors also point to varied forms of femininity, ranging from the "emphasized" (a term they have chosen because masculinity claims ultimate hegemony over femininity) to less visible forms.[30] Connell and his colleagues observe that although powerfully symbolic, "hegemonic masculinity" and "emphasized femininity" are not necessarily the most common patterns. This useful approach pries open unitary notions of masculinity and femininity and raises the question of why and how some forms come to be seen as masculinity and femininity in general.

Kids of various ages themselves recognize varied, albeit stereotyped, ways of being a boy or a girl. I overheard two first-grade boys arguing about whether it's better to be "mean" or "nice." They sorted themselves and other boys into the typology; the self-professed "nice" boy also used the term "machos" and "show-offs" for the ones who were "mean." A woman of college age described three types of girls she remembered from her year in fifth grade: "cootie kissers," "ugly girls," and "nerdy girls." Another woman distinguished "fast," "pretty," "smart," and "tough" girls. A man recalled that in his fifth-grade class the boys fell into three types: "intellectual," "athletes," or "troublemakers."

By junior high and high school, named cliques, or "groups," as kids call them, consolidate; some are same-gender and others include both girls and boys. Joyce Canaan, an anthropologist who did extensive participant-observation in the middle school and high school of a suburban U.S. community, found that from sixth to eighth grade, kids' social relations became increasingly hierarchical. Middle-school girls and boys enacted a three-tiered ranking system: "popular" (with two "cool" subgroups, "jocks" and "freaks"), "middle," and "low" ("scums," "wimps," and "fags"—the latter two terms used for boys; "brains," including both boys and girls, had an ambiguous status). Students more often labeled and talked about the "popular" than other groups. Canaan found that over the course of high school the group system became more open and ambiguous; it was both present and not present as kids manipulated contradictory values.[31] Research of this kind helps challenge overly coherent and monolithic portrayals of "boys' culture" versus "girls' culture." (As I discuss later in this chapter, metaphors like "culture" and "world" are themselves part of the problem.)

*What about Girls?* The different-cultures portrayal is as problematic for girls as it is for boys, although in both cases the conventional picture does illuminate some recurring patterns. Among the girls in Miss Bailey's classroom there were no large, bonded groups of the sort that John led.[32] And there indeed were "tense triangles" and shifting alliances, notably the axis of Kathryn, Jessie, and Judy. Judy also had strong ties to Connie, and Jessie bridged to John's group. Another shifting threesome, rife with conflict, encompassed Nancy, Jessica, and Shelly. Shelly was also friends with Lenore from the other fourth-grade classroom; together they formed the core of a wandering playground troupe. Sheila and Tracy, another pair, often hung out together, especially during baseball season when they journeyed across the playground to seek entry into the boys' games. Neera, Beth, Rosie, and Rita didn't seem to have close friends, at least not at school. As with the more isolated boys, their experiences spill beyond the generalizations.

The conventional emphasis on friendship pairs and shifting alliances masks not only the experience of those without intense affiliations, but also the complex range of girls' interactions. In some activities girls interact in large groups. For example, the playground troupes I described in the preceding chapter sometimes included as many as five or six girls, and shifting groups of six to eight girls often played on the bars, talking, doing tricks, and sometimes lining up in a row to twirl their bodies in unison. Although games of jump rope and foursquare involved only three or four active players at any one time, other girls lined up waiting for a turn and joined in the general and often contentious disputes about whether a given player was out.

Drawing on a detailed study of fourth- and fifth-grade girls on a school playground, Linda Hughes has challenged the depiction of foursquare as a simple, turn-taking type of play. She notes that within the formal rules of the game, the focus of Lever's generalizations about turn-taking, there may be varied ways of playing. (When the Ocean-side girls said that boys "slammed the ball" and didn't play foursquare "our way," they recognized this point.) Hughes found—and, alerted by her insights, I could also see this in my observations—that in their playing of foursquare, girls created "complex, large-group activity," elaborating a complicated structure of rules.[33] These patterns cannot be grasped if one adheres to Lever's contrast between the play of boys (large-scale, competitive, with complex rules) and that of girls (small-scale, cooperative, with a simple structure).[34] Girls, and not just boys, sometimes play in larger groups and negotiate and argue about rules.[35] In short, *separate-worlds dichotomies gloss the fact that interaction varies by activity and context.*[36]

This point is also central to Goodwin's research in an urban neighborhood. The girls who used collaborative language like "let's" and "we gotta" when they were engaged in the shared task of mak-ing rings out of bottles, shifted to hierarchical interaction, repeatedly giving and obeying direct commands, when they played house.[37] And while these girls used more mitigated and indirect (e.g., gossip) forms of conflict among themselves, they used aggravated verbal forms, includ-ing insults, when they argued with boys.[38] Other researchers have also found that African-American girls, as well as boys, tend to be skilled in direct verbal conflict, and several studies also report insult exchanges among white working-class girls who value "being tough."[39] *General-izations about "girls' culture" come primarily from research done with girls who are class-privileged and white; the experiences of girls of other class, race, and ethnic backgrounds tend to be marginalized.*

My own fieldnotes contain enough instances of girls using insults, threats, and physical fighting to make me uncomfortable with the assertion that these behaviors are somehow distinctively "male." Girls directly insulted boys, as in some of the borderwork incidents described in the previous chapter, and occasionally they insulted one another. One day on the Oceanside playground, Nancy held her legs apart, jumped up and down, and yelled, "Jessica goes to the toilet." Jessica bent her head, fighting off tears. Nancy then ran around Jessica saying, "Bye, hot dog. Jessica is Mr. Hot Dog." Jessica walked away, and Nancy ran behind her, jumping up and down like an ape. Then the bell rang and cut off the barrage of insults.

On another occasion, as Miss Bailey's class was gathering by the classroom door at the end of recess, Matt yelled, "You faggot!" at Nancy. Nancy, who was taller and bigger, ran after and knocked Matt down, pulled at his hair while she kicked him hard, and then walked away with a triumphant look on her face. Matt crumpled over and sobbed, "She pulled my hair." A group gathered round, discussing how "a girl beat him up."

Nancy was white. Jessie, who was Black, also didn't shrink from physical fights with boys; in fact, it was widely acknowledged that she could beat up any boy in the school. Both Nancy and Jessie were skilled at insulting and threatening ("Shut up or I'll punch you out"). It's true that these two girls were relatively exceptional compared with others in Miss Bailey's class. But either by ignoring the occasions when girls hurled insults, made threats, and got into serious physical fights, or by rendering them as forms of gender deviance, the different-cultures framework diverts us from examining important sources of complexity.

## What Does It Mean to Have Different Cultures?

As the difficulties multiply, I find myself wanting to return to fundamentals: What does it *mean* to claim, as Deborah Tannen does, that "boys and girls grow up in what are essentially different cultures?"[40] The literature is often ambiguous. Sometimes the claims—for example, that girls' groups tend to be smaller than those of boys or that boys use more direct insults—clearly refer to the relative frequency of various patterns of behavior or social action. At other points, the claims seem to refer to the symbolic (normative, ideological, or discursive) dimensions of gender. For example, boys talk about "being tough" and girls' talk about "being nice," and these discourses bring somewhat different meanings to what is sometimes similar behavior. When boys got into physical fights, kids talked differently than when a girl was involved; "a girl beat him up" added extra significance to Nancy's triumph over Matt.

Assertions about gender differences in actual behavior refer, at best, to *average* differences between girls and boys, or between groups of girls and groups of boys. The issue of relative frequency appears in words like "on average," "more than," and "tend to" that sprinkle through the contrastive rhetoric of different-worlds stories. Since qualitative researchers generally avoid careful counting, our "tend to"s and "more often"s are, at best, general impressions or perhaps "quasi statistics" gleaned from counting up descriptions in fieldnotes. But some of the evidence cited in the different-cultures literature comes from quantitative studies. The patterns are instructive.

For example, in a widely cited study of sex differences in rough-and-tumble play, Janet DiPietro coded observations of preschool girls and boys at play. Comparing boys and girls as groups, she found an unusually large difference: 15 to 20 percent of boys scored higher than any of the girls on the measure of rough-and-tumble play.[41] Nonetheless, as Carol Jacklin has observed, in this study "80 to 85 percent of the boys remain indistinguishable from 80 to 85 percent of the girls."[42] Rough-and-tumble play may be a "sex-related difference," but it is *not* a dichotomous difference since the behavior of most of the boys and girls overlapped.

Other studies show not only commonalities between girls and boys, taken as a whole, but also complex variation within and across those groups. For example, Elliott Medrich and his colleagues interviewed 764 children from different racial-ethnic backgrounds about how they spent their time outside school.[43] Forty-five percent of the boys and 26 percent of the girls reported playing team sports (note the sizable overlaps between boys and girls who did, and boys and girls who did not, play team sports). There was no gender difference in the median number of reported close friends (three), but African-American girls and boys reported more friends than either whites or those of other ethnic backgrounds. For all racial-ethnic groups and for both genders, being involved in team sports correlated with reporting more friends. African-American boys had the highest rates of sports participation, and number of friends, and African-American girls had higher rates than white girls. It is a serious distortion to reduce this complex variation into dichotomous claims, like "boys play team sports and girls engage in turn-taking play" or "boys organize into large groups and girls into dyads and triads."[44]

In these studies, as in other statistically based research on sex/gender differences, *within-gender variation is greater than differences between boys and girls taken as groups*. Although the variation may be dutifully reported, the point gets lost when the conclusions and secondary reports fall into the binary language of "boys versus girls." Some methodological writings caution against translating statistical complexity into a discourse of "the pinks and the blues," the tellingly dichotomous title of a popular television documentary on sex differences among children.[45] And they note another distortion in the literature on sex differences: although this is not "good science," findings of difference are much more often reported and published than findings of no difference. These problems seriously qualify general assertions that boys have a different "culture" than girls, if "culture" is taken to mean clearly differentiated patterns of behavior.

Claims that boys and girls have different cultures sometimes seem to refer not to externally observable behavior, like the amount of rough-and-tumble play, but to the *symbolic dimension of experience*— patterns of meaning, stereotypes, beliefs, ideologies, metaphor, discourses. (Each of these concepts has a different twist, but they cluster at the symbolic level. Note also that in daily experience "behavior" and "meanings" are not easily separable; human conduct is always infused with meanings.) As feminist scholars have thoroughly demonstrated, gendered meanings are deeply embedded in many of the discourses we draw on to make sense of the world. As Valerie Walkerdine has written, femininity and masculinity are powerful fictions or ideas, "imbued with fantasy and lived as fact."[46] The discourses of "girls are nice" and "boys are tough" enter kids' experiences, but so do other, sometimes contradictory discourses, like the argument of a boy who insisted that boys could be "nice," or the talk of girls who value being "tough."

An ambiguous mixing of the symbolic with claims about differences in behavior can be found in Carol Gilligan's research on gender and moral reasoning. After close and respectful listening to girls and, to a lesser degree, boys as they discussed moral problems, Gilligan concluded that girls have a "different voice," emphasizing relationships and care, in contrast with boys' preoccupation with individual rights and abstract principles of justice.[47] There is some ambiguity about what Gilligan intends to claim. In some statements she seems to be arguing that there are actual empirical gender differences in modes of moral reasoning, but the evidence for this has been much contested.[48] In her more recent work, however, Gilligan acknowledges that the same individual (male or female) may use both voices, mixing them as "contrapuntal" themes.[49] The voices may be gendered nonetheless because themes of "connection and care" are historically and symbolically associated with girls and women, and "rights and justice," with boys and men.

Once they are identified, systems of meaning—for example, the belief that caring and connection are "feminine"—can be studied in the context of social action. In her research on girls playing foursquare, Hughes pressed beyond the imagery of girls as cooperative and seeking intimacy by situating girls' talk about "being nice" within their ongoing interaction. She found that the girls "competed in a cooperative mode," using a language of "being friends" and "being nice" while aggressively getting others out so their friends could enter the game. The girls did not seem to experience "nice" and "mean" as sharply dichotomous; they maneuvered their rhetoric (associated with symbolic notions of femininity) and expressed nuances through mixed phrases like "nice-mean" and "not really mean."[50]

In a related vein, Amy Sheldon, who analyzed conversations among preschoolers, describes the girls as using a "double-voice style" that enmeshed or masked self-assertion within an orientation to relationships and maintaining group harmony. In interacting with one another, girls tried to avoid the appearance of hierarchy and overt conflict, but much else—conflict, self-assertion, sometimes aggression—went on beneath the surface. Sheldon found that boys sometimes used this double-voice style, although she argues that it is more often a feature of girls' talk because they are constrained by gender prescriptions to display themselves as egalitarian and harmonious.[51]

Sensitivity to gender meanings within varied social contexts and practices may enrich our understanding of boys as well as girls. In an interpretive study of the sex talk of a group of boys in a London secondary school, Julian Wood observes that "masculinity has at its heart not unproblematic strength but often weakness, self-doubt, and confusion." The outward face may be brash and full of "presence," or the promise of power, but the inward face is often the reverse.[52]

In short, a given piece of social interaction may be simultaneously cooperative and competitive, self-assertive and oriented to others, and brash and vulnerable. And these qualities do not sharply divide by gender. This subtlety and complexity become lost when analysis proceeds through a series of gender-linked contrasts (e.g., competitive versus cooperative, agency versus communion), and when varied dimensions of gender are compressed into static dualisms.

Ethnographers of education who work within "social reproduction" or "resistance" theory have also provided insight into multiple gender ideologies (the former emphasize the reproduction of inequalities of social class and gender through schooling; the latter give more attention to how individuals and groups resist this process).[53] For example, Connell and his colleagues argue that although dominant ideals of masculinity and femininity may exert powerful influence, they do not simply determine individual behavior. Individuals and groups develop varied forms of accommodation, reinterpretation, and resistance to ideologically hegemonic patterns.[54]

Joan Anyon, who interviewed and observed fifth-grade girls in the United States, found that some girls acquiesced in one kind of prescribed femininity: they wore dresses and skirts, were quiet in class, and avoided aggressive physical activities. Others used exaggerated feminine behavior (giggling, whispering; being coy and flirting with a male teacher) to resist schoolwork. Some girls actively resisted stereotyped femininity by refusing to wear skirts and frilly clothing, and by playing sports and engaging in verbal aggression.[55]

Rather than casting children as "objects of socialization," this approach grants them agency, tracing varied responses to and interpretations of gender prescriptions. By positing a complex and plural approach to gender, these ethnographies also challenge simplistic dualisms like girls' culture versus boys' culture. On the other hand, the "reproduction and resistance" literature analyzes gender primarily by emphasizing separation between boys and girls and by comparing the dynamics of varied same-gender groups or styles. While the groups and subcultures are multiple, a sense of deep division between girls and boys persists; how far such divisions may vary by situation or context is not made clear. Dualistic assumptions poke through the multiplicity.

## Beyond Dualisms

The separate-and-different-cultures model has clearly outlived its usefulness. But before I draw together alternative approaches, I want to briefly celebrate a breakthrough that was, I believe, facilitated by feminist work within the model of different cultures. Prior to the mid-1970s the experiences of girls were excluded from or devalued in most of the research on the social relations of children and youth. Within the United States, the child development literature on "peer relations" was based primarily on research on boys, as were historical studies of childhood and adolescence.[56] And, as Angela McRobbie observed in a trenchant critique, British youth culture studies either ignored or marginalized girls; for example, in Willis's study, girls are seen through the eyes of the "lads," as objects to be possessed.[57] Although Lever paid close attention to girls in her extensive research on sex differences in children's play, her work still suffered from a tendency to see them as deficient; for example, she described girls' play as "immature" and claimed that their groups had a "vacuum of leadership."[58]

The feminist movement has helped scholars focus more directly on girls, to be critical of the many ways in which they have been

stereotyped and devalued, and to grant girls voice and agency in knowledge. The different-worlds framework, animated by feminist revalu-
ing of "things female," cleared space to learn directly about girls and
their interactions with one another.[59] One valuable result, exemplified
by Gilligan's work, has been the articulation of dimensions of experience, such as relationality and caring, that were previously trivialized
or ignored. Once these experiences have been conceptualized, they can
then be studied in the context of the lives of boys and men, as well as girls
and women, leaving open the issue of empirical gender difference.

But the contrastive framework has outlived its usefulness, as
has the gender ideology that it builds on and perpetuates. The view
of gender as difference and binary opposition has been used to but-
tress male domination and to perpetuate related ideologies like the division between public and private.[60] A sense of the whole, and of the
texture and dynamism of interaction, become lost when collapsed into
dualisms like large versus small, hierarchical versus intimate, agency
vs. communion, and competitive versus cooperative. (The portrayals
often sound like a Victorian world of "separate spheres," writ small and
contemporary.)

Furthermore, by relying on a series of contrasts to depict the
whole, the approach of girls' culture versus boys' culture exaggerates
the coherence of same-gender interaction. Terms like "culture" and
"subculture" are too often used to reify contrastive images; as R. W.
Connell argues, these terms suggest a place which people inhabit rather
than an "aspect of what they do."[61] We need, instead, to develop concepts that will help us grasp the diversity, overlap, contradictions, and
ambiguities in the larger cultural fields in which gender relations,
and the dynamics of power, are constructed.[62]

If the separate-cultures story has lost its narrative force, how
can we grasp the gendered nature of kids' social relations? To move
our research wagons out of the dualistic rut, we can, first of all, try
to *start with a sense of the whole rather than with an assumption of gender as separation and difference.* If we begin by assuming different cultures, separate spheres, or contrastive differences, we will also end with
a sharp sense of dichotomy rather than attending to multiple differences and sources of commonality.

One way to grasp this complexity is by *examining gender in context* rather than fixing binary abstractions like "boys emphasize status,
and girls emphasize intimacy." Instead we should ask "which boys
or girls, where, when, under what circumstances?" As I have shown
throughout this book, the organization and meanings of gender vary

from schools to neighborhoods to families, and from classroom to playground to lunchroom settings. Some situations, like cross-gender chasing and invasions, evoke a sense of gender as dualism, but other situations undermine and spread out that view. Furthermore, gender takes shape in complex interaction with other social divisions and grounds of inequality, such as age, class, race, ethnicity, and religion. As Joan Scott suggests, we should "treat the opposition between male and female as problematic rather than known, as something contextually defined, repeatedly constructed."[63] An emphasis on social context shifts analysis from fixing abstract and binary differences to examining the social relations in which multiple differences are constructed and given meaning.

# CHAPTER 7

# Crossing the Gender Divide

In exploring the spectrum of children's gender relations, one must grapple not only with images of dualism, but also of deviance. "The tomboy" and "the sissy" stand at and help define the symbolic margins of dichotomous and asymmetric gender difference; the label "sissy" suggests that a boy has ventured too far into the contaminating "feminine," while "tomboys" are girls who claim some of the positive qualities associated with the "masculine." The images condense many cultural messages about gender, in part through their striking asymmetry: "tomboy" holds mixed, and often quite positive meanings, while "sissy" is an unmitigated word of contempt.

"Tomboys" and "sissies" are enduring figures in popular culture, inscribed in everyday talk, children's fiction, and adult recollections of childhood. The imagery of "sissies" and "tomboys" returns us to issues of boundary that were raised in Chapter 5, and to questions about the internal life of same-gender groups, the focus of Chapter 6. The topic here concerns passage: When gender boundaries are in force, how, and with what consequences, do individuals seek to cross the "gender divide" and gain access to groups and activities of the other gender? After critically examining cultural representations, I recenter the analysis within the social relations and collective practices of the kids I got to know in the Oceanside and Ashton schools. I argue that although they exert social force, narratives of individual deviance obscure a complicated continuum of crossing.


## "Tomboy" Lore

The term "tomboy" goes back as far as the sixteenth century, when it was used to refer to a "wild romping girl" who "behaves like a spirited or boisterous boy."[1] At least since Jo March in *Little Women*, first published in 1871, the tomboy has been a staple character in U.S. children's literature.[2] Fictional tomboys have included Caddie Woodlawn, living with her family on the nineteenth-century frontier; Charlie Boy (Charlotte) Carter, a 1920s "Texas tomboy," and Grace Jones, who wears an old Navy middy over her dress and climbs trees in a story set just after the Depression.[3] In stories of the 1960s and 1970s, Ellen Grae Derrybery wears "impossible" clothes and goes fishing with boys, and Toe (Antonia) organizes a "tomboy club" whose members like sports, wear jeans with flies in front, and distinguish themselves from "girly girls" who wear pull-on slacks.[4] Since the late 1960s the tomboy theme has been eclipsed by new, more complex coming-of-age stories, like those of Harriet the Spy and of Judy Blume's Margaret.[5] But, as Elizabeth Segel has observed, in the 1980s tomboy themes made a comeback, although without the label, in the form of characters like Gwyn, in *Jackaroo*, who disguises herself as a Robin Hood figure in feudal times, and Aerin, in *The Hero and the Crown*, who battles with dragons in a mythic past.[6] In short, "tomboy" characters have been created in different decades, and they span varied regions and specific concerns. But they all tap into, and have helped construct, a persistent cultural figure.

Fictional tomboys chafe at the restrictions of imposed femininity and "girly-girl" ways. Spirited and adventuresome, they like to move freely and to be outdoors. They dislike dresses and feminine adornments, and they are drawn to activities associated with boys. As friends and "pardners," as Charlie Boy's father calls her, most of these literary tomboys prefer the company of boys, although Toe forms a club limited to girls who call themselves tomboys. Fictional tomboys struggle with those, usually including their mothers, who would tie them down, keep them indoors, and put them into the confines of dresses, housework, and "manners." Others, usually fathers and/or boy companions, support tomboys in their struggles.

Although the authors root for their fictional tomboys, they provide an ultimately mixed message. The stories always conclude with the girl's entry into adolescence and young womanhood, when she ultimately succumbs, at least partially, to that which she has struggled against and begins to value traits and activities associated with "the feminine." For example, the Texas tomboy learns to be more "considerate" and finally recognizes that her houseworking sister has helped their family survive on the ranch; and Ellen Grae begins to understand the virtues of nicer clothes, manners, and "culture." For all these fictional girls, the transition out of childhood means leaving behind the full status of tomboy. They keep some of their spirit and independence, but they become softened, both more affirming of, and reconciled to, definitions of their gender that they had previously opposed.[7]

Because she resists the constraints of stereotyped "feminine" behavior, the tomboy can be seen as a vehicle of cultural criticism. But the term "tomboy" also has sexist overtones, implying that an independent and energetic girl is abnormal.[8] The term confuses other qualities with gender identity. Why call a girl a quasi boy just because she likes to dress comfortably, play sports, climb trees, go on adventures, or have boys as companions? The term may protest against, but it also helps perpetuate, gender stereotypes.[9]

Furthermore, like the backhandedly respectful "she thinks like a man," tomboy imagery pits females against one another. The mothers of Caddie Woodlawn and Charlotte Carter (as Charlie Boy's mother insistently calls her) disapprove of their daughters' tomboy ways and try to make them into "ladies." In many of these books, the tomboy's foil, and the target of her derision, is a "femme" girl of the same age. Ellen Grae ridicules the ladylike manners of her cousin, Laura; Charlie Boy looks down on her sister, Grace, who stays in the house, cooks, and likes to wear dresses; Toe and her friends define themselves in opposition to "girly girls." Pitted against her mother, and against other girls, the tomboy sets herself apart from others of her gender, becoming an exception to a group that is otherwise disparaged. At the conclusion of these stories, when the tomboys make the passage into adolescence and young womanhood, they come to see other girls and women in a more positive light. This change entails loss of freedom, and compromise with dominant types of femininity, but the transition also brings reconciliation with other girls and women.

## THE TOMBOY THEME IN ADULT
## NARRATIVES OF CHILDHOOD

In lived as well as fictional experience, "tomboy" is a popular term for depicting a trajectory through childhood. When asked to write or tell about their childhoods, a large number of undergraduate women,

well over half in most of my large university classes, spontaneously
describe themselves as having been tomboys; a few use qualifications
like "I sort of was a tomboy" or "I really was a tomboy."[10] The auto-
biographical narratives volunteered by my students resemble those
of fictional tomboys. As girls, they liked freedom, movement, the
out-of-doors; they preferred comfortable clothes and didn't mind getting dirty. At least some of the time, they played with boys and in
"boys' activities" like ice hockey, baseball, or climbing trees; some had
close friends who were boys. Several reported that as girls they dis-
dained stereotyped feminine dress and activities, and they used vivid
language—"pris"; "the boy-chasing, nylon-wearing, fluttery group";
"silly, twittery, girly stuff"—to convey remembered distaste for more
"feminine" girls and their ways.

    Narratives of childhood convey assertions about one's present
self. This seems particularly true of tomboy narratives, which adult
women tell with a hint of pride as if to suggest: I was (and am) independent and active; I held (and hold) my own with boys and men and have
earned their respect and friendship; I resisted (and continue to resist)
gender stereotypes. A twelve-year-old boy told me, "My mother was a
tomboy; she did things they said only boys could do." There is always
a gap between stereotypes and the complexity of lived experience. Perhaps some women say they were tomboys because their remembered
experiences didn't fit clichéd images of girlhood.[11] Now that gender
stereotypes have come under critical scrutiny, adult women may have
added reasons to claim "tomboy" childhoods and to make narrative
assertions about their independence.

CONTEMPORARY CHILDREN AND THE TOMBOY LABEL
What about present, rather than recollected or fictional, experiences
of children? Do contemporary kids speak of being tomboys? During
my eleven months of observing in the Oceanside and Ashton schools,
I heard kids use the word "tomboy" only twice, and teachers or playground aides use "tomboy" four times and "tomgirl" (a variant of "tomboy") once, always in conversation with other adults. Some kids were
clearly unfamiliar with the term. One day some of the fourth-graders in
Miss Bailey's class labored over a page of a reading workbook that asked
the word for "a girl who likes to play boys' games." Several of the students said they had never even heard the word "tomboy." In a study of
fourth- and fifth-graders in two schools in Massachusetts, Zella Luria
also found that many children—nearly half in interviews with twenty-
seven of them—were unfamiliar with the term.[12]

    The gap is quite striking: a majority of contemporary adult women report that they were tomboys in childhood, and yet contemporary kids rarely use the term. It is not that kids have an aversion to labels; in daily school life they frequently use terms like "jerk," "dummy," "loud-mouth," "nerd," and "fag." But "tomboy" is not a full-fledged insult. Although it sometimes has a derogating edge, it often purports to be a compliment, and when I heard adults and kids use the word, it was in moments of musing description. For example, on the Ashton playground I stood next to Julie, a fifth-grader, as we watched a girl and a boy embroiled in a physical fight. I asked Julie, "Do girls fight a lot? Do they beat up boys?" She replied, "Margaret does; she's sort of a tomboy. I don't fight 'em, but they don't mess with me."

Adults also take up a mode of musing description when they construct narratives about their own childhoods, a context that may invite the use of the word "tomboy." In addition, "tomboy" may be an identity that consolidates more in retrospect than in the present. Reflecting back in time, adults use the term to describe a pathway through the stereotyped and real gender arrangements of their childhoods, and to make claims about their present selves, for example, about their independence and flexibility. For kids navigating those arrangements in the present, however, the situation is far more complex and open-ended and a single trajectory less clear.

Contemporary kids may rarely use the term "tomboy," not only for generational reasons but also because of social change. Some adults remember that in their own childhoods, kids as well as adults often used the term, and some say that when they were girls, they thought of themselves, usually quite positively, as tomboys. In short, in earlier times—childhoods of the 1940s, 1950s, and 1960s were the focus of these recollections—"tomboy" may have had more widespread use among children both as a social category and as a label for the self. Kids' use of the term may have been undermined by changes of the past two decades, such as challenges of gender stereotypes, more acceptance of girls in team sports (in some contexts the term "jock" seems to have supplanted "tomboy"), loosened dress codes, and a general lessening of pressure on girls to be "ladylike." The terms "lady" and "tomboy" are linked, and the undermining of one leads the other to falter.[13]

## "Sissy" Lore

"Sissy," like "tomboy," alludes to gender deviance, but with relent-lessly negative connotations. The major contemporary definition, "an effeminate boy or man," has eclipsed the word's earlier, more neutral use as a term of address for girls ("sissy" was originally derived from "sister").[14] Put simply, a sissy is a person whose character, interests, and behavior partake too much of qualities, such as timidity, passivity, and dependence, that are stereotyped as childish, and as female. Kids and adults mostly use the term to refer to boys, but when they display fear or weakness, girls may also be called sissy. When an Oceanside fifth-grade girl said she was too scared to climb to the top rung of the bars, one of her female climbing companions laughed derisively and said, "You sissy!"[15] In this context, "sissy" is related to epithets like "baby," "crybaby," and "scaredy-cat." Qualities of immaturity and weakness lie at the despised core of "feminine" meanings, a core from which girls as well as boys often seek to distance themselves.[16]

When applied to boys, "sissy" conveys not only immaturity but also gender and sexual deviance. Kids use the term and its loose array of synonyms ("girl," "fag," "faggot," "wimp," and sometimes "nerd") to label boys who seem effeminate in dress and mannerisms, who avoid or perform poorly at sports, and/or who frequently play with girls. Kids also draw more generally on this repertoire of insults, as in the episode of gender antagonism, described in Chapter 5, when a group of girls taunted "Bratty boys! Sissy boys!" as a game of team handball unraveled.

In short, a "sissy" is a failed male. Indeed, one of its synonyms is, quite simply, "girl." Kids never used "boy" as a straightforward insult to a girl, but they sometimes derided a boy by calling him "girl." Freddy, an Ashton kindergarten boy who bragged about being "tough," repeatedly and sarcastically called Jimmy "you girl." Jimmy, who had soft curly hair and a babyish face, tried to avoid his tormenter. On the Oceanside playground three older boys came up to Steve, a fourth-grader, and leaned at him in a threatening way. "We heard you called us girls," one of them said in an accusing tone. "No I didn't," Steve quickly and defensively replied. "You better not," another said sternly as the three departed.

The words "fag" and "faggot" are also part of the collection of insults loosely interchangeable with "sissy." (This is probably a more contemporary meaning, indicative of the use of explicitly sexual meanings by and about people of younger and younger ages.)[17] I could sometimes tell from the context that younger kids didn't know the adult meaning of "fag" and "faggot," but they certainly picked up on and used the powerful allusion of deviance. "Fag" and "faggot" are fighting words, most often hurled at boys, but occasionally also at girls, as in the incident described in the previous chapter when Nancy physically attacked Matt after he called her "faggot." Older kids understand the sexual meanings, and they use the specter of homosexuality as a vehicle for enforcing dominant notions of masculinity. A boy who seems "girlish," for example, because he plays "girls' games" and/or likes to be with girls in a way that is not flirtatious or teasing, may be called "fag" or "faggot," as well as "sissy."[18]

When asked about their elementary school experiences, male college students sometimes recall occasions when they were called "sissy," "nerd," "wimp," or "fag." The memories are painful, and the men I talked with remember trying to avoid or cope with the stinging insult. Unlike the many women who reminisce quite positively about having been called a "tomboy," very few men affirm "sissy" as the core of an earlier (or present) identity. The one exception in the narratives I collected was a college student, an active participant in the gay rights movement, who said that as a boy he never liked to play sports; instead he preferred to play with girls and to play "girls' things." He mused about his growing sense of defiance: "People called me 'sissy' a lot; I knew it was an insult, and it hurt my feelings, but I was determined to stick with it."

The use of "tomboy" and "sissy" as terms of deviant identity has been reinforced by clinicians who write about the small number of children, many more boys than girls, referred for counseling because of "extreme cross-gender behavior" that leads to social ostracism and parental concern.[19] This literature is written in a tone of pragmatic compassion; the goal of treatment is to lessen the child's uncomfortable isolation from peers and to smooth out rocky family relations. But the clinicians remain remarkably unreflective about larger social circumstances and cultural meanings. They use "sissy" and "tomboy" without much critical reflection, and they have even medicalized the terms with derivations like "the sissy-boy syndrome" and "tomboyism."[20] Thus, social labels get turned into psychiatric conditions that are presumed to have a unitary character and to be located within the child. The authors do not reflect on the rigid notions of "masculinity" and "femininity," and the homophobia, that lie behind the labels, nor do they examine social processes of labeling, including referral for psychiatric treatment.

In his book on "the sissy-boy syndrome," Richard Green describes boys who have been stigmatized, in part, because they preferred to play with girls; they also occasionally cross-dressed and said they wanted to be girls. He designed interventions to help the boys become more comfortable with other boys, but, as one critic observed, Green did not ask why other boys avoid peers they see as "effeminate," nor did he work out interventions to alter this kind of prejudice.[21] Green mostly takes for granted the homophobia, the contempt for girls (playing with them is taken as a symptom of pathology!), and the avoidance of things "feminine" that are central to conventional notions of masculinity. In passing, Green observes that "'sissiness' causes social problems for boys while 'tomboyism' does not cause problems for girls."[22] But he does not query the asymmetric experiences of boys and of girls who cross symbolic boundaries of gender.

THE SISSY THEME IN CHILDREN'S FICTION

In the history of U.S. children's literature there have been few males who parallel the stock figure of the tomboy, that is, who affirm their right to engage in "feminine" pursuits and who thereby question dominant notions of masculinity. The exceptions are a handful of fictional characters who began to appear in the 1970s in the wake of the contemporary feminist movement. Perhaps the best known is William, the protagonist of a children's picture book called *William's Doll*. William begs his parents for a baby doll to "hug, cradle, give a bath, and kiss." His brother and a neighbor boy call William a "creep" and a "sissy"; his father, who also disapproves, refuses to give William a doll and instead gives him a basketball and a train. But William still wants a doll, and his grandmother finally buys him one, arguing that it will help him "practice being a father."[23]

Another set of books, clearly designed to challenge gender stereotypes, centers on boys who like to dance tap or ballet. In *Oliver Button Is a Sissy*, a picture book for younger children, the central character likes to read books, dress up, play paper dolls, jump rope, and dance.[24] Uncomfortable with his son's interests, Oliver's father tells him, "Don't be such a sissy! Go out and play baseball or football or basketball. Any kind of ball." (The father is a key oppositional figure in all these books, as is the mother in the tomboy literature.) But Oliver doesn't like to play ball, and he isn't any good at it. At school the boys tease him and write "Oliver Button is a Sissy" on the wall. Oliver goes to tap-dancing school, practices and practices, and finally performs in a talent show. He doesn't win, but his father is proud of his son's performance and takes him out for pizza. When Oliver returns to school, he finds the boys have crossed out "Sissy" and replaced it with "Star," so the wall message reads, "Oliver Button is a Star."

In an innovative research project, Bronwyn Davies read this and other feminist children's books to preschoolers in Australia and talked to them about their understandings. Many of the children missed the feminist lesson of *Oliver Button*; the story seemed to ratify their investment in the distinction between "girls' things" and "boys' things." The children couldn't figure out why the boys who at first teased Oliver then changed their minds; several suggested that a teacher probably told the boys to replace "sissy" with "star"; and most concluded that Oliver Button was wrong to do girls' things. One girl, Anika, explained: "when people, when the wrong kind of human being does that, I get a tickle in my brain." Davies probed, "And what about if a girl does a boy thing?" Anika replied, "I get the same thing . . . and it makes me laugh . . . it's like a little man is in my brain tickling my brain . . . it's like a piece of string like this tickling from side to side."[25] Davies concludes that conventional discursive practices of gender are more deeply entrenched than the authors of feminist children's books may assume.

A variant of the same plot—a boy who likes to dance, who persists in the face of opposition from his father and teasing from other boys, and who finally gains public acceptance for his skill—also appears in 1970s books for older children, such as *The Nutcracker* and *Nobody's Family Is Going to Change*.[26] It seems significant that in most of these books, publicly valued art forms such as tap and ballet dancing are the focus of the boy's unusual interests, and that his persistence, talent, and skill, which can be seen as "masculine" qualities, soften up his father and other male critics. While girls may lend an occasional helping hand (a group of them tell the teasing boys to leave Oliver Button's tap shoes alone), girls do not enter into these books as close companions or good friends of the boy protagonist. Unlike literary tomboys, who often have male, and sometimes female, companions, literary sissies remain relatively isolated as they pursue their interests and successfully weather criticism from their fathers and other boys. But while fictional sissies triumph and gain some acceptance for who they are, fictional tomboys experience eventual loss and resignation.

## From Deviant Individual Types
## to Processes of Crossing

Sissy and tomboy lore provide insight into cultural representations of gender: an obsession with oppositional dichotomies (not only boy/girl, but also tomboy/girly girl); persistent devaluing of girls; the policing of dominant notions of "masculinity" and, to a lesser degree, "femininity"; a language of identity; and the connection of gender deviance with sexual deviance. Terms like "the tomboy" and "the sissy" abstract from complex social relations to construct unitary categories of individual identity. These deviant types constitute the youthful, less overtly sexualized side of a roster of singular sexual/gender identities: "the homosexual," "the lesbian," "the prostitute" (note how use of the definite article, *the*, fixes a sense of unitary meaning). In his classic work on the history of sexuality, Michel Foucault argues that these identities have been created by modern discursive practices that stress individual essences as a means of social control.[27] Paradoxically, once these labels are in force, they sometimes become a basis for resisting social control, as the labeled, for example, lesbians and gay men, unite to challenge their oppression.

The taxonomy of deviant types can be situated in changing historical contexts; "the tomboy" and "the sissy" consolidated as reified images in the last two centuries.[28] Both terms now seem to be on the wane, perhaps because gender stereotypes have been challenged, but also because more contemporary terms ("jock," "fag") have begun to supplant the older labels. But the cultural slots—being labeled as deviant because one has trespassed symbolic gender boundaries—remain fairly sturdy, especially for boys. As does the tendency, honed by experts like psychiatrists as well as by everyday folk, to create labels, "conditions," and stigmatized identities, partly as a means of social control.

The world of lived experience does not, except in cultural categories, sort into tidy and essentialized types of identity. But the symbolism of "tomboys" and "sissies" raises questions about passage in gender-divided situations in elementary schools. Returning to the earlier metaphor of gender boundaries as fences that are continually built up and dismantled: when the fences are in place, how, when, and with what consequences do individuals of the "wrong gender" seek to cross them? The answer, I will argue, does *not* lie in the essence of individual character, as suggested by the imagery of "tomboys" and "sissies." It is more fruitful to examine a continuum of "crossing" and a complex process through which crossing is more or less likely to happen, and to fail or succeed. Furthermore, labeling is more likely in some circumstances than in others. Labels exist, but they should be understood in social and historical context.

THE CONTINUUM OF CROSSING

I have carefully chosen the word "crossing" to allude to the process through which a girl or a boy may seek access to groups and activities of the other gender. The word "passing" is inappropriate because in the situations I observed, boys and girls did *not* pretend to be of the other gender. Nor were they claiming a sort of "third-gender" status found in some other cultures, although they may have been blending attributes stereotypically associated with various forms of masculinity and femininity.[29] *The process of crossing is complex and often contradictory, affected by matters of definition, activity, and the extent to which an individual has developed a regular place in social networks of the other gender.*

*Varied Frameworks of Meaning.* Crossing is, first of all, a matter of *definition.* Earnest crossing, with the intent of full participation in the activities and on the terms of groups of the other gender, can be distinguished from "playing at," where one maintains distance and brings in other definitions of the situation. As elaborated earlier, boys are much more likely than girls to "play at" the activities of the other gender with the intent of invading or disrupting, and hence, of altering the terms of the encounter. "Borderwork" situations are antithetical to "crossing."

For example, two Ashton third-grade boys approached a group of girls who were playing jump rope and asked, seemingly in earnest, if they could join. The boys offered to "twirl the rope," the least desired positions in the game. After some hesitation, the girls finally agreed and handed the ends of the long rope to the newcomers. The boy twirlers picked up the rhythm of the previous game, turning the rope slowly while one girl jumped and the others chanted, "Sea-shells, cockle bells." After a few verses, with the twirlers providing an appropriately slow, rocking motion of the rope, the boys suddenly, and without announcement, switched to "hot peppers," spinning the rope very fast and tangling the unprepared jumper in the rope. Having used a Trojan-horse scenario to disrupt the game, the two boys ran away laughing.

That incident can be contrasted with one of the few occasions when I saw a boy join a game of jump rope in earnest, without altering the ongoing interaction. Brian, a white Ashton fourth-grader, joined an ongoing jump rope game at recess by getting into line behind two girls and waiting his turn to jump. He had on cowboy boots, a T-shirt, and jeans; the girls were taller, and all wore pants except for one of

the twirlers who wore a long skirt. The twirlers, also all white, maneuvered with two ropes, working hard to get both into the air and in
synchronous rhythm. Brian watched with an eager expression; by the
time the ropes were in motion, two more girls had gotten in line behind
him. Brian joined knowledgeably in the collective chant, "Cin-der-el-la
dressed in yel-la, went down-town to meet her fel-la," until Marcia, the
jumper, stumbled and lost her turn, and the next two girls came forward to jump. "Let me go too," Brian urged, and he ran to join them.
The twirlers got the ropes back in motion, and the three jumped skillfully through several verses of "Cinderella dressed in yella," until one of
the girls accidentally caught her foot in the rope and made it sag. Then,
as the rules prescribed, she, Brian, and the other jumper left and went
to the back of the line. Brian continued in the jump rope game, waiting
his turn in line, joining in the chants, and taking a turn at twirling,
until the buzzer sounded the end of recess.

Experimental forays across the gender divide lie between disruptive and earnest forms of crossing. John, the unofficial king of
Miss Bailey's classroom (he was tall, blonde, athletically and verbally
skilled, widely respected, the leader of the largest clique in the classroom), specialized in this mode. One day a visitor introduced Miss
Bailey's class to a dance from the Philippines, which involved rhythmically holding pairs of long sticks. Only girls moved forward to take
turns trying out the movements to the rhythm of music. Several boys
watched but didn't join in, and Eddie sealed up their reluctance by
announcing loudly, "That's for girls." But then John, who had been
watching from a distance, moved into the action, trying out the sticks
and the movements along with a group of girls. No one commented on
his involvement.

John joined groups of girls on other occasions as well. Once during PE when Miss Bailey was organizing boys against girls for a game
of kickball, she observed that there weren't enough girls to make the
teams numerically even. John came forward, "I'll play with the girls,"
he said. Saying, "I'm after you," his buddy, Nick, followed John to the
area by the fence where the girls were standing. John and Nick more or
less organized the team, working out strategies to compensate for the
generally lesser skill of girls.

John felt free to violate age as well as gender taboos. During one
noontime recess he organized a group of fourth- and fifth-grade boys
and girls to play "baby games" like "Red Rover" and "red light, green
light." The large mixed-gender group played with an edge of merri-
ment that seemed related to doing the unexpected. When the bell rang

and I was walking back to the classroom with Tracy, I commented, "I never saw you kids play Red Rover before." "Me neither," Tracy replied. "Whose idea was it?" "John. He had us playing all those baby games, 'red light-green light,' 'Father-may-I.' John and Nick were the father."

Why did John feel free to break expectations about gender- and age-appropriate behavior? Because of his extensive social resources, John could occasionally cross into girls' activities without being stigmatized. His unquestioned masculinity as one of the best athletes and most popular boys in the school was like money in the bank; he could take the risk of spending, because there was plenty where it came from.[30] And other kids seemed to admire his temerity. When Eddie came out late to the PE session and the kickball game was already in progress, he asked, "How come John's on the girls' team?" "He wanted to," Matt said. Eddie did not reply. As the highest-status boy, not only did John have extensive social leeway; he could also enter forbidden activities in a leadership and experimental mode, drawing others along with him, as in the lark of once again playing "baby games" that fourth- and fifth-graders felt they had otherwise outgrown.

Girls also cross into boys' groups and activities within varied frameworks of meaning. As I elaborated in Chapter 5, girls rarely enter boys' groups with the intention of disrupting. Girls' more typical form of "playing at" involves being physically present but self-consciously hanging back and maintaining distance from the activity.[31] The contrast between earnest and playing-at forms of involvement was evident in a kickball game on the Oceanside playground. One team included ten boys; the other, eight boys and three girls. One of the girls was Jessie, who covered second base as a skilled and serious player. Standing with her legs and arms loose and apart, she moved in the center of the action, keeping a careful eye on the progress of the game, pushing to the front of a group, running after the ball, grabbing with annoyance at a boy who edged her out and caught the ball. The other two girls, Kimberly and Cheryl (both sixth-graders), moved as a pair, which helped create distance and an alternative envelope of reality. They played positions in the outfield, occasionally catching or picking up on the ball when it came their way. But they generally stayed on the periphery of the game, only loosely following the action. They kept up a stream of talk with each other and now and then rhythmically clapped their hands and danced around. Several times they left the game and then returned.

Boys who seek out team sports generally "play hard." They don't join kickball, basketball, baseball, or soccer unless they intend to put

out earnest effort, and nonathletic boys avoid the playing field and
basketball court. Girls more often join predominately male games in
a "playing at," not-trying-very-hard mode that seems related to feeling
self-conscious, perhaps because of having lesser skill. When I asked kids
why girls so rarely played games like soccer or basketball, the answer
usually had to do with skill—"girls aren't good at it." But absence of
skill was *not* the reason most often given for boys' avoidance of jump
rope or hopscotch; instead, kids said that the problem was that these are
"girls' games."

No one, child or adult, doubts that team sports, the playground activities where boys predominate, require skill; the media
even amplify baseball, football, and basketball into epic proportions.
In contrast, the skill that goes into "girls' games" like jump rope and
playing on the bars remains, like the skill of adult "women's work"
compared with "men's work," more obscured. When boys occasionally
experiment with "girls' games," they expect it to be easy. Once Phil
and James, two Oceanside fifth-grade boys, wandered over to the jungle gym where a group of girls were taking turns doing named tricks
like Half Moon Bay and Around the World. "I can do it," Phil said, as
he tried to pull his legs up and around the bar; the girls on either side
did that movement with ease, and Phil kept looking at and copying
their postures. When Phil found he couldn't manage the maneuver, he
said to James, "Give me a little push." "Okay, ready," James said, helping Phil lift himself up. Phil finally got his legs up and over the bar and
tried swinging his body clear around, as the girls were doing in rapid
sequence. He managed it once and then swung down to the ground. "I
almost killed myself," he said to James. In the meantime Sherry spun
around the bars with agility. Phil watched her and then said to James,
"How do they do that? I tried and I couldn't." In this quiet admission,
which the girls did not seem to hear, Phil voiced his discovery that
playing on the bars requires considerable skill.

***Variation by Location and Activity.*** Crossing can be understood as a continuum of *location* and *activity*, as well as definition.
Many adult women who say they were childhood tomboys reminisce
almost exclusively about having played with boys and in "boys' activities" in neighborhood settings. When asked about school experiences,
many say that at recess they mostly played with girls, and some say that
their neighborhood male companions shunned them at school. As discussed in Chapter 4, it is often easier for girls and boys to voluntarily
associate in neighborhoods—which, although this may vary by class and
ethnicity, are typically less crowded and more private—than in school.

Some girls seek access to groups of boys only when a specific activity is under way, such as a sixth-grade Oceanside girl who regularly played with boys in the skateboard area, but not in other predominantly male activities. In the Ashton kindergarten, several boys liked to play in the "house" corner, but they otherwise didn't seek out groups of girls or activities associated with the other gender.

Tracy and Sheila, fifth-graders in Miss Bailey's classroom, frequently and skillfully played group sports—handball, dodgeball, and kickball—that were less divided by gender. During the spring season, they joined predominantly male games of baseball out on the grassy diamond, and they carried their mitts around school as a kind of badge of involvement. Tracy and Sheila, along with Jessie and six or seven boys in Miss Bailey's classroom, participated in the city's predominantly male youth baseball league, with practices after school and games on weekends. Tracy and Sheila sought out games of baseball as serious players, and they played hard. But I never saw them play basketball, soccer, or football, and in the classroom and lunchroom, they usually sat with groups of girls.

## The Vicissitudes of Brian's Crossing

By the fifth grade an extreme asymmetry becomes evident in patterns of crossing: girls, much more often than boys, seek access to groups and activities of the other gender.[32] In the younger grades, as discussed in Chapter 4, girls and boys more often play together. By fifth grade the majority of boys spend recess playing team sports like basketball, football, and baseball rather than the more informal activities (chasing, scenarios of "pretend") that engage many younger boys. A few older girls, like Tracy, Sheila, and Jessie, also play team sports, but it is rare, and much more stigmatizing, for an older boy to routinely seek access to the activities like jump rope or playing on the bars that are associated with girls and their groups.

Brian was the only boy in the upper grades of either school who routinely tried to enter girls' activities as a serious participant rather than with the intention of disrupting or in an experimental mode like John in the Filipino dance, or Phil and James at the bars. With practiced skill and an involved demeanor, Brian often played jump rope (I earlier described a game in which he was centrally involved). Brian also liked to do tricks on the bars, and, unlike Phil and James, he had learned the requisite skills.

One day after he had been playing kickball, Brian walked over and lined up behind two girls waiting turns on the two tall metal bars at the edge of the grassy playing field. Two more girls got in line behind him. (I wrote as an aside in my fieldnotes, "I almost gasped when I saw Brian join the row of girls; I've never seen a boy do that.") Two girls at the top of the bars took turns swinging by one leg; then one of them jumped off the taller bar. "Now somebody can get on the high bar," she said. "Me," Brian volunteered. Becky, who was in front of him, protested, "No, you ain't in line." "I am too," Brian retorted. Becky got up on the bar (the girl ahead of her had walked away), and Brian and the two remaining girls continued to await their turns. Then Valerie, the girl on the lower bar, lost her momentum. Brian went over and gently pushed the heel of her foot so she could turn around on one leg. Valerie regained momentum and spun around, calling, "Watch me!" When she finished and dropped down, she tacitly ceded her turn to the next person in line, who was Brian. He came forward and pulled himself onto the bar, swinging around with one leg as he called out, "Watch me!" Brian and Becky, who was still on the higher bar, then swung in unison. After a spell of serious and skilled playing, Brian dropped down and left the area. His involvement showed no hint of holding back, buffoonery, or hassling. He joined in the activity on the terms the girls had established, and with a skillful sense of nuance, as when he gave Valerie a needed gentle push.

However, Brian's participation in girls' activities had a tenuous quality. Girls sometimes challenged his efforts to enter their activities, and one day I saw a group of jump ropers chase him away from their games three different times. Since I did not have access to Brian's classroom, I saw him maneuver only in playground settings, where he was unusually versatile. In addition to playing jump rope and on the bars, he was interested in and fairly good at playing soccer and kickball. And he traversed age as well as gender lines. Arriving on the noontime playground, I came upon a mixed-gender kickball game on the fifth- and sixth-grade playground. Brian, who was in fourth grade, and notably shorter than most of the other players, was pitching. I sometimes scanned the playground, wondering where Brian would show up next. It was like looking for Waldo, who appears in an unusual place on each busy page of a series of picture books for children.

Although he found his way into a wide assortment of groups and activities, Brian did so essentially as a loner. In the cafeteria he often sat by himself. On the playground he didn't have a "crossing partner," as Tracy had in Sheila; nor, unlike Jessie, did he have a stable place in the apparent friendship networks of the other gender. There was some indication that other kids labeled him as deviant. One day I watched a group of boys choose sides for a game of kickball in a process laced with evaluation ("C'mon you dummy, us three"; "He's better 'n Jack; he's good"; "Get Jason, Jason's good"). The two newly-sorted teams ran toward the playing field, leaving behind four boys, including Brian. Looking unhappy, Brian, who wore a one-piece brown snowsuit (the other boys had on shorter jackets or coats), walked away. Another boy, standing nearby, yelled at Brian, "Why are you wearing that sissy snow-suit?" Brian angrily exploded, "Cause my mom wants me to, I told you a million times."

## Jessie's Patterns of Crossing

It was not unusual for girls to participate in playground groups where boys predominated, but Jessie, a fifth-grader in Miss Bailey's class-room, was at the extreme of the continuum of definition, activity, and frequency of crossing. Active in the team sports of every season, Jessie was one of the most talented and practiced players of soccer, base-ball, football, basketball, dodgeball, and kickball. She frequently rode bikes and hung out with groups of boys outside school, and she par-ticipated in the mostly male city baseball and soccer leagues. Girls like Tracy and Sheila, who joined boys' activities in more episodic ways, did not have a stable niche in the networks of boys. But Jessie did. She was an active member of the athletically involved, other-wise all-male clique in Miss Bailey's classroom. She called John, Nick, Kevin, Allen, and Tony her "buddies," and they included her in plan-ning conversations and in rituals of food sharing, such as splitting a twinkie or an orange, that marked membership in the group. Not only did Jessie play with boys; for most of the year she chose a seat in the "boys' side" of the classroom, and she often sat with boys when cafeteria table arrangements were largely gender-divided. At the same time, Jessie maintained ongoing ties with a group of fourth- and fifth-grade girls, claiming Kathryn as her "best friend," and sometimes joining games of jump rope.

    Jessie was the only African-American student in Miss Bailey's classroom, and one of only 5 percent in the school overall. That token racial status, and perhaps experience in less gender-divided social rela-tions among African-American children, may help account for Jessie's minimal investment in the notion of gender as a basis of "opposite sides."[33] It should be noted that the two other girls who were visibly "nonwhite" did not bridge in this way. Neera, whose parents were East Indian, and Rosie, who was a Filipina-American, stayed mostly with girls when they had a choice, although Neera was active in the mixed-gender terrain of handball.

There are deep cultural barriers to romantic connections between white males and Black females, which may have contributed to Jessie's avoidance of heterosexual definitions in interactions with her classmates, although she may simply not have been interested in heterosexual romance. (I return to this theme later in the chapter.) Furthermore, Jessie's physical and verbal self-assertion, which helped her maneuver in and between same-gender groups, may have had roots in African-American culture.[34] Her unusual navigation of the field of gender relations was also a navigation of race relations in a situation of tokenism; gender and race were being mutually constructed.

Miss Bailey once observed to me, "Jessie wants action with both groups." Indeed, Jessie showed unusual social versatility in moving back and forth between groups of girls and groups of boys in every school setting. When her classroom desk was on the boys' side, Jessie sometimes went over to the girls' side, pulling up a chair to join a conversation or activity; boys did that quite rarely, and mostly when an adult was present. During the part of the year when she had a desk with the girls, Jessie often went to the boys' side of the room to join an informal cluster or to find a spelling partner. Only one other girl, Tracy, ever practiced spelling with a boy. Jessie kept a continual eye on happenings in both sides of the room. One day when Miss Bailey was moving from student to student, checking a spelling test, Jessie, who was then sitting with the girls, whispered loudly, "Kevin got his all right; me and him got one hundred." Making eye contact with John from across the room, she added, "I was watching you make mistakes."

When girls and boys were formally separated into different teams or lines, Jessie stayed with the girls. But, as shown by her readiness to sit with the boys in the classroom and to weather the occasional observation that the class had a "girls' side" and a "boys' side except for Jessie," she was active at the margins. Her skill in moving across the gender divide was evident one day when the class lined up, girls on one side and boys on the other, to go to the auditorium to see a play. Jessie, who was a little late leaving the room, ran to the front of the girls' line. When the two lines entered the crowded scene of the auditorium and began to disperse, she easily joined John, Nick, Kevin, and other boys in a group moving to find seats together.

The extent of Jessie's connection with both boys and girls was also evident when kids negotiated recess and lunchtime groups and activities ahead of time ("Let's sit together at lunch"; "Wanna play soccer at recess?"). This ahead-of-time staging, where talk maps future action, almost always divided by gender, but Jessie laid plans with groups of boys *and* groups of girls. One day when Miss Bailey told students to get ready for recess, three boys knelt beneath the coat hangers where they kept their skateboards, readying their equipment and talking about tricks they intended to do. Kathryn, Connie, Judy, and Jessie (who was then sitting on the girls' side) put papers away in their desks and whispered together. "Just us four will play jump rope," Judy said. Kathryn grabbed the yellow jump rope as they got in the girls' line, and when the moving row dispersed at the boundary of the playground, the four girls set up a game near the chain link fence. They played for the whole ten-minute recess. At one point a boy came over and repeatedly yelled, "Turkeys! Turkeys!" Jessie hit at him, and he ran off. Later two boys came up and stood so close the rope couldn't be turned. Standing with her hands on her hips, Jessie faced off the boys and exchanged hostile words until they moved. Then she and Connie, who was also turning, started up the rope and resumed the chant of "S-C-H-O-O-L and don't for-get the gol-den rule." During this sequence Jessie was part of a group of girls who plotted recess activities in advance, and she stayed with them the whole time, actively defending their turf against boys who came to disrupt.

On other occasions, Jessie laid plans and moved through recess with a group of boys. For example, at the opening of one recess period Jessie talked at the doorway with John and Nick, who were a few feet away in the boys' line. When the lines dispersed, Jessie, John, and Nick walked along. John split an orange and handed pieces to the other two; then they shared popping candy while watching a baseball game forming. Jessie had grabbed a soccer ball as they left the room, and she began to dribble it and then kicked it to John, who kicked it on to Nick. The three constructed an informal kicking game, with John announcing a few rules: "You can use anything except your hands. That's the boundary." When the bell rang, John, Nick, and Jessie walked back to the classroom together.

## The Components of Successful Crossing

What does it take to gain access to groups and activities of the other gender, without notably disrupting or altering what goes on? This relatively unusual accomplishment points to barriers that sustain gender separation for the majority of kids. First of all, successful "crossers" like Tracy, Sheila, Jessie, and Brian *want* to participate in activities stereotypically associated with the other gender. Just why Tracy loved baseball and Brian loved jump rope is beyond the scope of my knowledge, although it is clear that what engages different imaginations spills far beyond the narrow cultural channeling of "appropriate" activities for boys and for girls. Tracy, Sheila, Brian, and Jessie not only wanted to play activities associated with the other gender, but also *persisted* in the attempt. Other kids got discouraged when their requests for access were turned down. For example, when a third-grade Oceanside boy asked a group of girls if he could join their game, the girls said a curt "no," and he turned away. Brian, in contrast, was remarkably persistent; even when denied entry into jump rope games, he kept returning.

Those successful at crossing persevere in spite of the risk of being labeled or teased. Kids target their most severe teasing at boys like Brian who repeatedly seek access to girls' activities in a respectful and serious rather than hassling or experimenting style. Unlike John, who was a very occasional "crosser," Brian did not have the protection of high status or an experimental stance. Girls who cross are labeled less often than boys, although I heard occasional comments about Tracy's and Jessie's unusual behavior.

One day on the Oceanside playground, Janet, a third-grader who didn't know Tracy's name but was trying to describe her to me, said, "You know, that girl who looks like a boy." Having figured out that Janet was referring to Tracy, I observed that Tracy had long hair. "Well, she still looks like a boy," Janet insisted, perhaps having picked up on other dimensions of Tracy's appearance (she always wore pants and dressed without feminine adornments) and on her sports involvement. On another occasion when I stood near an Oceanside handball court, where Tracy was vigorously hitting the ball, a playground aide commented, "Look at that tomgirl, every time she misses, she has to give an excuse." I asked the aide why she called Tracy a "tomgirl." The aide responded, "she's the only girl who's really getting into the game and hitting the balls hard" (Neera, Rita, Alejandro, and two other boys were also in that particular game). Thus, I twice heard Tracy labeled in terms of gender deviance, although I have no idea if she was aware of the labeling or what her reaction might have been.

Jessie's participation in boys' groups and activities was also the focus of occasional comment. Although I never heard Jessie called "tomboy" or "tomgirl," Miss Bailey privately observed to me, "All year Jessie thought she was a boy." Several times I heard kids say that Jessie was "the toughest girl in the school." Her skills in athletics and in verbal and physical confrontation (it was widely acknowledged that she could beat up any boy in the school) gained Jessie a kind of wary respect. She was not teased for playing with boys, although kids sometimes insulted her with words that had racist allusions. Once on the playground Jessie and Kevin got into an angry argument, and she finally pushed him to the ground. Kevin yelled, "Chungo!" "You're a chungo, not me," Jessie said, walking away. Freddy came over and asked Kevin, "What's a chungo?" Kevin replied, "A name I made up, like gorilla." During a social studies lesson on hieroglyphics, Miss Bailey had the students invent their own "picture writing" on the blackboard. Tony, who was sitting at his desk, yelled out, "Jessie's King Kong," while other boys laughed. Jessie, who was drawing at the blackboard, briefly looked around with a good-natured smile. Jessie's position as the only African-American in an almost all-white classroom, and as the only girl to consistently bridge back and forth across the gender divide, made her highly visible and set her apart from other kids.

Jessie, Brian, Tracy, and Sheila were successful at crossing the gender divide not only because of persistence but also because of *skill*. They were adept at negotiating the junctures of social interaction—initiating activities, forming new groups, and securing access to groups already formed.[35] During transition to regular or lunchtime recess, Brian and Jessie often made bids for equipment; arriving with the jump rope or soccer ball ensured their participation in newly forming games. During baseball season Sheila and Tracy brought their own mitts and ball to school, which enhanced their chances of being included in the game. Brian knew how to gain access to jump rope games by patiently standing in line, chanting the rhymes, and claiming and arguing about turns.

Jessie's athletic skills guaranteed her inclusion in games of soccer or baseball; the reputed skill of each player ("Jessie's good") figured centrally in processes of choosing-up. The fact that, as several different boys said to me, "Jessie can beat up any boy in the school," also gave her credibility on the playing field. She had the further resource of being "buddies" with a large, athletically oriented group of older boys. Jessie's access to games of jump rope was probably based less on skill than on friendship ties. Indeed, there is some evidence that even when they play team sports, girls more often choose players according to who is friends with whom rather than who is more skilled at the game.[36]

When she wanted to play jump rope with Kathryn, Judy, and Connie, Jessie could draw on her friendship ties. In contrast, Brian did not, as far as I could see, have strong friendship ties with either boys or girls. His persistence and skill (evident in jumping two ropes at once, knowing all the chants, spinning his body around a bar in agile unison with another player) helped validate his presence in girls' games of jump rope and gymnastics. But he was there more as a visitor than a core participant, and girls sometimes challenged his presence, calling him a "nuisance," which was their term for boys who sought access to girls' games with the intention of disrupting.

## Heterosexual Meanings as a Barrier to Crossing

When kids successfully cross into groups of the other gender, they have, in effect, avoided the meanings that accompany borderwork situations. Gender remains relatively low in salience; the gender tokens (Jessie in a soccer game; Brian in a jump rope game) participate on the terms of the majority, and not as "the other sex." This can only be accomplished if gender-marking is minimized and heterosexual meanings are avoided.

Tracy and Sheila played seriously and hard in games of baseball, and the male players seemed to accept them. In other situations (but never, so far as I could tell, on the baseball diamond) the two girls whispered about which boys they "liked," and for two weeks Tracy "went with" Allen in a public and widely-talked-about romance. Jessie hung out with boys and girls who were moving into the "goin' with" world, but she largely managed to avoid heterosexual definitions. When Miss Bailey gave the class a choice of dividing or mixing by gender for gift-giving at the holiday party, Jessie actively argued in favor of girls giving only to girls. Jessie never played chasing games, and when kids talked about who "liked" whom, she acted as a kibbitzer and teasing witness, thereby exempting herself from becoming a target of verbal matchmaking.

Jessie may have avoided heterosexual definitions for several reasons. One cannot be "goin' with," or paired off heterosexually, *and* a "buddy," with relaxed and accepted presence in boys' groups and activities, at the same time, and Jessie clearly preferred to be a "buddy."[37] Jessie may simply not have been interested in heterosexual romance. But even if she were interested, her position as the only African

American in the classroom pushed her to the margins of the developing heterosexual market; definitions of attractiveness are deeply shaped by race, and this was a white system.[38]

## Does Crossing Challenge
## Gender Boundaries?

When girls and boys cross into groups and activities of the other gender, especially at the earnest end of the continuum, they challenge the oppositional structure of traditional gender arrangements. Teasing and labeling can be seen as strategies for containing the subversive potential. But incidents of crossing may chip away at traditional ideologies and hold out new possibilities. (Note that the arenas, like handball, dodgeball, and many classroom situations, where girls and boys mix in relatively even numbers and on shared turf, also undermine the notion of gender as oppositional dichotomy.)

Once I asked Rita why girls didn't play soccer. "Jessie does," she promptly replied, implying open possibilities for herself and for girls in general. When Jessie or Nancy beat up a boy, a ripple of excitement moved among the girls, including me; I think it gave us a sense that one of our kind could resist and even herself exert physical dominance over boys. Through such processes of identification, the accomplishments of girls who cross the gender divide may challenge familiar stereotypes and even the boundaries themselves. However, I saw no evidence that Brian's crossing grabbed the imagination of other boys; the barriers to movement in the other direction are heavy indeed.

On the other hand, when Jessie joined groups of boys by herself and on the boys' terms, she left existing gender boundaries intact. She was a token, a kind of "fictive boy," not unlike many women tokens in predominantly male settings, whose presence does little to challenge existing arrangements. In such token situations, groups of men often define the woman as a sexual object, thereby highlighting difference, turning her into the "Other," and exerting control over her presence in their group.[39] Although not well developed in elementary school, this kind of control is incipient in the expanding use of heterosexual meanings in the upper grades. By junior high or middle school, it becomes much more difficult for girls to cross into boys' groups and activities with the ease that Jessie demonstrated.

Heterosexual meanings also pose strong barriers to crossing by boys, with the added obstacle of homophobic insults. By fourth grade, definitions of acceptably masculine pursuit have settled around team sports, and playing with girls, especially in games like jump rope or gymnastics, is seen, simultaneously, as a sign of immaturity, being "girlish," and being "a fag." Homophobia, as Lynne Segal has written, represses "the 'feminine' in all men as a way of keeping men separated off from women and keeping women subordinate to men."[40] These lines of separation and inequality, which have already begun to appear in elementary school, consolidate as kids enter adolescence and the institution of heterosexuality. The next chapter focuses on this transition; as kids move from "child" to "teen" meanings and arrangements, their constructions of gender also shift.

# CHAPTER 8

# Lip Gloss and "Goin' With": Becoming Teens

*Firecracker, firecracker, boom, boom, ba boom.*
*Boys got the muscles, Teachers got the brains.*
*Girls got the sexiness, so they win the game.*
—Chanted by a group of Oceanside kindergarten girls

Thus far, my analysis of kids' gender relations has relied on spatial metaphors, showing how kids mark, cross, undermine, and challenge boundaries between girls and boys. This chapter, which examines fluctuating and uneven transitions from "child" to "teen," adds temporal and bodily dimensions. The transition—for some, it starts as young as fourth grade—not only involves dramatic bodily change, but also entails striking shifts in kids' gender relations and systems of meaning. Kids mark teen meanings through modes of dress and adornment, and through group-mediated pairing that they call "goin' with" ("Judy and Nick are goin' with each other"). I conclude by assessing the shift from the relatively asexual gender system of childhood to the overtly sexualized gender systems of adolescence and adulthood. Symbolically, older girls, as the kindergarten ditty observes, may have "got the sexiness," but there is ample evidence that they hardly "win the game."

## Schools and Bodies

Like Valerie Walkerdine, I have been struck by the gap between the physicality and sexuality of childhood and the "sanitized and idealized images of innocence and safety" found in much of the research on schools.[1] In fact, when I stand in a crowded area of a school playground, I am often overwhelmed by a sense of the physical: the din of noisy voices and the surround of rapidly moving bodies; constant poking, grabbing, and pinning from behind; chanting and swearing with sexual themes; occasional eruptions of violence. School lunchrooms are also noisy, bodily places, dominated by the talk and motions of speedy eating. Although more subdued, classrooms, too, have strikingly physical dimensions. Seating and movement are subjects of continual negotiation; kids sneak food from their desks, and they sometimes whisper and giggle about eating boogers and the smell of farts. In the kindergarten classroom Mrs. Smith and her students dealt with loose teeth, wet pants, tying shoes, and fastening zippers. And in the underground economy of Miss Bailey's fourth-fifth grade, kids sometimes exchanged plastic body parts—a little pink hand, a rubber fingertip with a long red nail.

Keenly aware of physical size, kids tease the unusually large ("Ricardo's a blubber butt"; "fat Carol"), stand face-to-face or back-to-back and use a flattened hand to compare heights, and compete to see who is tallest. They sometimes rib those who wear braces ("railroad tracks") or glasses ("four eyes"). The sheer number of kids in a school provides much grist for commentary about bodily variation, as does their rapid and uneven growth, symbolized by the mouth of an average third-grader: small pearly baby-teeth mixed with large jagged-edged regular teeth, and gaps here and there where transitions are underway.

A dramatic period of bodily change starts, for a few, in third or fourth grade and expands over the course of fifth and sixth grades, generally consolidating in middle school or junior high. The names for this transition—"pubescence," "sexual maturation," "entering adolescence"—feel awkward and unpleasant, expressing a prevalent attitude toward this socially defined period of life. As eleven- and twelve-year-olds, many sixth-graders are in transition, but even the most advanced have not, by general reckoning, moved fully into the status of "teens." In any case, as R. W. Connell and his colleagues have observed, the category "adolescent" continually dissolves into "adult," and, I would add for the early end, it also dissolves into "child."[2]

## DIVERSE SHAPES AND SIZES

The lunchtime rows marching from the Ashton cafeteria to the playground provided me with a frequent visual scan of the diverse shapes and sizes of elementary school kids. The marchers were organized by classroom and thus by age, which made each line loosely homogeneous since third-graders are, on the whole, much shorter than sixth-graders. But within each line there was great variation, especially among the fourth-, fifth-, and sixth-graders. A few, nearly all of them girls, had the full height and bodily development of adults; others were so short and small, they could be mistaken for second-graders. And when fifth- and sixth-grade girls and boys lined up separately, girls were, on the average, notably taller and bigger than boys, reversing the adult pattern of sexual dimorphism (the average man is taller and bigger than the average woman).

Biologists and physicians have measured differential rates of physical development at puberty and condensed them into patterns. James M. Tanner, whose charts are used to map individual growth, summarized the changes: "There is a swift increase in body size, a change in the shape and body composition, and a rapid development of the gonads, the reproductive organs, and the characters [e.g., female breasts and male facial hair] signalling sexual maturity."[3] On average, girls develop two years earlier than boys; their spurt of height peaks at age twelve, while boys peak at age fourteen. But within this general pattern, there is enormous variation; according to Tanner, girls who are ages eleven, twelve, and thirteen, or boys who are thirteen, fourteen, and fifteen may range from "practically complete maturity to absolute preadolescence."[4] Some girls and boys go through puberty in a relatively short time, while others may take as long as six years.

Across the life course only the rapid growth of infants surpasses this period of dramatic physical change, a fact adults recognize in their ways of talking. Fifth- and sixth-grade teachers sometimes speak of "hormones coming out" and driving the behavior of their students. A newspaper article about junior high schools emphasizes "the extraordinary difficulty of teaching boys and girls in whom the fires of puberty are starting to rage."[5] In our culture we surround this phase of life, more than many others, with an aura of biological causation.

But even when striking physical changes, like spurts of height and the emergence of breasts, are underway, they are shaped by social practices and cultural meanings. Cultures organize the life cycle in different ways. Some downplay and others dramatize the changes of puberty, for example, with initiation rituals that involve tattooing or cutting scars on the body. Furthermore, male and female bodily changes are often handled quite differently.[6] In our culture we take the physical changes of puberty as signs that an individual is entering adolescence, a transitional period between the other named stages of "child" and "adult." (Although this period of physical transition was recognized in earlier centuries in Europe, "adolescence" was named and, in a sense, invented, in the early part of this century and became institutionalized as a separate phase of life when commercial teen culture spread across social classes in the 1940s and 1950s.[7])

Popular beliefs suggest direct biological causation—the hormones rage and *then* girls get interested in cosmetics and dating. But adolescence is *not* a given of biology. Like other age categories, adolescence is deeply cultural; collective beliefs and practices organize and give meaning to bodily changes, and they redefine the contours of gender. In our culture we have few if any rituals to mark passage from "child" to "adolescent," and the transition is surrounded by negotiation and ambiguity.

In my fieldwork I tried to be alert to the cultural handling of physical variation, especially the social practices that help create, amplify, or override gender as an individually embodied form of difference. I watched to see how kids and adults dealt with the changes of puberty, examining bodily processes within the context of social relations and cultural meanings.[8] My approach resonates with an observation made by Sandra Kessler and her colleagues, who did research on secondary schools in Australia:

> In the process of growing up—and this is very clearly shown in the experience of puberty—the bodily process becomes an object of social practice. The social relations of gender become embodied, quite literally, in the construction of masculinity and femininity. The gender regime of a high school is not an expression of sexual biology so much as a social means of dealing with it. In many respects it contradicts, rather than expresses, the biological statute. The result is a dialectic of biosocial development rather than an expressive relationship.[9]

THE EXPERIENCES OF "EARLY DEVELOPERS"

Like other institutions, schools make basic assumptions about the life cycles of their participants.[10] The age-grading of schools assumes that individuals of the same chronological age, who move together step-by-step through the institution, will remain similar in cognitive and physical development. This assumption, of course, is often proven wrong since individuals of the same age differ in rates of maturation. Schools adjust to disjunctures by internally dividing classrooms, for example, into reading groups for those of varying skill, and by "skipping" and "holding back."[11] But the sheer variety may slip beyond these institutional adjustments and become defined as individual deviance. And there lies the fate of some of the kids, mostly girls, who are at the "early developing" end of the normal bell curve of physical maturation.

Soon after I began doing fieldwork in the Oceanside School, I noticed a tall, heavyset Latina with full breasts and rounded hips—she had the figure of a woman and the face of a child—standing in line outside a fourth-grade classroom. Several members of the school staff pointed her out to me and, with cluck-clucking voices, noted that "she's only nine years old." A week later her family moved, and she left the school. The staff talked in the same mildly amazed and disapproving way about Lenore, a white, tall, and "well-developed" (their euphemism for "big-breasted") fourth-grader who wore short tight sweaters and often chased and flirted with boys. One of the staff told me, "Lenore isn't getting adult guidance; she should wear a loose-fitting smock or something." Adults felt uneasy around girls who "had their development," especially big breasts, way ahead of their peers.[12]

Kids also gossiped about girls with big breasts, like an Ashton, white third-grader whom other kids called "cow." After an episode of teasing, the girl came crying to her teacher, who counseled, "Just tell them your body has a reason."[13] College women who were early developers recall being teased and stigmatized by both girls and boys. One remembered that in third grade her peers repeatedly snapped her bra; "this girl asked me in a loud voice in class, 'Why are you wearing a bra?' I was so mortified, I stopped wearing a bra and instead wore layers of clothes under a tunic."

Early-developing boys also stand out: their greater height and musculature visibly set them apart from other boys. But, in contrast with early-developing girls, who, especially if they have large breasts, are treated almost as if they are physically handicapped, early-developing boys reap social advantages. John and Nick, the tallest boys in Miss Bailey's classroom, were also the most popular, and other kids spoke admiringly of their athletic prowess and sheer size ("We call John the Empire State Building," Rosie told me in a praising way). In contrast, kids occasionally teased Don and Scott about their short stature, tousling their hair and repeatedly pinning their arms from behind. The two boys used various strategies, like joking and squirming away, to get out of these physically subordinating positions. Kevin was also short, but he did not receive these ritual reminders, perhaps because he was unusually skilled in athletics and a member of the group of boys with the highest status.

My observations echo the findings of survey research on the consequences of different rates of physical maturation. Several longitudinal studies have found that early-maturing girls tend to have less prestige with their peers and to be less satisfied with their bodies than are other girls of the same chronological age.[14] On the other hand, boys who enter puberty early tend to have higher self-esteem and prestige, and a more positive body image, than other boys of the same age. Early-maturing boys tend, more often than other boys, to become outstanding athletes and student leaders, although some early-maturing boys, perhaps because they form friendships with older boys, may be more likely to get involved in truancy and minor forms of delinquency.[15] By junior high or middle school, some physically small and weak boys may be labeled "wimps" and "fags"; social hierarchies have a loose relationship to somatic type.[16]

The striking difference in the experiences of early-developing girls and boys points to key features of our sex/gender system and the dynamics of male dominance. Height is valued in boys, but for girls the judgment is relative because they are "supposed" to be shorter than boys. Since the average girl physically matures two years before the average boy, a fourth- or fifth-grade girl who has begun the growth spurt of puberty towers over most of the boys in her class. Furthermore, while boys' growth tends to be more muscular, a form that is positively regarded in males, "pubescing" girls tend to put on body fat; their physicality often violates the cultural ideal of the thin female, as well as the ideal of being shorter than boys.

On several occasions during my fieldwork, kids conveyed a sense that a world in which females are taller than males is out of kilter. During a school assembly when a group of Oceanside fourth-graders had paused in the middle of a square dance, a boy stood straight and moved his flattened hand back and forth toward his much taller female partner. "Whew," he said, publicly displaying amazement at the disparity in size. On the playground two tall sixth-grade girls who were watching a group of boys playing on skateboards engaged in a wistful verbal exchange: "I wish there were more guys who were taller"; "I wish there were more *good* guys." On the other hand, girls sometimes enjoyed their bigger size, like Nancy, the Oceanside fifth-grader who, in a moment of anger, was able to physically overpower Matt, who was much smaller. But the talk afterward, about a girl beating up a boy, suggested this was not the way things are supposed to be.

The literature on gender differences in experiences of early pubescence discusses the fact that height and musculature are valued in males, while height and greater body fat violate standards of appearance for girls.[17] But the authors tiptoe around an obvious point: height and breasts (which have overt sexual connotations) are the most visible early changes of puberty, and only girls grow breasts. The breaking and lowering of boys' voices and the emergence of facial hair are also public phenomena, but these transitions happen well after elementary school. Other physical changes of early puberty—menstruation, the development of ejaculate sperm (wet dreams), the growth of underarm and pubic hair, the expansion of genitals—are much more private, except in locker rooms, a scene of junior high trepidation over issues of differential development.

In our culture, breasts are a key signifier of puberty and of female sexuality; in contrast, height is less loaded with sexual meanings. "She has all her development," a typical phrase in the language of school staff, means not only that she has grown taller, but also, and especially, that she has grown full breasts. "He has his development" refers mostly to height, with a connotation of greater athletic ability and generally enhanced power.[18] The kindergarten chant sums up the asymmetry: "Boys got the muscles . . . girls got the sexiness."

Third-, fourth-, and fifth-grade girls with "figures" (big breasts and rounded hips) are treated as deviant and even polluting because they violate the cultural ordering of age categories. As Frigga Haug states, "Female breasts are never innocent," for as soon as they appear, they signal sexuality.[19] In our culture we draw sharp divisions between "child" and "adult," defining the child as relatively asexual (although the media sexualize children of younger and younger ages) and the adult as sexual. "Teen," a third, transitional category, is also sexualized. Charged with sexual meaning, fully developed breasts seem uncomfortably out of place on the body of individuals who are still defined as children. A sense of pollution derives, as Mary Douglas has argued, from the violation of basic lines of social structure.[20]

KIDS' TALK ABOUT THEIR CHANGING BODIES

The physical events of puberty—a girl's first menstruation, the budding of breasts, a boy's wet dreams, the emergence of pubic and

underarm hair—are intensely private and often surrounded by feelings of secrecy and shame. Moments of public revelation may be dramatic, couched in humor, teasing, and experiences of embarrassment.
Kids sometimes shame early-developing girls, whose breasts cannot be
hidden from view. But even those whose development is paced with
the majority remember moments when their personal bodily changes
became the stuff of public commentary.

Some of this commentary, like bra-snapping, takes ritual form.
Once in a classroom and several times on the playground I saw a girl
or boy reach over and pull on the elastic back of a bra, letting it go
with a loud snap followed by laughter. Some college women remember
that this shaming ritual was accompanied by little jokes, like "I see
you're wearing a Band-Aid" or "Did you grow up overnight?" Others
remember being teased for *not* having breasts; one woman recalled that
when she was in sixth grade, a boy taunted her with, "A pirate's dream:
a sunken chest."[21]

Kids are often curious about one another's bodily changes, which
they may transform into public news. When I attended summer camp
between sixth and seventh grades, two girls sneaked into everyone else's
suitcases and then announced who had or had not packed sanitary
napkins. Melanie, a sixth-grade Ashton girl, told me that other girls
kept asking her if her period had come; "it hasn't, but even if it did, I
wouldn't tell them; it's none of their business."

Some girls report having private conversations with their friends
about subjects like menstruation and breast development. Several of my
women students who pooled their memories of fourth, fifth, and sixth
grades in different schools, concluded that if the most popular girls
started menstruating or wearing bras (even if they didn't "need to"),
then other girls wanted those changes too. But if the popular didn't
wear bras and hadn't, at least to general knowledge, gotten their periods, then these developments were seen as less desirable. I have heard
of two instances where groups of sixth-grade girls who had read Judy
Blume's popular book, *Are You There God? It's Me, Margaret*, formed
clubs to talk about their developing bodies; "we did it just like the girls
in the book," one woman remembered.

In Judy Blume's book, Margaret and several other sixth-grade
girls form a secret club where they talk about menstruation and make
lists of boys ranked by desirability. They do exercises to try to grow
breasts, and one by one they get their mothers to buy them bras, even
though they are still flat. The girls in the club gossip about Laura
Danker ("the big blonde with the big *you know what's*!") who has been
wearing a bra since fourth grade and who, they say, goes behind the

A&P with boys. When Margaret confronts Laura with that bit of scandal, Laura expresses hurt and anger, and a rueful Margaret realizes that her friend, Nancy, made it up. This incident points to a broader theme: females with breasts may be automatically suspected of being sexually active. Margaret starts wearing deodorant, gets teased by a boy for being flat-chested, plays "Two Minutes in the Closet," a kissing game, at a mixed-gender party, and finally, after months of worrying ("let me be like everybody else"), she gets her period.

Another of Judy Blume's books, *Then Again, Maybe I Won't*, tells the story of a thirteen-year-old boy, Tony Miglione, and his entrance into puberty. Tony begins to fantasize about Lisa, a girl who lives next door, and he uses binoculars to watch her through her bedroom window. He then dreams about Lisa and has his first wet dream. Tony keeps these events, which are surrounded by guilt and anguish, to himself.

The contrast between these representations—a girl sharing her vulnerability, but a boy going through changes in relative isolation—may or may not tap into the variety of actual experiences.[22] Margaret and her friends talk about brands of sanitary napkins and types of bras, and their mothers guide them into these technologies. In contrast, boys' early bodily changes (a spurt of height; wet dreams) do not require the purchases and equipment that accompany menstruation and breasts, although male college students have told me about how vulnerable they felt when they got an erection in class, were first told they should buy a jockstrap for PE, or discovered their first whiskers. A father, brother, or in the case of a young man raised by his mother, a male neighbor, helped them purchase jockstraps and learn how to shave.

Girls may more readily share their private vulnerabilities, but boys also discuss matters of the body in same-gender contexts, with, some evidence suggests, emphasis on genital sexuality. Gary Fine has described vivid, often bragging talk about sex among boys on Little League teams who used words like "blow job," "header," and "pusslick."[23] As school-based observers, Zella Luria and I (who have jointly written elsewhere about these themes) heard less of this kind of talk, but we both noted that boys more often flaunted rules against using "dirty words," and Luria observed fifth-grade boys playing "Mad Lib," which involved substituting "shit," "fuck," and "cunt" for words in a paragraph about the U.S. Constitution.[24] We each learned of instances where boys secretly shared pornographic magazines on school playgrounds.

Luria and I observed that elementary school girls' sexually related talk focused less on actual sex than on themes of romance, for example, in conversations about which boys are "cute" and about who "likes" whom. Jump rope rhymes often celebrate heterosexual love. An Ashton favorite was "Down in the Valley Where the Green Grass Grows," a saga of romance that concludes: ". . . along came Jason, and kissed her on the cheek. First comes love, then comes marriage, then along comes Cindy with a baby carriage." The chanters would ask the jumper (in this case, Cindy) "Who do you want to be your boyfriend?" and then tailor the chant according to her matter-of-fact or coy response (in this case, "Jason"). Sometimes they changed "kissed her on the cheek" to "kissed her on the lips."

John Gagnon and William Simon have suggested that adolescent boys and girls emphasize two different strands of sexuality.[25] Boys more often learn about sexual acts before they pick up the rhetoric of romantic love and commitment. The sequence for girls is more often the reverse: they emphasize the emotional and romantic before the explicitly sexual. Same-gender groups carry and circulate these meanings, and when heterosexual dating ensues, males and females teach each other about what they want and expect, a process that does not always go smoothly.

Lest the contrastive difference be taken too far, however, I would add examples of elementary school girls engaging in sexually explicit talk. An Oceanside staff member overheard a group of sixth-grade girls discussing "blow jobs," and Margaret Blume, who also observed on the Oceanside playground, reported that she saw one girl ask another, who was passing by, "Mona, do you like Jeff?" "Jeff who?" Mona responded. "Jeff hard-on."

## THE OFFICIAL AGENDA: SEX EDUCATION

While kids talk about and deal with bodily changes in both same- and mixed-gender contexts, school staff generally ignore these topics unless circumstances press them to respond. The adult staff at both schools mostly ignored bra-snapping and snippets of folklore with sexual content, although they sometimes punished kids for saying "dirty words." Several times I heard the staff privately discuss the pubescing bodies of students, but in the course of my fieldwork I saw only one official acknowledgment of sexually maturing bodies: the menstruation movie. Annually shown to Oceanside fifth-graders near the end of the school year, the film was the first step in the school system's sex education curriculum; the next step was a film about the facts of sexual reproduction, shown to sixth-graders. Nervous constraints related to the subject matter and to community and state controversy over sex education surrounded the event: only fifth-graders could attend, and a parent or guardian had to sign a prior note of permission. As she set up the projector, Miss Bailey joked to me, "You can be a witness if they try to take my teaching credential away."

In previous years the movie was shown only to girls, but afterward boys had repeatedly asked girls what the film was about and even offered to pay money for copies of the booklet the girls received at the end. The staff decided that in the future, boys should also see the film. The movie was preceded by rustles of anticipation. Jeremy came over and asked me, "You gonna see the film?" "What's it about?" I asked. "Sex education for fifth-graders," he replied. The two Oceanside fifth grades crowded into Miss Bailey's classroom, the girls choosing seats on one side of the room, and the boys on the other; Jessie sat with the boys, at the edge by the girls. Miss Bailey asked the students to vote on how they wanted to divide for questions after the movie—into their two classes, or with all the boys in one group and all the girls in another. Four boys raised their hands for the former, and the rest of the students voted for gender separation.

The film, which was a new one produced by a sanitary napkin company, described the changes of puberty ("soft growth of hair under your arms and in the pubic area, both boys and girls" . . . "girls' breasts become tender and fuller" . . . "girls start to menstruate"). It defined menstruation, showed a diagram of female anatomy, and then girls of varied ethnicities told their experiences ("I got mine when I was twelve"; "eleven"; "summer of sixth grade"; "when I was ten"). A female voice-over concluded, "Whenever it happens is the right time for you." The movie then showed sanitary napkins and belts and talked about how often to change and about forms of disposal. (At this point, giggles burst out around the room.) There were shots of girls talking about how it felt, about cramps and ways to relieve them, and, as evidence that "there is no way anyone can know," a sequence in which a girl put a sanitary napkin into a little folder and tucked it into her purse, which she then carried to a boy-girl party. The film concluded with a series of pictures of young women—the same ones who were earlier shown as girls—in different occupational scenes, including motherhood, and a woman's voice said, "Being a woman is one of the best things." A little girl's voice got the last chiming word: "It's better than being a boy." The last line brought laughter from around the room.

After the movie Mrs. Sorenson, the other fifth-grade teacher, led the girls to her classroom for a discussion, and I followed; the boys stayed with Miss Bailey. The ensuing half hour went very slowly; when various girls turned around to look at the clock, they expressed what I was also feeling. Mrs. Sorenson opened by telling the girls that she was not supposed to volunteer information but only answer questions raised by students. (This nervous gesture left a hanging sense of deep secrets that would not be revealed.) There was a long pause with giggles, but no questions. Mrs. Sorenson talked about the importance of "keeping clean" (thereby implying that something quite dirty was involved). Still no questions. She then talked about how "everyone is different; some flow longer, some cramp; some get pimples." "No questions? No questions?" She looked around.

Finally Helen spoke up, "Why didn't the girls see it alone? Some boys were serious, but some laughed and everything." Mrs. Sorenson responded, "Why do you think they laughed? They were nervous about it too; boys go through changes at that age too." Julia loudly added, "Their sperms." Nancy giggled and quietly repeated to Sherry, "Their sperms." The classroom aide volunteered, "You should carry a little packet all the time, just in case." Mrs. Sorenson looked slowly around the room, pleading for questions. "Any questions? Jessie?" Jessie shook her head no. "Fine." (There were still ten minutes to go.) Mrs. Sorenson: "This is the quietest I've seen many of you." A long pause, and then she had a new thought, "How many of you have sisters? You can ask sisters questions." Helen, still worrying about the boys' responses, said, "I wonder how Miss Bailey is doing? I wonder if the boys have questions? They're probably embarrassed because she's a lady."

Mrs. Sorenson began another spate of talk: "The sixth-grade film will take care of more questions; this just tells a little bit. You don't need to know it all." She paused, "Sherry, what's wrong, are you embarrassed?" Sherry gestured toward Nancy, "She hit me on the head." Then Mrs. Sorenson picked up the issue Helen had raised; "I realize it's different seeing it with boys; don't you think it's better if the boys know and can understand? If they don't understand, they might be afraid of it. I live in a family of men; I have two boys and a forty-seven-year-old boy, my husband; men are like boys, so I can tell you, boys are unsure themselves; that's why they are nervous themselves. . . . Now we know it's okay for boys to cry, to say what they want to say; we didn't used to think that. The person you should marry should be your best friend."

Julia piped up, "I can't marry Helen," and the room broke into laughter. Mrs. Sorenson turned to Jessie, "Jessie, did you like the film?" "Nope," Jessie said in a curt small voice, her body turned to the side. There were giggles. "Neera, did you think it was okay?" "A little bit," she said, looking picked-upon and uncomfortable. "Diana, was it a good film?" "I don't know." At last, as several girls turned around to look at the clock, the bell rang. Mrs. Sorenson concluded, "I'd appreciate your not discussing this on the playground."

As I participated in this uncomfortable event, I wondered how many girls had already started menstruating and how the official messages related to their varied experiences, anxieties, knowledge, and conversations with friends and family. In spite of the matter-of-fact, upbeat tone of the movie, several themes reverberated: menstruation is a secret, emotionally loaded, and shame-filled topic; adults and kids don't feel very comfortable discussing these matters; these issues are charged with tension, awkwardness, and mistrust between girls and boys. Mrs. Sorenson twice put Jessie on the spot in what I felt was a punitive mode, in effect reminding her that although she hung out with boys and preferred their activities, her body was marked by sexual difference. Julia's observation that she couldn't marry her best friend showed insight, although she would not have recognized this language, into the mismatch between the heterosexual imperative and the fact that boys and girls are rarely close friends. Finally, the fact that official sex education begins with such a central emphasis on girls reinforces their definition in terms of sexuality.[26]

## Uneven Transitions to Teen Culture

The menstruation movie put forth a saga of change from girl to young woman, but the boundaries between age categories are not clearly marked by bodily difference. Some girls and boys who have entered physical puberty stay in the social and cultural spaces of children, playing jump rope or with toy cars, and some, as in reminiscences of several professed childhood tomboys, actively resist being defined as "teens." On the other hand, some kids who physically still look like children embrace the symbols of adolescence, participating in the heterosexual rituals of "goin' with," and wearing the clothes (e.g., short tight sweaters), carrying the props (e.g., portable radios tuned into rock stations), and engaging in the movements (e.g. stylized dance steps) of commercial teen culture.[27] In short, being a child or a teenager is not dictated by the degree of one's physical maturity or the state of one's hormones; social practices shape the transition. Some kids actively display themselves as teens, in a kind of public performance, while others hang back or avoid that whole arena of activity.[28]

At both Oceanside and Ashton a disjuncture between the physical and cultural dimensions of adolescence was evident in the groups of girls (described in Chapter 5) who actively displayed teen symbols in their dress, demeanor, and activities. (In these elementary schools fewer boys participated in the public symbols of adolescence, except for "goin' with.") Lenore was one of the most physically developed of the Oceanside girls, and, as a fourth-grader, the youngest with a "figure." Some of the other full-breasted girls wore loose overblouses and spent their recesses playing jump rope. But Lenore embraced teen culture. She wore tight sweaters and pants, lip gloss, and rouge, and she often chased and flirted with boys. Lenore was part of a troupe of five or six girls who went around the playground looking for heterosexual action and who practiced dance and cheerleading steps, sometimes in rhythm with rock music on a radio they managed to smuggle into school.

The members of the troupe shared forms of stylized dress, movement, and activity associated with being teenagers, but their bodies ranged widely in size and shape. The least physically developed was Sherry, a fifth-grader in Miss Bailey's class, who was short and flatchested. From a distance, Lenore looked like an adult woman (about five and a half feet tall) and Sherry, who was older than Lenore, looked like a child (she was around three and a half feet tall). But they were close friends with neighborhood and family connections, and they shared the interests and artifacts of cultural adolescence. Sherry was also friends with Nancy; when they were together, Sherry engaged in more child-associated activities like playing on the bars or pretend games like "animals" and "statue buyer." One day when Lenore, Sherry, Nancy, and Jessica were standing together on the playground, Nancy suggested, "Let's play statue buyer." "Yes," Jessica agreed. "Are you kidding?" Lenore said with loud sarcasm, and she walked away, leaving the other three to play what Lenore contemptuously regarded as a game she had outgrown. In moments like this, kids negotiate and mark the boundaries between "child" and "teen."[29]

## COSMETIC CULTURE

Cosmetics have powerful symbolic status in the gendered marking of age-grades. When young children "dress up," they often use makeup; preschool girls, and sometimes boys, use red felt pens and crayons to paint their lips and nails. By fourth and fifth grades some girls own their own cosmetics, which they often freely share. Most adults disapprove of elementary school girls using makeup, and some schools have formal rules against the wearing of lipstick or eye shadow; the forbidden nature of makeup, of course, may heighten its allure.

One day when Miss Bailey was explaining antonyms, I noticed Nancy reach into a small leather purse and pull out a clear plastic container with pink contents. Holding her hands beneath her desk, she screwed off the lid and held it out; Rosie reached over and put her finger in, smelled the dab of pink, and, lowering her head, quickly rubbed it around her lips. Nancy smoothed some around her lips. Then Jessica got a dab and rubbed it around her mouth. Seeing that Miss Bailey was beginning to notice, Nancy screwed on the lid and tucked it back in her purse.

Elementary school girls may favor lip gloss because its shiny trace is less detectable than bright lipstick. Some brands, designed for younger girls, feature the smells and flavors of commercialized childhood. In the Ashton lunchroom a third-grade girl showed me a tube of lip gloss packaged to look like a pink Crayola; she flashed it under my nose, saying, "Smell it; strawberry. I got chocolate too." Another version that circulated in Miss Bailey's class came in a tube and had a strong grape smell; "Lip Smackers, Bonne Bell" was printed on the side.

At these ages there is still ambiguity about whether the use of cosmetics is "pretend" or "real," a vacillating line that assumed interesting proportions on Halloween. Ashton School had an annual Halloween parade; students brought in costumes and, after lunch, changed for the event. Before the parade was due to begin, I went into the girls' bathroom and discovered a group of sixth-graders in the throes of preparation. Two girls, each holding an elaborate makeup kit with many colors of eye shadow and rouge, had cornered the mirror above the sinks. One, a short white girl with small breasts, had changed into a black leotard cat costume with a tail and a cap with perky ears. The other, a Black girl, wore a long white dress with ribbons threaded through it, high heels with open backs, and an aluminum foil crown kept in place by a row of bobby pins. Side by side they leaned over the two sinks and into the mirror, applying eyeliner, eye shadow, mascara, lipstick, and rouge. They wielded various tools—sponges, Q-tips, tubes, and wands—with expert gestures. I was struck by how much more these girls knew than I about the world of cosmetics.

Other girls watched with admiring faces. One of them, a white girl, wiggled into a long printed nylon dress and then took a small makeup kit out of her brown paper bag, turned to me in a hesitating manner, and asked, "Would you put this on me?" "Can't you do it?" I asked. "I don't know how, I'm scared." She first handed me a wand of mascara. "Pretty or garish?" I asked. "Pretty," she said, so I did my best, getting some on her skin. Then she gave me a small sponge of pale eye shadow to apply, and then a tube of lipstick. Another white girl who wore bobbysocks and a flared felt skirt decorated with a cutout poodle (I flashed on the fact that her costume was what I wore "for real" when I was in junior high) said to a girl near her, "I've never worn makeup before. I have to put on gobs." She went to the mirror and worked on eyeliner, smeared it, and then asked my help in getting it off. "It looks dark under my eye. I need some blush!" she exclaimed, coming up with a cosmetic solution.

Other girls, dressed as clowns and a vampire, used makeup in a slapstick mode. "I'm getting lipstick all over," the vampire announced as she outlined her mouth and smeared the lipstick on her prominent plastic teeth. Two white girls dressed as men, one in a suit, coat, and tie and a false mustache, and another in faded blue jeans and a flannel shirt with a false beard and mustache fastened from her ears. There were crossings of race and ethnic lines, as well as of the gender line. An African-American girl wore a Wonder Woman costume, including a mask with pinkish skin. Wilma, who wore an elaborate feathered Native American costume, was, in fact, Ojibwa. "She's dressed like an Indian; she *is* an Indian," two different girls explained to me in appreciative tones. Wilma later told me her mother made the costume at the Indian Center and that it was "a boy costume; a girl's would have beads not feathers."

I wasn't able to watch the boys getting into costume, but they also wore garb that crossed boundaries between real and fantasy (monsters, ghosts, robots, superheroes), historical eras (pirates, hobos), ages (professional football players), body sizes (with pillows to add bulk), but *not* between genders. In Halloweens over the years I've noticed that boys don't costume up as females until they are in junior high. However, boy vampires did wear lipstick, which they applied in outlandish fashion and called "blood."

Halloween exemplifies what anthropologists call a "ritual of reversal," when rules are loosened and one can dress and behave in usually forbidden ways—females as males, younger as older, humans as monsters.[30] Among the youngest girls, cosmetics are full-blown pretend; the second-graders all asked adults to help with their lipstick or mascara. But as girls get older, the line between child and adult, between innocent and knowing, becomes increasingly ambiguous. Some of the sixth-grade girls demonstrated the skills of cosmeticized women, which brought admiration from other girls. Others were amateurs, and one confessed that the unfamiliar challenge of applying one's own makeup was scary.

## "GOIN' WITH"

In addition to wearing makeup and other details of personal style, dating is central to our cultural conception of teenagers. As earlier chapters have suggested, younger children sometimes invoke hetero-sexual meanings: kindergartners may chant about "sexiness," play chase-and-kiss, and tease that "Billy likes Jean." However, in the upper grades of elementary school these meanings begin to eclipse other definitions of cross-gender relations, and some kids start to pub-licly affirm themselves as sexual or at least romantic actors. By fifth and especially sixth grades the rituals of "goin' with" become a central activity.

Although pairs are the focus, "goin' with" is a group activity that bridges from moments of teasing to the construction of more last-ing and self-proclaimed couples. On the day when a substitute teacher tried in vain to bring order to Miss Bailey's classroom, the kids spent some of their time launching couples on the blackboard. Mike drew a heart, and inside he wrote, "Rita + Bert" (Rita and Bert were both on the social margins, and the gesture compounded their humiliation). Kevin erased "Rita" and replaced it with "Kathryn," the name of the most popular girl, thereby insulting Kathryn by linking her with a stigmatized boy. Then Rita erased "Kathryn" and wrote "Allen + Bert," venturing a homophobic insult, perhaps to deflect attention from the insult she had received. Allen quickly ran up and erased it. Picking up on a couple who were widely said to be "goin' with" each other, Freddy wrote "Nick + Judy," and the heart-circled inscription remained on the board.

Much effort goes into calibrating publicly named couples with actual, but hidden patterns of desire; a mutually acknowledged fit dis-tinguishes full-fledged "goin' with" relationships from those that are teasingly ventured. Sometimes an individual who "likes" another will directly inquire to see if the feeling is reciprocated. Joan, an Ashton fifth-grader, told me, "Wally sent me a note asking me to go with him. I said yes, and now we talk on the phone." David, another fifth-grader, explained, "I hired a messenger, a friend; he asked Pam if she'd go with me, and she said yes." Sometimes "goin' with" requests are turned down. Early in the year in Miss Bailey's classroom, Bill sent Tracy a note asking "Will you go with me? yes—no—." She checked "no" and silently sent it back.

Although they more often invite through indirection, girls may also be turned down. Mary, a college student, described a complex sequence of events that unfolded when she was in sixth grade. She told Janet, her best friend, that she liked Vincent, and the word was passed on to him. Then Vincent told Jack to tell Mary that he didn't like her because she was flat-chested and had a mole on her face. Mary was crushed, and she began to stuff her bra with cotton until a teacher told her to "give it up." Kristine also remembered a sixth-grade "crush"; "my stomach would turn when I saw him; I would walk behind him in the hopes that he'd stop and notice me, and I ripped out a page of my diary and sent it to him, but he ignored me."

Third parties play a busy role in discovering and circulating news about who "likes" whom and declaring a "goin' with" pair when they find a match. Both Ashton and Oceanside kids would come up to one another on the playground with queries like "Craig likes you; do you like him?" "Do you like Jane?" When there was "liking" affirmation from both parties, the news traveled widely. At Oceanside there was a wave of gossip about Judy going with Nick, a pairing that three different kids went out of their way to report to me. I asked one of the gossipers if the pair went on dates; "Nick asked her to the movies, but her mom wouldn't let her go" was the reply, from a girl who wasn't a close friend of either party.

Tracy and Allen, another Oceanside couple who started going together in May, were the focus of much gossip and teasing. One day in the classroom Jessie loudly asked Allen, "Having fun with Tracy?" Then she added, "Tomorrow Allen and Tracy are going to get married." Sheila ran over to the boys' side of the classroom and whispered and laughed with them, gesturing toward Tracy. Tracy looked a little embarrassed, and Allen slumped in a chair by the back table. As they lined up for recess, Kevin told Allen, "We won't bug you anymore." But then Sheila came over and said, "Kevin's best man." Tracy grabbed Sheila's sleeve and urgently whispered, "Why is it such a big deal?"

Although that teasing episode bothered her, Tracy took pride in her romantic relationship with Allen. A week later she came up to me and announced, "Did you know I'm goin' with Allen?" "Did you go on a date?" I asked. "One, last Sunday; we went to the movies." "Was it fun?" "Yeah, except RJ tried to spoil it; he's Sheila's old boyfriend. He poured ice on Allen." Jessica, who was standing next to us, started to tease, "I'm gonna tell Allen." Tracy retorted matter-of-factly, "He doesn't care. At first they really teased him 'til Miss Bailey said if they bugged us anymore she'd send them to the principal."

Most of the elementary school "goin' with" relationships I learned about were fairly distant. Various couples sent notes, talked on the phone, exchanged gifts on birthdays and holidays, and sat, danced, or skated together at group parties. Few went on dates. One college woman remembered that she and her fifth-grade boyfriend "barely talked to each other, but we held hands a few times; we didn't do much for fear of teasing." On the other hand, several college students remember kissing their elementary school boyfriend or girlfriend, sometimes at parties ("we had a contest to see who could kiss the longest and couples competed"). There is no doubt more extensive sexual activity than I uncovered in short interviews and by observing in relatively public, school settings.

The "goin' with" relationships of fourth-, fifth-, and sixth-graders usually last only a few days, or at most, a few weeks. Third parties often carry out their dissolution, as well as their formation. David, who "hired" a messenger to ask if Pam would go with him, said that after a few days, "Pam's friend Jennie told me that Pam wanted to break up," and that was the end of the liaison.

Several college students told me that in elementary school they wanted a girlfriend or boyfriend because it was the popular thing to do, and they wanted partners who were generally considered desirable and sought after by others. They frequently switched partners and remember an element of competition in "goin' with" circles. In her memoirs Susan Allen Toth muses upon the impersonal dimension of these practices: "'Boyfriends' weren't friends at all; they were prizes, escorts, symbols of achievement, fascinating strangers, the Other. It is simpler to regard people as the Other; it means you don't have to think of them as human beings like yourself, with any hopes, fears, or vulnerabilities. They can be pasted into position like movie stills or pictures into an album."[31] In some cases, having a boyfriend or girlfriend may express personal desire and connection, but it may also be a way of claiming status with one's peers, and a qualitatively different, more mature ("teenage") form of femininity or masculinity.

By high school, when full-fledged dating becomes prevalent, the collective structure—groups assessing patterns of desire, ranking desirability, and constructing, launching, and dissolving couples— consolidates into a kind of market. Although groups may be less involved in the direct creation and dissolution of couples, they continue to rank desirability and to shape understandings about "how far" a couple should "go." Social status enters into competition for dates, and "attractiveness" becomes a kind of commodity. Willard Waller and other sociologists of dating describe the mix of vulnerability and self-protectiveness that individuals bring to a process in which they risk exposure, rejection, and exploitation.[32] Both males and females take a calculating approach, viewing the other gender with wariness and even antagonism.

## Gender, Age, and Sexual Meanings

The transition from childhood to adolescence is uneven and fluctuating, the focus of negotiation and occasional conflict. Many of the struggles are between kids and adults, and the dynamics focus issues of generational boundaries and inequality. But the transition is also gendered. It is in same-gender groups (with occasional, often loaded mixed-gender moments) that many girls and boys assess and give meaning to the physical changes of puberty, teaching one another new meanings and skills partly gleaned from the larger worlds of the media and market. Same- and mixed-gender groups structure the early forms of active heterosexuality, and they assert an increasingly vocal taboo against other forms of sexuality. By fourth and fifth grades, "fag" has become a widespread and serious term of insult. Unlike those who are heterosexual, lesbian and gay adolescents have no public, school-based rituals to codify and validate their desires; "there are no affirming public markers about what they are feeling and thinking."[33]

Our culture organizes the contrast between "child" and "adult" ("teen" vacillates between these major age categories) around a series of dualisms: irresponsible/responsible; dependent/autonomous; play/ work; asexual/sexual.[34] The last is especially charged and increasingly contested. As a culture we have been invested in the notion of childhood innocence and the belief that children should be kept apart from sexual knowledge and action.[35] The taboo surrounding children and sex is tenuous; many, at least in theory, accept the notion of children as sexual beings, and children sometimes engage in practices (some leading to orgasm) that adults call "sexual." Adult sexual abuse of children is increasingly visible, and advertisements and films eroticize children of younger and younger ages. But special taboos and tensions continue to surround relationships of children to sexuality, taboos which many kids actively challenge as they enter adolescence.

In contrast with the relatively, or ambivalently, asexual gender meanings of childhood, "teen" and "adult" styles of femininity and masculinity are overtly sexual. This has not been the case in other times and places. Some traditional Native American cultures defined gender meanings by occupational pursuits, dress, and demeanor, but not by sexuality.[36] And in Euro-American culture before the late nineteenth century, sexuality was not, as it is now, defined as an essential core of individual adult identity.[37] In this century heterosexual meanings have come to saturate dominant notions of adult "femininity" and "masculinity," and, especially with the expansion of commercialized teen culture, heterosexual meanings have also become central to gender symbolism geared to teens. Within the large categories of "child," "teen," and "adult" lie many variations and contradictions. But a major symbolic disjuncture is bound up in the transition from the "sexually innocent" child to the "publicly sexual" teen. (Because the students in Oceanside and Ashton were predominantly white and working-class, and because I gathered more fragmentary information about the transition to adolescence than about other topics, I have paid too little attention to race, ethnicity, and social class as they enter into age and gender transitions.)

Drawing on Adrienne Rich's conceptualization, the transition to adolescence can be understood as a period of entry into the institution of heterosexuality.[38] While this transition brings new constraints and vulnerabilities for boys as well as girls, girls are particularly disadvantaged. Disturbing national statistics paint an overall picture of adolescence as "the fall" for girls: compared with boys of the same age, and with themselves at earlier ages, girls who are twelve, thirteen, and fourteen have higher rates of depression, lower self-esteem, more negative images of their own bodies, and declining academic performance in areas like math and science.[39] These, of course, are statistical patterns; many girls fare well through this period of change, and some boys experience serious problems. But larger institutional forces, bound up in structures of gender, sexuality, and age, make this an especially difficult period for girls.

During adolescence both boys and girls come to be seen, and to see themselves, as sexual actors, but girls are more pervasively sexualized than boys. Athletics provides a continuous arena where at least some boys can perform and gain status as they move from primary through secondary schooling. But for many girls, appearance and relationships with boys begin to take primacy over other activities. In middle school or junior high the status of girls with other girls begins to be shaped by their popularity with boys; same-gender relations among boys are less affected by relationships with the other gender.[40] In short, the social position of girls increasingly derives from their romantic relationships with boys, but not vice versa.

The sixth-grade girls' Halloween preparations were a microcosm of a vast project that absorbs many teenage girls: bringing their personal appearance into line with idealized and sexual images of femininity. This involves learning the skills and practices of cosmetic culture, new modes of dress (pantyhose, heels, dangling earrings), and heterosexualized ways of moving and holding one's body. Propelled by strong cultural and commercial forces, many teenage girls learn to turn themselves into, and regard themselves as, objects.[41]

The Halloween scene also showed that there can be pleasure and creativity in this process. And sexual meanings can be a source of new forms of power. In their sexualized troupes, girls like Lenore and Sherry claimed space and exuded strength and energy. Girls may use cosmetics, discussions of boyfriends, dressing sexually, and other forms of exaggerated "teen" femininity to challenge adult, and class- and race-based, authority in schools.[42] But the pleasurable and powerful dimensions of heterosexual femininity contain a series of traps and double binds. The double standard persists, and girls who are too overtly sexual run the risk of being labeled "sluts."[43] As Rosalind Petchesky has observed, teenage girls "are in the anomalous position of being at once infantalized by the cult of virginity (codified, for example, in statutory rape and 'age of consent' laws) and objectified by the media's cult of 'Lolita'; at the same time, they have few real resources for independence."[44] Sexual harassment and rape are persistent dangers, and if they are heterosexually active, girls also run the risks of pregnancy and disease. In gestures that mix protection with punishment, parents and other adults often tighten their control of girls when they become adolescents, and sexuality becomes a terrain of struggle between generations. While some girls use active sexuality to declare their independence from parental and school authority, this challenge (if they are heterosexual) may "ultimately and paradoxically" bring them under more direct control by boys; as Mica Nava remarks, "girls' most common form of rebellion serves only to bind them more tightly to their subordination as women."[45]

# CHAPTER 9

# Lessons for Adults

*In the schoolroom more than any other place, does the
difference of sex, if there is any, need to be forgotten.*
—Susan B. Anthony, 1856

In this ethnographic study of kids' daily lives in school, I have sought
to ground and develop, with detailed substance and a sense of process
and activity, the claim that gender is socially constructed. I have argued
that kids, as well as adults, take an active hand in constructing gender,
and that collective practices—forming lines, choosing seats, teasing,
gossiping, seeking access to or avoiding particular activities—animate
the process. I have explored the subject of children and gender without being limited by notions of "socialization" and "development." As a
result, I have been able to give full attention to children as social actors
living in the abundant present, although influenced by larger social
forces. One of my goals is to bring children more fully into sociological
thought.

I have pushed for fresh thinking not only about children but
also about gender. The last two decades of feminist theory have moved
the analysis of gender beyond unexamined dualisms and toward much
greater complexity. But these insights have not, by and large, been

extended to research on children. Relatively static and dichotomous notions of individual and group gender difference sit, like a gigantic magnet, at the core of much of the research on children and gender, shaping orienting questions, research designs, and frameworks of interpretation.

In this study I have repeatedly returned to this force field, trying to understand its powerful attraction, analyze its effects, and to break away from its limitations. Thus, I showed how kids construct "the girls" and "the boys" as boundaried and rival groups through practices that uphold a sense of gender as an oppositional dichotomy. But I also examined practices that have the effect of neutralizing, or, as in situations of "crossing," even challenging the significance of gender. Coming at the magnet from another direction, I deconstructed and moved beyond a popular but limiting narrative of group gender difference: the claim that boys and girls have essentially different cultures.

My thinking has benefited enormously from the realization that gender has analytically separable dimensions.[1] At the *individual* level, gender, indeed, takes dichotomous form. Each newborn is declared to be either "a boy" or "a girl," and although a few later migrate, for the vast majority the initial assignment remains lifelong. Through patterns of naming, dress, and many other concrete details, we daily mark and give life to the dichotomous gender categories, girl/ boy, female/male, man/woman.

The dichotomous nature of individual gender categories and identity—one is *either* a boy or a girl, never both—may help account for the deep hold of dualisms on our ways of thinking about gender.[2] But while dichotomous in form, these categories fill with complicated, shifting, and sometimes contradictory *gender meanings.* Those who use a discourse of "the pinks and the blues," continually searching for contrastive differences, may assume that girls and boys sharply divide as two separate and unitary types of beings. But the social world is not that simple. There are many ways of being a boy or girl, some of them overlapping, some varying by context, some shifting along lines of race, ethnicity, class, and age. Throughout the book I have examined varied gender discourses, and the social practices that evoke or undermine them, including kids' talk about boys as "tough" and girls as "nice"; narratives and labels associated with "tomboys" and "sissies"; and the contested and gendered divisions between "child," "teen," and "adult."

Gender is not only a category of individual identity and the focus of symbolic constructions, but also a dimension of *social relations and social organization.* I have traced the weaving of gender in the creation of groups, encounters, and, at a more abstract level, institutions. The organization and meanings of gender vary from one social context to another, from families to neighborhoods to schools, and, within schools, from foursquare to scenes of chasing to classrooms and lunchrooms. Gender varies in degree and mode of relevance. When they form separate girls' and boys' tables in the lunchroom, kids make individual gender categories highly relevant to their social relations. But when boys and girls get together to work on a classroom project or in situations where age or ethnicity is at the fore, gender becomes less or differently significant. In short, at the level of social situations, gender has a fluid quality.

Finally, power is central to the social relations of gender. Both boys and girls operate from a position of subordination to adults; age relations, like those of class and race, alter the dynamics of gender. However, boys—who control more space, more often violate girls' activities, and treat girls as contaminating—participate in larger structures of male dominance. Girls often contest boys' exertions of power, and other lines of inequality add to the complexity. The dynamics of power, like those of gender, are fluid and contextual.

## Implications for Social Change

This fluid and contextual approach, this sense of a play of possibilities, has concrete implications for social change. The kinds of change I generally support fit with the visions of many of the writers about and practitioners of nonsexist, or antisexist, education, including Susan B. Anthony, who in 1856 argued that in schooling, "the difference of sex, if there is any" should be forgotten.[3] I share the long-range goal of eliminating the gender typing of tasks and activities, of allocating opportunities, resources, and teacher attention without regard to the social categories of students.[4] I also believe that school staff should try to open, rather than diminish, opportunities for boys and girls, and students of different class, racial, and ethnic backgrounds, and physical abilities, to get to know one another as individuals and friends. Adults can help kids build relationships based on mutuality and respect.

When I take this vision and line it up with gender-marked occasions—when girls and boys avoid one another, trade insults, or tease those who try to enter "gender-inappropriate" groups and activities—the path to change looks extremely difficult. But other moments offer encouragement and suggest clues for action. These are the occasions when boys and girls play together in amicable games of handball or dodgeball, when mixed-gender groups comfortably interact in classrooms and lunchrooms, when individuals join groups of the other gender without commentary. One of the most hopeful lessons I have drawn from research on schooling is that gender-related patterns, such as boys participating more actively and receiving more teacher attention than girls in classroom settings, are, at the most, a matter of statistical difference. There is wide individual variation in patterns like readiness to talk in class, and classrooms vary in patterns of teacher-student interaction. Comparing kids' gender relations in different kindergartens, Goodenough found that informal interactions in some classrooms were far less male dominated than in others.[5] *Understanding that gender relations are not fixed and invariant but vary by context can help teachers and aides reflect on their practices and extend those that seem to promote equitable interactions.*

Only one of the teachers whose practices I observed was explicitly concerned about sexism. Mrs. Smith, the Ashton kindergarten teacher, told me that several years before when she was teaching at another school, she had students line up by gender because it was "convenient," but the other kindergarten teacher told her she should discontinue the practice because of Title IX. Soon after, Mrs. Smith attended a Title IX workshop and gave more thought to grouping practices. She shifted to having students form single lines or sort themselves according to criteria like what they liked to eat or the color of their shoes, which, she observed, was a useful way to teach classification. Mrs. Smith occasionally talked to her colleagues about their practices. For example, as they were preparing for the opening of school, she noticed that another teacher was making pink name tags for girls and blue name tags for boys. "That's sexist," she told her colleague, who reflected on it and then shifted to yellow for everyone.[6]

Mrs. Johnson, the Ashton second-grade teacher, was unconcerned about and somewhat dismissive of gender issues. "They're just kids," she said when I first met her and she learned of my interest in gender. But her practices were far from neutral. The graphics on her walls were quite stereotyped, and she verbally separated girls and boys with repeated admonitions like "you girls should get busy." On the other hand, although I doubt this was her intent, some of Mrs. Johnson's practices did lessen the salience of gender. For example, she organized permanent classroom seating according to principles like "hearing, sight, height" and thereby increased communication between girls and boys. In contrast, Miss Bailey, the Oceanside fourth-fifth–grade teacher, let her students choose their own seating, which resulted in almost total gender separation. And she ratified the gender divide by pitting boys against girls in math and spelling contests. But when she formed reading groups based on ability and organized lines according to the principle of "hot lunch versus cold lunch," her practices drew girls and boys together.

By setting up contests that pitted boys against girls, Miss Bailey tried to harness gender rivalry as a motivation for learning. The resulting group antagonism sometimes spilled beyond the academic purposes at hand. When kids defined "the girls" and "the boys" as separate and antagonistic groups, primarily in the lunchrooms and on the playgrounds where they were freer to shape the grounds of interaction, they created pockets of trouble for adults intent on maintaining order.

In both schools a few noontime aides were responsible for a large number of students. These were part-time, working-class women employees, some of them mothers or aunts of the students. Students called the aides by their first names and were more familiar and informal with them than with most teachers. The aides often had to respond to the combustible, angry feelings and the yelling, taunting, and complaining that accompanied scenes of cross-gender chasing and invasion. Several Ashton aides tried to solve problems of cross-gender hassling by keeping boys and girls totally apart from one another, for example, by banning boys to the grassy playing fields and telling girls to stay near the building. Ironically, efforts to maintain order by separating girls and boys perpetuate the very polarization, the sense of being opposite and antagonistic sides, that sets spirals of hostility into motion in the first place.

After a particularly difficult lunch period when a small number of boys continually raised a ruckus, Betty, an Ashton aide, told all the second-grade boys that for the rest of the week they had to sit at a separate table so she could "keep an eye on" them. Talking above the noisy eaters, Betty loudly said to me, "This is my boys' table. I made them sit here. They're wild, but I love every one." When I went over to the girls' table, formed by default when the aide pulled out all the boys, one of the girls volunteered, "The boys have to sit over there; they're naughty." "Yeah, boys are naughty," echoed several other girls with self-righteous tones.

Separating all boys from all girls perpetuates an image of dichotomous difference (all boys as "naughty" and "wild"; all girls as better behaved) and encourages psychological splitting. Pressed by cultural ideals to display themselves as "good" and "nice," girls may displace anger and conflict onto boys, defining them as "naughty." Boys, in turn, may project forbidden feelings of vulnerability and dependence when they taunt girls as "crybabies" and "tattletales."[7] More cross-gender interaction, of the relaxed rather than borderworking kind, would undermine these cycles of projection. When girls and boys are separated, it is easier to objectify and stereotype the other gender.

A few researchers have examined the gender-related practices, and thinking, of teachers, aides, and principals, including the ways in which they think about interactions among gender, race/ethnicity, social class, and age.[8] Clearly the same individual may engage in contradictory actions, and beliefs and actual practices do not always coincide. Within one school, as at Ashton and Oceanside, there will no doubt be an array of beliefs and practices.[9] For example, compared with staff who work mostly in classrooms, playground aides may deal with a different sort of gender imagery, with more emphasis on the physical, such as connections between sports and dominant forms of masculinity. Overall, however, school staff may be less likely to engage in practices that polarize boys and girls if they question the notion of "natural" and dichotomized gender differences (the empirical evidence overwhelmingly counters that notion) and become aware of alternative ways of grouping and interacting with students.

## How to Promote Cooperative Relations between Boys and Girls

In Chapter 4 I discussed the conditions that encourage girls and boys to interact with one another without engaging in the social distancing of borderwork. Relaxed mixed-gender interaction is more likely when an adult sets up the activities, when access is routinely structured, when there are few potential witnesses, and when individuals have the skills an activity requires. Analysis of the "how"s of gender integration, along with the insights of observant teachers who have developed techniques to challenge separation and antagonism between boys and girls, lead to the following practical suggestions for promoting cooperative cross-gender interaction. Some of these practices have been developed by teachers and researchers trying to challenge racial separation and inequality, and in this brief review I will try to encompass some of the interactive dynamics of race and gender. The ideas may also apply to the handling of other differences, such as religion or disability.

*1. In grouping students, use criteria other than gender or race.*[10] When teachers and aides divide girls and boys into competing teams or tell them to sit at different tables, they ratify the dynamics of separation, differential treatment, stereotyping, and antagonism. Organizing students on other grounds, such as random sorting, and using terms of address like "class" or "students" rather than the ubiquitous "boys and girls" will help undermine gender marking.

This suggestion raises a basic dilemma. When granted autonomy and left on their own, kids tend to separate by gender and sometimes also by race. Should school staff determine all seating, even in lunchrooms? Should playground aides bustle into situations kids have set up and urge girls and boys to play together? Obviously this is neither practical or desirable. In my emphasis on promoting cooperative relations between boys and girls, I don't want to neglect the value of same-gender relationships, and of kids having some autonomy to structure their own activities. Kids do not flourish when they are perpetually watched and controlled; they need, and will struggle to claim, at least some independence from adults. Trying to see the world through kids' eyes can help adults act more effectively, in part by tempering our impulses to control.

On the other hand, freedom from adult intervention does not open a realm of unlimited choice, and the dynamics of kids' social relations, such as patterns of teasing, may actually foreclose possibilities. If teachers leave classroom seating up to students, as Miss Bailey did, the result may be extreme separation by gender, and, depending on the composition of the school, also separation by race. When adults form mixed-gender groups, I have observed that some kids look a little relieved; the adult action takes away the risk of teasing and makes girl-boy interactions possible. "That's the advantage of assigned seating," one boy told me; "you get to talk to kids you usually wouldn't get to know." When they do choose to form groups, for whatever purpose, I believe that school staff should try, self-consciously, to maximize heterogeneity.

*2. Affirm and reinforce the values of cooperation among all kids regardless of social categories.* A fifth-grade teacher recently told me about her efforts to undermine "girl-boy stuff" and foster more cooperative cross-gender relations among her students. At the beginning of the year when the students formed gender-separated lines, she told them there would be one line, the "class line." "We're one class, not boys and girls; we're going to get together as a class," she repeatedly told them. By emphasizing "the class," she affirmed a more inclusive basis of solidarity.

To be effective, affirmation of the value of mixed-gender, and mixed-race, interaction may need to be explicit and continual. Lisa Serbin and her colleagues, who found extensive gender separation among children in a preschool, trained the teachers to positively reinforce cooperative cross-gender play, for example, with comments like "John and Cathy are working hard together on their project." This behavior-modification effort lasted for two weeks, during which the amount of cross-gender play increased significantly. But when the program was discontinued, the children returned to the earlier pattern.[11]

Barbara Porro describes a "processual" approach to nonsexist education that she developed while teaching a first-grade class. She deliberately integrated girls and boys in seating arrangements, small group instruction, lining up, and supervised team games, but she found that when they were together, some boys and girls continued to interact in hostile ways. Porro then worked to explicitly promote the value of cooperative interaction between girls and boys. She read her students stories in which boys and girls approached one another and made friends. Heated discussions sometimes followed, in which the kids talked about how girls and boys who played together were called "tomboys," "sissies," and "in love." Porro encouraged the students to explore these loaded words and the unfairness of the labeling. "Children began to admit that it was possible for boys and girls to play together just because they liked each other. The stories and the talks helped to establish a new classroom value: Boys and girls can be friends."[12]

Kevin Karkau, a fourth-grade student teacher, has also written about strategies for lessening the amount of gender separation in the classroom and on the playground. He used exercises to raise the students' awareness of gender stereotyping and asked the class why boys and girls were so reluctant to associate with each other, for example, why so few girls played soccer at recess. The boys said girls could play if they wanted, but they didn't want to. But one of the girls observed, "The boys never ask us to play. Then when we do play, only boys are chosen to be captains. And girls don't get the ball passed to them very often, and when a girl scores a goal, the boys don't cheer." After much discussion, some of the boys agreed these were legitimate complaints. The class also discussed talk about "being in love," "cooties," and "girl-touch" and how it kept boys and girls apart. After a number of these discussions, Karkau asked the students to think of specific activities that would reduce separation between girls and boys. The list included inviting girls to play soccer, mixing in line, and not laughing or teasing when people associate with someone of the other gender. Some of the students implemented these suggestions, and Karkau helped facilitate a shift to more mixed-gender seating. By the end of the year, he observed that there was an increase in the amount of communication and interaction between girls and boys.[13]

3. *Whenever possible, organize students into small, heterogeneous, and cooperative work groups.* Unfortunately, we can't lessen the crowding of most schools, but small group instruction may create pockets of less public and thus, perhaps, more cooperative interaction. Indeed, social psychologists who study the dynamics of intergroup relations have found that when people from different racial or gender groups interact in smaller groups focused on a shared goal requiring interdependence, they are more likely to see one another as individuals rather than through the lens of "us-versus-them."

Elliot Aronson and his colleagues entered desegregated classrooms and organized small multiracial groups to work together on reports, studying for quizzes, and other collaborative tasks. They called this a "jigsaw classroom," referring to the principle of a jigsaw puzzle in which each person has pieces of information the entire group needs to complete the task. The result was a deemphasis on racial divisions and an increase in friendships among African-American, Chicano, and white students. Marlaine Lockheed reviewed similar classroom experiments in which small group instructional methods created more amicable relationships between boys and girls.[14] In line with this, I noticed that some of the most comfortable cross-gender encounters in the Oceanside fourth-fifth–grade classroom took place when a smaller group of girls and boys worked together on tasks like creating a radio play or building a papier-mâché map.[15]

4. *Facilitate kids' access to all activities.* On one rare day on the Ashton "little kids" playground, an aide organized a mixed-gender group into a game of "London Bridge." The kids played with cooperative enthusiasm, in contrast to the usual separation and antagonism between groups of boys and groups of girls. Probably without realizing it, the aide had chosen an innovation that had multiple possibilities for enhancing amicable cross-gender interaction. London Bridge is a cooperative activity; both girls and boys had access to the game; and she taught the words and skills to everyone. Many activities, especially on playgrounds, do not fit these criteria, and even in classrooms girls and boys may not have equal access to particular activities; for example,

in some classrooms boys have been found to have more access than girls to computers.[16]

To broaden access to gender-typed activities, school staff can make a point of teaching the skills to everyone and, if possible, setting an example by challenging stereotypes. Barbara Porro played soccer with her first-grade students and found that her active presence encouraged girls to join the game.[17] A teacher in Michigan told me about one of her colleagues, a male first-grade teacher, who energetically taught his entire class to jump rope, drawing in boys as well as girls.

Lessons can also be drawn from playground activities where girls and boys most often mix. A few years before I arrived at Oceanside, the physical education teacher introduced the game of handball. Wooden backboards were installed on the playground, and all students were taught the rules and given a chance to play during physical education classes. The ease of access to handball (lining up rather than having to be chosen and thus being vulnerable to teasing and exclusion) also encouraged heterogeneity among the players. A large proportion of gender-mixed play in the Massachusetts private school where Zella Luria observed took place in "ghost," a type of volleyball. Easy and routinized access was, Luria believes, the key to the game's success in promoting cross-gender play. According to the rules of the game, teams could be any size as long as each side had the same number. When a group (say, three girls) arrived to play, each individual had to go to the side with the fewest players, which divided them up. While more boys than girls played ghost, it was easy for girls to join; they couldn't be excluded, as they sometimes were from team games like soccer.[18]

School staff might consider introducing games, like handball and ghost, that have the potential to increase the amount of cross-gender play. A playground rule that would-be players cannot be "locked out" of a game unless there are already too many players can also lessen opportunities for exclusion and may embolden more kids to join activities stereotypically associated with the other gender. By introducing new activities and teaching relevant skills in a gender-neutral way, teachers and aides can create conditions in which kids themselves may more often form mixed-gender groups. The transformative elements of play—a sense of the voluntary and of control over the terms of interaction—can be drawn on to facilitate social change.[19]

*5. Actively intervene to challenge the dynamics of stereotyping and power.* Proximity does not necessarily lead to equality, as critics of the philosophies of assimilation and integration have long pointed out. Boys and girls and kids of different racial and ethnic backgrounds may be encouraged to interact more frequently, but on whose terms? Groups may be formally integrated, but tensions and inequalities may persist. In the desegregated middle school where Schofield observed, the teachers by and large affirmed a neutral or color-blind ideology, trying to ignore the presence of race divisions (the teachers more readily marked gender in their interaction with students). But the students often divided and sometimes hassled one another along lines of both race and gender, and there was persistent mistrust and fear between Black and white students. The teaching staff were so intent on pretending that race made no difference that they did little to help white and Black students learn how to interact with one another or explore the nature and meaning of cultural difference and the dynamics of racism.[20] In some situations it may be important for teachers to openly deal with rather than ignore social divisions.

My observations of antagonistic mixed-gender interactions at Oceanside and Ashton also suggest that drawing boys and girls together is only one step; the dynamics of stereotyping and power may have to be explicitly confronted. Barbara Porro and Kevin Karkau engaged their classes in discussions about gender stereotyping, persistent separation between girls and boys, and the teasing ("sissies," "tomboys," "you're in love") that kept them apart. Porro explained sexism to her students by finding terms that six-year-olds could understand; the class began to label sexist ideas (e.g., that women could not be doctors, or men could not be nurses) as old-fashioned.[21] Raphaella Best, a reading teacher, both observed and intervened in the interactions of a group of students as they moved through elementary school. She encouraged them to challenge stereotypes, especially the one boys had of themselves as superior and girls as inferior, and she tried to help boys and girls relate to one another as friends rather than potential romantic partners.[22] These accounts suggest ways in which teachers can engage their students, even first-graders, in critical thinking about and collaborative ways of transcending social divisions and inequalities.

## The Problems of Aggressive Masculinity

When asked about the gender situations they find most troubling, teachers and parents of young children often talk about boys. The troubling behaviors lie at opposite ends of a continuum. At one end is the aggressive masculine bonding in evidence when groups of boys disrupt classrooms, derogate girls and invade their play, and make fun of subordinated "weaker" boys. Boys who engage in this sort of behavior take center stage in many school ethnographies; in fact, as I earlier observed, their style is often equated with masculinity itself. At the other extreme, adults express concern about boys who do not uphold dominant notions of masculinity, who avoid the tough and aggressive, don't like sports, and are therefore vulnerable to ostracism, teasing, and being labeled "sissy," "nerd," or "fag."

Women often seem far more troubled by boys' aggressive masculine bonding than are men. Vivian Paley's saga of a kindergarten "super-hero clique" starts with her discomfort and ends with her acceptance of their rambunctuous and invasive style of play. Paley queries her discomfort with uninhibited movement and "aggressive tumble-and-wrestle," relating her uneasiness to her gender.[23] After several months of field-work I also became aware of my discomfort with physical roughhous-ing, which I far too quickly framed as fighting, and I began to suspect that my response was anchored in my background as an upper-middle-class woman. To creatively deal with gender, especially in settings with students from varied class and ethnic backgrounds, school staff might want to reflect on their responses to and develop more tolerance of dif-ferent styles of self-expression.[24]

There is, however, a point at which differences of style shade into patterns of harassment or domination. Paley's self-reflectiveness is admirable, but I find her much too accepting of male dominance among her students. In contrast, Goodenough remains troubled by the sexism of more macho kindergarten boys because, especially in the classroom where such a group set the overall tone, their harrassment and verbal put-downs "reined in the spontaneity and limited the par-ticipation of the girls."[25] Her concerns contrast with the relatively uncritical acceptance of sexist masculine bonding found in Gary Fine's ethnography of U.S. Little League teams and Paul Willis's study of working-class "lads" in England.[26]

Some adults excuse boys' displays of masculine superiority because they detect a defensive edge in the contempt for things femi-nine and because they figure it's just a stage, in spite of obvious links to adult male privilege and sexism. Adults may even feel quietly reas-sured that a boy who behaves in aggressively sexist ways is affirming "normal" masculinity; after all, dominance and control, in less harass-ing and more modified forms, are valued in adult men. In contrast, parents of "good," quiet boys sometimes worry that their sons are too "feminine" and will be taunted by other kids. As an antidote, some push their sons into sports programs and urge them away from playing with girls or engaging in female-typed activities. The specter of "sissies," "nerds," and "fags" helps sustain hegemonic masculinity and the structuring of gender as opposition and inequality. At both ends of the spectrum of masculinity lies a devaluing of things feminine, and ultimately of girls and women.

Ellen Jordan has perceptively explored these issues, drawing on many years of experience as a teacher in an Australian "infants school," encompassing kindergarten through second grade. The staff of the school were committed to nonsexist education, and they implemented gender-neutral practices such as mixing girls and boys in all activities, using gender-inclusive language, and challenging the definition of particular jobs and games as "for boys" or "for girls." Jordan observed that while these practices opened up a range of options, especially for girls, they did not challenge a negative cycle of behavior involving boys. The teachers valued cooperative and gentle behavior, and when children (nearly all of them boys) were loud and disruptive, the teachers said they were "naughty." Boys who were labeled "naughty" began to define themselves in opposition to girls and to official school authority, adopting an idiom of masculine bonding and, in effect, defining masculinity for the children as a whole. "Good" boys, who were not disruptive, risked being ridiculed.[27]

Teaching practices that ignore or try to play down gender differences, Jordan argues, may have unintended negative consequences. Without guidance and positive intervention, boys adopt definitions that set masculinity in opposition to femininity and reproduce male dominance. Jordan proposes that adults should demonstrate to kids that there are a "variety of ways of being male, many of them admirable" and that "none need depend on being different from and superior to girls and women."[28] I would add that we should challenge labels like "sissy," "nerd," and "fag," and, when they are old enough to understand the issues, discuss with students not only the dynamics of sexism and racism, but also homophobia.

## The Problems of Heterosexualized Femininity

Perhaps because no specter comparable to "sissy" and "fag" reins in imagined alternatives for girls, teachers and parents of young children seem far less ambivalent about encouraging androgyny in their young daughters than in their sons. Jordan observes that because girls have more leeway to begin with, nonsexist educational strategies have been more successful in challenging conventional gender definitions for younger girls than for younger boys.

But the leeway begins to tighten as girls approach adolescence and move into the heterosexualized gender system of teens and adults. Statistics about "the fall"—the decline in self-confidence, self-esteem, body image, and ambition that many girls experience as they enter adolescence—have begun to raise widespread concern. As I suggested in the preceding chapter, it is during the transition from "child" to "teen" that girls start negotiating the forces of adult femininity, a set of structures and meanings that more fully inscribe their subordination on the basis of gender. "Emphasized femininity" (Connell's term for the most culturally valued form) is based on accommodating to the desires and interests of men.[29] Girls are pressured to make themselves "attractive," to get a boyfriend, to define themselves and other girls in terms of their positions in the heterosexual market. Although boys also enter into this market, it is less defining of their status and presumed futures, and, given the structuring of heterosexuality, it is they who tend to have the upper hand.

Many teenage girls enter into heterosexualized femininity through popular culture (music, teen magazines and fiction, movies, soap operas) and through interaction with their peers, including the "goin' with" rituals discussed in the previous chapter. They may dream of intimacy and love, of relationships based on mutuality, but the heterosexual marketplace all too often involves exploitation. Active efforts to get and keep a boyfriend lead many young women to lower their ambitions, and the culture of romance perpetuates male privilege.[30]

The rituals and desires of heterosexual romance may undermine friendship among young women. In an ethnographic study of peer groups on two university campuses, one primarily African-American and the other primarily white, Dorothy Holland and Margaret Eisenhart found that for many women students, heterosexual relationships were primary. At the predominantly white campus women friends "tended to be turned into a support group for orchestrating the main activities—activities with men."[31] When a woman got a boyfriend, she often turned her attention to him and left her women friends behind. At the predominantly African-American campus, relationships among women were also fragile; intent on protecting themselves from gossip, they maintained distance from each other, especially when they were involved in heterosexual relationships.

The older elementary school girls that I got to know during the course of my fieldwork were just starting to negotiate the pressures of heterosexual femininity. One healthy counterpressure, it seemed to me, came from bonds with other girls that helped them sustain self-respect in the face of being devalued. I'm thinking here of girls who collectively protested boys' invasions, who turned "cootie" contamination into a mode of resistance, and who formed friendships and created worlds of meaning out of shared experiences.

Solidarity among women, not as background chorus for hetero-sexual romance, but as a primary form of bonding, has been crucial to women's struggles for equality with men. The gender-based conscious-ness and solidarity of girls may foster adult women's willingness to say "we," to identify themselves and act collectively *as* women, and *for* women. Of course, this bonding is often contextual and momentary. Girls, like women, do not consistently unite as a group; they engage in conflict, divide along other lines, and sometimes oppress one another. But I believe that bonding among girls, when enacted out of shared self-respect and a spirit of support, can be a powerful force not only for sur-viving within but also, potentially, for challenging conventional gender arrangements and female subordination.

In the long run, I would prefer schooling, and a society, in which gender is of minimal importance. But in the world as it exists, everyone does not start out with the same value and resources. To chal-lenge male dominance in its overt and subtle forms, we have to change the organization and content of masculinities and femininities, rec-ognizing their complexity and plurality, and altering forms based on opposition and domination. Paradoxically, to create an equal world, we may sometimes need to emphasize gender, for example, by promot-ing strategic solidarity among girls or legitimizing alternative forms of masculinity among boys. This "gender-sensitive perspective," as Jane Martin calls it, recognizes that in some situations and circumstances we may need to emphasize gender in order to promote equality.[32] Strat-egies for social change are most fruitfully pursued with close attention to context. But these strategies also need to be tied to a broader type of imagining.

## Imagining a Different Future

Twenty years ago, when the second wave of feminism was just begin-ning, we were preoccupied with countering biological arguments that had long been used to justify gender divisions and inequalities.

Now many of us are concerned less about biology than about the hold of existing arrangements on our imaginations and desires. How do we become invested in particular forms of femininity and masculinity, in oppositional gender, in arrangements based on domination? What are sources of resistance, of opposition, of alternative arrangements based on equality and mutuality? How can we imagine, and realize, other possibilities?

When I grasp for a concrete image to hold an abstraction like gender equality and mutuality, I sometimes think about Hansel and Gretel, extracted, if they can be, from the adults of the story—the wicked stepmother, the witch, the irresponsible father. Gretel and Hansel (I exchange the order of their names to animate the image of equality) provide mutual support as they go through the dangers of the forest. They each take the lead, Hansel in gathering and scattering the pebbles and, later, the bread crumbs to mark their path, and Gretel in tricking the witch. They confront the vicissitudes of life as brother and sister, as caring friends.

In fact, in our culture the model of sisters and brothers offers one of the few powerful images of relatively equal relationships between girls and boys, and between adult men and women.[33] It is not by chance that relationships between brothers and sisters begin in childhood, a period in which gender relations are relatively egalitarian. Boys of elementary school age lack major sources of adult male privilege, such as access to greater income and material resources, control of political and other forms of public power, and the legal and labor entitlements of husbands compared with wives.[34] The "protected" status of children (which, from another vantage point, constitutes a pattern of legal, economic, and political subordination) cuts across gender and mutes male privilege. The dominance of boys over girls may, as a result, be more anxious, but it also has a weaker material and legal base than the dominance of men over women.

The painfully sparse language that kids have for relationships between girls and boys—"like" charged with romantic connotations, "hate" as a quick nullification—underscores the need for more images of, and more experiences with, cross-gender relationships based on friendship and collegiality. The culture of heterosexual romance needs fundamental reconstruction so that it no longer overshadows other possibilities for intimacy and sexuality. Friendship and equality are a much better basis for intimate relationships than mistrust and a sense of being strangers.

As adults, we can help kids, as well as ourselves, imagine and realize different futures, alter institutions, craft new life stories. A more complex understanding of the dynamics of gender, of tensions and contradictions, and of the hopeful moments that lie within present arrangements, can help broaden our sense of the possible.

# *Afterword*

C. J. PASCOE

---

I've thought about *Gender Play* a lot over the years since I first read it in graduate school, but perhaps never more than I did during the 2020 school year. As I looked around my cozy home, nestled in the hills of Eugene, Oregon, I watched one fourth grader giggling into her iPad screen perched on the dining room table, another fourth grader altering their Zoom background as they leaned precariously back on their chair in front of the living room desk, and an eighth grader dashing up the stairs, his long legs taking them two at a time, so he wouldn't be late for his first period class, a class he attended from the comfort of his bedroom. That year our children, like so many others, perhaps including students at Oceanside and Ashton, no longer left home to learn in person alongside their classmates because schools across the globe had pivoted to online learning in response to the COVID-19 pandemic.

Suddenly and unexpectedly, parents like me spent multiple months witnessing a version of the events so beautifully and compassionately detailed by Barrie Thorne in *Gender Play*. Most mornings I'd hear and watch kids tumble into their Zoom squares shouting "Hi!" or "Look at my cat!" while awkwardly maneuvering a ball of fur toward a camera lens that was struggling to focus on the nonstop movement of child and animal. We bore witness as our kids did the stuff of the school day—the math problems, reading comprehension, and science quizzes.

We also heard the loud yawns and saw the stretches, the sketching of action figures, the jiggling legs, perhaps even the completion of a small jigsaw puzzle just out of sight of the computer camera. We could hear teachers try to draw attention back to the task at hand as they gently reminded one student that it wasn't nap time and another that if they were attending class from bed, they needed to sit up. Just like in the physical classroom, some kids were more talented than others at hiding their nonschool activities. Occasionally, we would get a glimpse of a flickering TV screen or a hand rapidly pushing buttons on a video game controller. From time to time, I would feel like a school staff member myself as my fourth graders expressed frustration with an assignment, were reduced to tears over friend disagreements, were again stuck in a "breakout room" with rowdy classmates and no adult supervision, or simply did not understand what was expected of them at a given moment. These screen-filled days would conclude with noisy good-byes as teachers relinquished control of the mute button and the simmering physicality and kid energy Barrie documents again and again burst through the computer screens, screens that both connected but also separated kids during that long year.

I was, and continue to be, so struck by how *familiar* the stories in this book feel, even more than three decades later, even in the context of online schooling, even in a world that has changed significantly (though perhaps not as significantly as we may have hoped) regarding gender and sexuality. This familiarity speaks not only to Barrie's gifted storytelling and analysis but to her claim that these experiences feel familiar because we all went through a childhood. When Barrie gets summoned to the principal's office, for instance, many of us can quite viscerally *feel* this summons—whether we were the child who was called, the one who lived in fear of it, or the one whose best friend was always headed that way while we giggled at their repeated misfortune. Barrie not only helps us remember those experiences, but her attention to the detail, the physicality, the feeling of being a kid, places us *in* those experiences. More than that, she helps us to reframe those moments, not as ones that prepared us for some far-off adult lives, the lives we are living as we read this book, but as moments that were "life itself." She brings us back to these childhood experiences with vulnerability and humility, reminding us of the helplessness, shame, and embarrassment that can color childhood memories with the curiosity of an ethnographer who sees value, humanity, and meaning-making in those moments.

For all the familiarity of stories in *Gender Play*, much has changed for young folks in and out of schools in the years since its publication. As my kids logged on to Zoom school, for instance, I watched as some of their classmates proudly displayed colorful rainbow or trans or bisexual or lesbian flags as their backgrounds and as others made sure their pronouns appeared next to their names. As a queer woman who is roughly the same age the kids from Ashton and Ocean-side are now, I marveled at how my own children and their classmates were and are living out identities that simply weren't available to us in the late '70s and early '80s (and quite frankly through the '90s as well!). Meanings and categories of gender and sexuality have shifted cultur-ally, legally, and definitionally in the intervening decades in ways many of us may have hoped for but few of us could have anticipated.

Research with youth, including my own, suggests that these shifting categories have opened up opportunities for some young folks. Youth, for instance, are increasingly identifying as something other than straight or cisgender.[1] And no longer are young folks saddled with one narrative about what it means to be queer or trans, a narrative characterized by loneliness, torment, or rejection. Instead, many young folks are attending schools with supportive teachers, clubs, and peers. Some are growing up in what sociologist Tey Meadow calls "facilitative families" or families that not only support and embrace their queer and trans children but advocate for them in schools and beyond.[2]

The way some young folks are embracing these gendered pos-sibilities continually underscores Barrie's insights about the multidirec-tionality of the socialization process. Kids push back against gender segregated bathrooms and adult demands that they identify neatly as boy or girl. Kids remind their teachers, parents, and other adults that there are more than two genders and that you can't just assume some-one's pronouns. My kids, for example, will yell with enthusiastic sup-port for their friends, "SHE!" from the back of the car when a friend or adult errs in using the correct pronoun for their buddy who recently transitioned. Some even encourage their teachers, as my middle child did, to buy new books for classroom libraries that reflect a range of gen-dered identities and relationships. It's no wonder that sociologist Trav-ers calls young folks a "trans generation" to capture the way that youth (and often their parents) are clearing space and developing language for a range of gendered possibilities, identities, and selves.[3] Even as conser-vative forces attempt to roll them back and there is still quite a journey ahead, gay and trans rights have expanded exponentially in the past few decades in a way that has fundamentally shifted identities and experi-ences for many kids (not to mention adults).

When I reflect on Barrie's analysis of kids' experiences in the late

'70s and early '80s, the other major shift I notice is in what Barrie calls the "landscapes of childhood"—families, neighborhoods, and schools. In the decades since she documented the worlds of Ashton and Ocean-side, children's unstructured play moved to arranged "playdates," pickup soccer games to organized sports, and coming home when the streetlights came on to ensuring one's cell phone location services were on so parents can locate them. With the increasing privatization (due in no small part to the moral panics of the 1980s about child safety and "stranger danger") of kids' worlds, young folks have been pushed out of public spaces—libraries, malls, parks, sidewalks. Their worlds became smaller, more structured, and especially for middle- and upper-middle-class kids, more future facing. Those parents, often parents of color or working-class parents, who did grant kids a degree of freedom came to be seen as neglectful, bad parents and sometimes suffered criminal penalties for their practices.

For many kids, the hanging out and socializing that used to happen across these three landscapes now happen in a fourth landscape, an online one. Kids now live much of their lives in online environments, from schooling during the pandemic, to hanging out with friends, to engaging in hobbies, to playing games, to economic activities. These mediated environments allow young folks to transcend the landscapes in which they are often constrained—home and school. These digitized environments allow them a space away from adult supervision as well as democratize access to information that has not always been easily accessible. Kids now, in Barrie's words, "act, resist, rework, and create" online much like they did offline in her research. In fact, whenever I see the cell phones tucked in kids' backpacks or sticking out of their jean pockets, I think of Barrie's insights about transitional objects. She says that these objects "bridge different spheres of life" and provide "materials for an oppositional underlife" (20). Cell phones are, in this sense, all-purpose transitional objects, bridging home, school, and social lives. They provide opportunities for moments of resistance throughout the school day—sending furtive texts, secretly playing digital games to break up the boredom, or taking pictures in the hallway to share with friends. While, as we learn in *Gender Play*, schools themselves structure gender difference, these digitized spaces may provide us a moment to see how kids might do and organize gender in less hierarchical environments. As Barrie notes, gendered patterning is a "choreography of separation and integration" (36), and I wonder, when looking at kids looking at their phones, what might this choreography look like in this newer, mediated landscape of childhood?

For all of these gendered and mediated changes, though, so much of what Barrie documents still feels shockingly familiar, not only because we all had childhoods, but because of what has changed so little over the years. These digitized spaces are, of course, gendered ones, not always so different from the offline spaces kids inhabit. Listening to my kids' stories about their friendships, watching online school, reading the news, and talking to other parents all indicate how *little* has changed in the intervening decades since the publication of *Gender Play*. Boys still make gay jokes, still take up the vast majority of space on the playground (whether that playground be digital or physical), still tease girls and other boys in ways that look a lot like sexual harassment, and still get more attention from teachers. Hallways and playgrounds still echo with gendered and sexualized slurs. Some teachers still use gender to organize their classrooms—referring to students as "boys and girls" or requiring that kids sit on the carpet "boy, girl, boy, girl." One day the now eighth grader arrived home incensed that not only did his teacher have boy and girl bathroom passes but the passes were bottles of hand sanitizer. Thinking about the stories of gendered pollution and "cooties" in *Gender Play*, I tried to explain to the teacher that attaching gendered labels to hand sanitizer was probably not the best idea. He did, however, grudgingly change them.

It is little wonder his change was grudging. The popularity of the "born that way" (2) discourse Barrie noted about gender difference has not meaningfully waned. She noted that every few years, national news magazines would post some sort of cover story about innate gendered differences. They still do. In fact, shortly before I wrote this piece, *The Atlantic* featured a story entitled "Redshirt the Boys" arguing that boys should start school a year later because of these inborn gendered differences. These contradictions characterize the moment in which *Gender Play* currently finds us. It is a moment of competing discourses about gender, youth, and inequality. It is a moment in which adults and young folks alike still enforce sexist notions and gendered behavior but also a moment in which young folks and their adult allies push for expanded notions of gendered identities and practices. It's a moment from which we can move into a more equal and just future, but it's also a moment that can lead us backward.

When it comes to the possibilities of this moment, I hear Barrie's voice and see her arm raise in a fist as she exhorts, "Onward!" like she so often would when I found myself in her office stymied by some research challenge or another. Now, I realize this is an afterword about Barrie's influential book and not about Barrie herself. But I cannot write about her book without writing about her. That I cannot call her anything but Barrie in this essay speaks to who she is as a researcher, a mentor, an academic, and a writer. The seriousness with which she takes children's experiences mirrors the seriousness with which she took my ideas as her advisee, even when they were underdeveloped and not well thought out. The feminist care, thoughtfulness, and insight she brought to children's lives is the same feminist care and thoughtfulness and insight she brought to her mentorship. Whether it be pulling out her fieldnotes to spend an afternoon teaching a group of us how to analyze our own jumbled ethnographic jottings, providing warm tea on a cold Berkeley day, a hug accompanied by an appropriate dose of feminist fury to counter sexism in our department, or her familiar encouragement to "sing your song!" Barrie's mentorship looks a lot like her writing—caring, attentive, fierce, feminist, and, perhaps most importantly, always seeking out the voices that are not being heard.

We still have work to do in answering Barrie's call to bring kids into the center of feminist and sociological thought. I think about what it would mean to put kids at the heart of social analysis every time I hear yet another claim about the "learning loss" that happened during online schooling. If we take *Gender Play*'s attention to kids seriously, then maybe what we need to attend to is not so much learning loss as it is "social loss." What happens, in other words, when kids' entire ecosystem is upended? When their traditions, their rituals, their norms, their friendships, and their routines are so drastically altered? To answer these questions, to attend to "social loss," we need to take kids seriously. We need to see kids as social actors in their own right. We cannot just focus on kids in the future tense because, as Barrie writes, to do so "distorts the vitality of children's present lives" (3). By taking kids seriously as social actors and social analysts, I hope we can build a future in which gender is more play and less power. After all, "children's interactions are not preparation for life; they are life itself" (3).

# *Notes*

## Chapter 1. Children and Gender

1. Recent examples include *Newsweek*, May 28, 1990, with a cover story titled "Guns and Dolls: Scientists Explore the Differences between Girls and Boys," and *Time*, January 20, 1992, with a cover that asks, "Why Are Men and Women Different: It Isn't Just Upbringing. New Studies Show They Are Born That Way."

2. Key insights into the socially constructed nature of gender can be found in R. W. Connell, *Gender and Power*; Anne Fausto-Sterling, *Myths of Gender: Biological Theories about Women and Men*; Suzanne J. Kessler and Wendy McKenna, *Gender: An Ethnomethodological Approach*; and Candace West and Don H. Zimmerman, "Doing Gender."

3. Nearly every textbook or anthology on the sociology of sex and gender contains a section on "gender socialization," which is often the only place where children appear.

4. This point is nicely developed by Beverly T. Purrington in *Effects of Children on Their Parents: Parents' Perceptions*. As Anthony Giddens observes: "The unfolding of childhood is not time elapsing just for the child; it is time elapsing for its parental figures, and for all other members of society; the socialization involved is not simply that of the child, but of the parents and others with whom the child is in contact, and whose conduct is influenced by the child just as the latter's is by theirs in the continuity of interaction" (*Central Problems in Social Theory*, p. 130).

5. For example, in *Friendship and Peer Culture in the Early Years*, William A. Corsaro draws on the theories of Jean Piaget, Lev Vygotsky, and George Herbert Mead to rework conventional notions of socialization. These theorists emphasize the activities of children who take the role of the other, discover and interpret the world, engage in practical activities, and hence help shape their own experiences of socialization or development.

   Inspired by this approach, a growing number of researchers have used the tools of ethnography, sociolinguistics, and open-ended interviewing to uncover the complexities of children's interactions. However, many continue to frame their analyses around the concept of socialization. For example, in "Sex Differences in the Games Children Play," Janet Lever takes the rich detail from observations of fifth-grade children's play and games and refers it to presumed adult futures. She argues that differences in types of play (e.g., team sports vs. turn-taking play) teach boys and girls different types of adult competence and orientation to organizations. Because studies like this are richly empirical and allow for the agency of children, the discoveries spill beyond the conceptual container of socialization. But the authors do not develop other lines of interpretation.

   As a result, research on children that might enhance more general understanding has remained on the margins of sociological and feminist scholarship. If more researchers conceptualized children not as adults-in-the-making, but as actors in present or past institutions, knowledge would be greatly extended. For additional discussion of this point, see Leena Alanen, "Rethinking Childhood"; Anne-Marie Ambert, "Sociology of Sociology: The Place of Children in North American Sociology"; Diana Leonard, "Persons in Their Own Right: Children and Sociology in the UK"; Enid Schildkrout, "Age and Gender in Hausa Society: Socio-Economic Roles of Children in Urban Kano"; and Barrie Thorne, "Re-visioning Women and Social Change: Where Are the Children?"

6. See Matthew Speier, "The Adult Ideological Viewpoint in Studies of Childhood," and Chris Jenks, "Introduction: Constituting the Child." For additional criticisms of the "socialization" framework, see Alanen, "Rethinking Childhood"; Arthur Brittan and Mary Maynard, *Sexism, Racism, and Oppression*; Thorne, "Re-visioning Women and Social Change"; and Frances Chaput Waksler, "Studying Children: Phenomenological Insights." For critical discussions of developmental psychology, see William Kessen, "The American Child and Other Cultural Inventions," and Valerie Polakow Suransky, *The Erosion of Childhood*.

7. This wording relies on a phrase in Brian Sutton-Smith, "A Performance Theory of Peer Relations," p. 75: "Peer interaction is not a preparation for life. It is life itself."

8. Rom Harré ("The Step to Social Constructionism") discusses individualism as a problem in theories of development, as does Kessen ("The

American Child and Other Cultural Inventions," p. 819) who argues that the field of child psychology is steeped in an American cultural view: "The child—like the Pilgrim, the cowboy, and the detective on television—is invariably seen as a free-standing isolable being who moves through development as a self-contained and complete individual. Other similarly self-contained people—parents and teachers—may influence the development of children, to be sure, but the proper unit of cultural analysis and the proper unit of developmental study is the child alone. The ubiquity of such radical individualism in our lives makes the consideration of alternative images of childhood extraordinarily difficult."

Although the concept of socialization resides at the border between sociology and psychology, it, too, ultimately focuses on individual processes, like internalization. Alanen ("Rethinking Childhood") sketches the historical shift from Durkheim's emphasis on socialization as a corollary to theories of society, to a more psychological view. For too long sociologists and anthropologists have ceded the study of children to developmental psychologists; it is time to broaden and diversify theoretical and empirical research on children.

9.  West and Zimmerman, "Doing Gender."
10. My thinking has been influenced by the work of postmodern feminist theorists, such as Jane Flax ("Postmodernism and Gender Relations in Feminist Theory"); Judith Butler (*Gender Trouble: Feminism and the Subversion of Identity*); and Joan Wallach Scott (*Gender and the Politics of History*). But I reached a deconstructive approach mostly through the contextual and interpretive methods of ethnography.
11. The phrase "grounded in the concept of possibility" is from Mihaly Csikszentmihalyi and Stith Bennett, "An Exploratory Model of Play," p. 45. For a review of the extensive literature on play, see Helen B. Schwartzman, *Transformations: The Anthropology of Children's Play.*
12. See Suransky, *The Erosion of Childhood*, for a critical discussion of the dichotomy between "play" and "work" and the structuring of childhood in contemporary U.S. society.
13. Even young children, who have to know a great deal in order to "act like children," display far more competence than adults may assume. See Robert W. MacKay, "Conceptions of Children and Models of Socialization"; David A. Goode, "Kids, Culture, and Innocents"; and Waksler, "Studying Children." For fascinating information on historical changes in conceptions of children and childhood, see Philippe Ariès, *Centuries of Childhood*, and Viviana A. Zelizer, *Pricing the Priceless Child: The Changing Social Value of Children.*
14. Reviewing other ethnographies, I found interesting variation in the choice of age-generics. With a few exceptions (such as Barry Glassner, "Kid Society"), ethnographies of preschools and elementary schools use "children." The pattern is more mixed for the next age-grade: Janet W. Schofield (*Black and White in School*) calls middle-school

students "children"; Gary Alan Fine (*With the Boys: Little League Baseball and Preadolescent Culture*) calls twelve- to fourteen-year-olds "preadolescents," and, significantly, he writes about "developmental imperatives." On the other hand, Joyce Canaan, who studied students in a middle school and in a high school, uses "kids" (see "A Comparative Analysis of American Suburban Middle Class, Middle School, and High School Teenage Cliques"), as do R. W. Connell and his colleagues in *Making the Difference: Schools, Families, and Social Division*, a study of high school students in Australia. The older the informants, the less "children" fits; "kids" proves serviceable for a wider range of ages.

15. A growing literature argues persuasively that gender should be understood in the context of other differences such as race, ethnicity, social class, sexuality, and age. See, for example, Patricia Hill Collins, *Black Feminist Thought*, and Elizabeth V. Spelman, *Inessential Woman: Problems of Exclusion in Feminist Thought*.

16. I capitalize "Black" and not "white," because "Black," often used as a synonym for "African-American," refers to a heritage and culture, whereas "white," a term of racial privilege, covers multiple capitalized ethnicities, such as Italian-American and Irish-American.

## Chapter 2. Learning from Kids

1. For interesting essays on uses of the self and personal experience in doing social science, see Susan Krieger, *Social Science and the Self: Personal Essays on an Art Form*.

2. Adrienne Rich, *Of Woman Born: Motherhood as Experience and Institution*, p. 50.

3. James Clifford and George E. Marcus, eds., *Writing Culture: The Poetics and Politics of Ethnography*; Frances E. Mascia-Lees et al., "The Postmodernist Turn in Anthropology: Cautions from a Feminist Perspective."

4. Alice Miller, *The Drama of the Gifted Child*.

5. Vivian Gussin Paley, a teacher who taped and then wrote about her interactions with young children, describes a similar effort of consciousness. See Paley, "On Listening to What the Children Say."

6. Speier, "The Adult Ideological Viewpoint in Studies of Children," p. 185.

7. Dorothy E. Smith, *The Everyday World as Problematic*; and Valerie Walkerdine, *Schoolgirl Fictions*.

8. Speier, "The Adult Ideological Viewpoint in Studies of Children," p. 172.

9. Nancy Mandell ("The Least-Adult Role in Studying Children") describes a similar shift of consciousness in her observations in a preschool.

10. In *The Prelude: Or Growth of a Poet's Mind*, William Wordsworth wrote about the creative power that comes from reliving childhood experience, with the outer world "striking upon what is found within." Examining

the biographical experiences of creative people, Edith Cobb (*The Ecology of Imagination in Childhood*) and Vera John-Steiner (*Notebooks of the Mind: Explorations of Thinking*) argue that adult creativity is nurtured by access to the child within. In a contribution from psychoanalytic theory, Ernest G. Schachtel (*Metamorphosis*) contends that children have unique access to sensory experience.

11. The ethical dilemmas of my fieldwork in the draft resistance movement are explored in Barrie Thorne, "Political Activist as Participant Observer: Conflicts of Commitment in a Study of the Draft Resistance Movement of the 1960s."

12. Mandell ("The Least-Adult Role in Studying Children") writes about her efforts to create a position of "least adult" in a preschool; similar strategies are reported by Corsaro (*Friendship and Peer Culture*) and by Bronwyn Davies (*Frogs and Snails and Feminist Tales: Preschool Children and Gender*). Gary Alan Fine, who was a participant-observer with ten- to twelve-year-old boys on Little League baseball teams, and Barry Glassner, who observed in an elementary school, tried to hang out, mixing friendliness with minimal authority (Gary Alan Fine and Barry Glassner, "Participant Observation with Children: Promise and Problems"). All these observers avoided intervening and disciplining, except when there was a chance of serious physical injury. For a review of these and other discussions of participant-observation with children, see Gary Alan Fine and Kent L. Sandstrom, *Knowing Children: Participant Observation with Minors*.

13. Corsaro (*Friendship and Peer Culture*), Mandell ("The Least-Adult Role in Studying Children"), and Fine and Glassner ("Participant Observation with Children") also describe their efforts to contain adult requests for help. These requests exemplify a recurring feature in our culture's organization of children's worlds: a low ratio of adults to children and an assumption that more adult hands are always welcome, and will readily be made available, in the managerial tasks.

14. Bronwyn Davies (*Life in the Classroom and Playground: The Accounts of Primary School Children*) also discusses the dual agendas of classrooms—one set by the teacher and another, running parallel and sometimes contradictory or complementary, set by students. Also see Philip A. Cusick, *Inside High School*.

15. Erving Goffman, *Asylums*. Corsaro (*Friendship and Peer Culture*) describes processes of sharing and dispute among preschool children who smuggled in forbidden objects from home.

16. For further analyses of ritualized exchanges among children, see Tamar Katriel ("*'Bexibudim!'*: Ritualized Sharing among Israeli Children"), who observed stylized sharing of treats by children on the way home from school, and Elliot Mishler, "Wou' You Trade Cookies with the Popcorn? Talk of Trades among Six Year Olds."

17. Social class was more inscribed in the appearance of girls than of boys. In

both schools boys wore mostly T-shirts and solid-colored jeans or pants, whereas girls' clothing ranged more widely in design, fit, materials, and colors, and hence could go more easily awry. Furthermore, standards of grooming are also more exacting for girls than for boys. Girls from more impoverished backgrounds, like Rita and Jessica, wore mismatched patterns and fabric, and pants whose seats bulged out from wear. In contrast, girls from more affluent families, like Kathryn, wore well-matched "outfits" (the word itself is telling).

18. In several evocative studies, adult women have drawn on their own memories as a research tool for learning about experiences of girlhood in a patriarchal culture. See Walkerdine, *Schoolgirl Fictions*, and Frigga Haug, *Female Sexualization: A Collective Work of Memory*, which explains an interesting methodology of collective "memory-work."

19. Jennifer C. Hunt, *Psychoanalytic Aspects of Fieldwork*.

20. Walkerdine (*Schoolgirl Fictions*) analyzes the "adult gaze" in teaching and in research with children.

## Chapter 3. Boys and Girls Together . . . but Mostly Apart

1. Philip W. Jackson (*Life in Classrooms*) highlights the centrality of *crowds*, *praise*, and *power* in the organization of schools.

   Children who have previously attended day-care centers or preschools have already made the transition from household and neighborhood to a more bureaucratic set of experiences, as ethnographically detailed by Suransky in *The Erosion of Childhood*. During the opening weeks of Ashton School, the kindergarten teacher told me that she could tell which children had come from "group" care; they made an easier transition to school than did children coming from home-based care.

2. Cusick, *Inside High School*.

3. An observation from Robert Dreeban, *On What Is Learned in School*.

4. See Jeannie Oakes, *Keeping Track: How Schools Structure Inequality*, for a thoughtful study of ways in which academic tracking further disadvantages poor and racial minority students.

5. The schools I studied had relatively small numbers of Chicanos/Latinos (around fifty out of four hundred students), African-Americans (twenty-five or thirty in each school), and a scattering from other racial/ethnic groups. Since these children spread across six different grade levels, there were not enough of any one age-grade to constitute a critical mass that might separate off.

   In contrast, Schofield (*Black and White in School*) studied a newly integrated urban middle-school with 1,500 students, two-thirds of them Black, and one-third white. She found that the staff mentioned race only on rare occasions when they urged students to ignore it. When they constructed their own groups, the students often divided along racial lines. These racially homogeneous groups also tended to divide by gender, although Schofield found less gender segregation among Black students than among white students.

6. In an informative history of gender practices in U.S. public schools, David Tyack and Elizabeth Hansot (*Learning Together: A History of Coeducation in American Schools*) trace complex relationships between official policies and the practices of school staff. Formal practices, which have changed over time, range from the gender-neutral to separating girls and boys into different classes and activities.

7. According to the *Oxford English Dictionary*, in the thirteenth and fourteenth centuries the word "girl" was used as a generic to refer to a child of either gender. Females were called "gay girls," and males were called "knave girls." "Girl" later lost the generic connotation and came to refer specifically to young females. The word "boy" appeared slightly later. "Child," a word never marked for gender, goes back to ancient times.

8. Margaret A. Eisenhart and Dorothy C. Holland, who observed in fifth- and sixth-grade classrooms in a school in the South, also found that teachers continually referred to "boys and girls," especially when directing them to start routines like reciting the Pledge of Allegiance or lining up. The authors observe that this generic usage (teachers were instructing boys and girls to do the same thing) emphasized student more than gender-differentiated identities. See Eisenhart and Holland, "Learning Gender from Peers: The Role of Peer Groups in the Cultural Transmission of Gender."

9. Spencer E. Cahill, "Language Practices and Self-Definition: The Case of Gender Identity Acquisition." Patricia M. Passuth ("Age Hierarchies within Children's Groups"), who observed in a summer day camp, also found the children were keenly aware of age differences and believed it was better to be older than younger.

10. Gregory Bateson, *Steps to an Ecology of Mind*, p. 453. Others have also called attention to social processes by which a given category may be rendered more or less salient. For example, Marilynn B. Brewer argues that "which differences are emphasized under what circumstances appears to be flexible and context dependent; this flexibility permits individuals to mobilize different group identities for different purposes" ("Ethnocentrism and Its Role in Interpersonal Trust," p. 350). In the same vein, Sandra Wallman observes that "a cultural or phenotypical difference which counts in one situation does not count in another" ("The Boundaries of 'Race': Processes of Ethnicity in England," p. 201). Also see Kay Deaux and Brenda Major, "Putting Gender into Context: An Interactive Model of Gender-related Behavior."

11. Erving Goffman, "The Arrangement between the Sexes," p. 316.

12. Cynthia A. Cone and Berta E. Perez ("Peer Groups and the Organization of Classroom Space") observed a similar pattern, including children

perceiving a girls' side and a boys' side, in elementary classrooms where teachers allowed students to choose their own seating. Steven T. Bossert (*Tasks and Social Relationships in Classrooms*) compared the organization of four different classrooms; in those where the teacher let students choose their own seats, friendship groups, usually of the same-gender, sat together.

13. See reviews of research in Barrie Thorne et al., eds., *Language, Gender, and Society*; Jere E. Brophy and Thomas L. Good, *Teacher-Student Relations*; and in the American Association of University Women Educational Foundation and the Wellesley College Center for Research on Women, *How Schools Shortchange Girls*. Educational researchers have also found that boys tend to receive more teacher attention, both positive and negative, than do girls, and that some teachers praise and reprimand boys and girls for different things. Several studies have found that boys are more often scolded for misbehavior and praised for their academic work, while girls are more often chastized for poor academic performance and praised for appearance, neatness, and being polite. For reviews of this research, see Marlaine S. Lockheed with Susan S. Klein, "Sex Equity in Classroom Organization and Climate," and Louise Cherry Wilkinson and Cora B. Marrett, eds., *Gender Influences in Classroom Interaction*.

14. See Tyack and Hansot, *Learning Together*, for photographs and floor plans of schools built in the early decades of this century with separate entrances and spaces designated for girls and boys

15. Robert B. Everhart, *Reading, Writing, and Resistance*, p. 51.

16. Goffman observes that this "parallel organization," in which similar activities are organized in a segregated manner, provides a "ready base for elaborating differential treatment," such as having a row of girls file in before a row of boys ("The Arrangement between the Sexes," p. 306).

17. My observations resemble those of Janet Lever, who recorded differences in the playground activities of fifth-graders in Connecticut. She found that boys most often engaged in team sports, whereas girls focused on turn-taking play. (See Lever, "Sex Differences in the Games Children Play" and "Sex Differences in the Complexity of Children's Play and Games.") John Evans ("Gender Differences in Children's Games: A Look at the Team Selection Process") observed during recess in an Illinois public school and found that of 238 team games, 78 percent were played by boys as a group; on only 52 occasions (22 percent) did team membership include both boys and girls. Of all team games, 193 (81 percent) were played by fifth- and sixth-graders.

18. While sex differences in children's game preferences are less extreme than in earlier times, Brian Sutton-Smith and B. G. Rosenberg found that between the late 1920s and the late 1950s there were some convergences in the game choices of girls and boys in fourth, fifth, and sixth grades. The change was due mostly to girls adopting interests

(swimming, tag, kites) previously limited to boys. On the other hand, boys drew away from some games (hopscotch, jacks, jump rope) that then became more typed as girls' play. The enhanced interest in organized sports for girls that emerged in the 1970s and 1980s has probably further increased the convergence of girls' and boys' game preferences, but the overall separation remains substantial. See Sutton-Smith and Rosenberg, "Sixty Years of Historical Change in the Game Preferences of American Children."

19. An early article by Carole Joffe ("As The Twig Is Bent") first alerted me to children's invocation of gender as an "ideology of control." For a detailed analysis of processes of access and exclusion among children at play in a day-care center, see William Corsaro, "We're Friends, Right? Children's Use of Access Rituals in a Nursery School."

20. This estimate comes from Willard W. Hartup, "Peer Relations."

21. Zella Luria and Eleanor W. Herzog, "Gender Segregation across and within Settings"; Marlaine S. Lockheed and Abigail M. Harris, "Cross-Sex Collaborative Learning in Elementary Classrooms." Also see reviews of research in Hartup, "Peer Relations"; Marlaine S. Lockheed, "Some Determinants and Consequences of Sex Segregation in the Classroom"; and Eleanor E. Maccoby and Carol Nagy Jacklin, "Gender Segregation in Childhood."

22. Luria and Herzog, "Gender Segregation across and within Settings."

23. For example, when Maureen Hallinan and Nancy B. Tuma ("Classroom Effects on Change in Children's Friendships") asked fourth-, fifth-, and sixth-graders to name their "best friend," 77 percent named someone of the same gender. Elliott A. Medrich and his colleagues (*The Serious Business of Growing Up: A Study of Children's Lives Outside School*) asked 764 sixth-graders to name their "close friends." The students named a median number of three, and more boys (91 percent) than girls (82 percent) named only people of their own gender; the girls who named at least one boy were more likely than other girls to play team sports.

24. Maureen Hallinan, "Structural Effects of Children's Friendships and Cliques."

25. Schofield, *Black and White in School*. Schofield found that race, as well as gender, was a barrier to the development of friendship; in the racially balanced middle school where she observed, close friendships between students of different genders *or* races were quite rare.

## Chapter 4. Gender Separation: Why and How

1. Observers in several other cultures have also found a great deal of separation in the social relations of girls and boys, especially in middle childhood. Drawing on observations of the daily lives of children, ages six

to ten, in the Philippines, Japan, India, Kenya, Mexico, and the United States, Beatrice B. Whiting and Carolyn P. Edwards conclude that "the emergence of same-sex preferences in childhood is a cross-cultural universal and robust phenomenon" (*Children of Different Worlds*, p. 81). They also observe, in a point I discuss later in this chapter, that gender separation emerges more among same-age peers than among groups of children of different ages.

2.  John Gottman ("The World of Coordinated Play: Same- and Cross-Sex Friendship in Young Children") reports similar cross-gender friendships in Urbana, Illinois. One of his research assistants canvassed two neighborhoods, asking parents about the "best friendships" of their children. Among three- and four-year-olds, 36 percent of "best friends" were of the other gender; the figure declined to 23 percent among five- and six-year-olds, and by age seven, girl-boy "best friendships" were almost nonexistent—there were only five in all. These five friendships had begun when the children were much younger, and by age seven the friendships had gone underground; the boy and girl played together at home, but in school they did not acknowledge their close tie.

3.  Lockheed ("Some Determinants and Consequences of Sex Segregation in the Classroom") found a notable inconsistency between students' self-reported preferences for work partners, which resulted overwhelmingly in same-gender choices, and the "rich world of cross-sex interaction" actually observed in twenty-nine fourth- and fifth-grade classrooms.

4.  Shari Ellis et al., "Age Segregation in Children's Social Interaction." In a qualitative study of children, ages four to fourteen in an urban African-American neighborhood, Marjorie Harness Goodwin (*He-Said-She-Said: Talk as Social Organization among Black Children*) found some gender and age separation in play groups, but she also found a great deal of interaction between girls and boys and among kids of different ages. Girls and boys usually interacted as friends rather than as potential romantic partners.

    Helena Wulff observed twelve- to sixteen-year-olds in a working-class area in London with a mix of whites and children of Black immigrants from the Caribbean. Girls and boys interacted regularly on a neighborhood street corner, in a group also mixed by age and ethnicity. But when they were on the schoolyard, the same kids divided into groups separated by gender, ethnicity, and age. See Wulff, *Twelve Girls: Growing Up, Ethnicity, and Excitement in a South London Microculture.*

    To further illuminate the dynamics of gender in the social relations of kids, we need more research on different kinds of neighborhoods—inner-city, suburban, rural—and in other settings, like churches and shopping malls. We also need more systematic inquiry into possible variation by race, ethnicity, and social class.

5.  Tyack and Hansot, *Learning Together.* In countries like France and England, with strong traditions of same-sex schooling, and in same- and mixed-sex Catholic schools in the United States, there is far more

institutionalized separation between girls and boys than in U.S. public schools.

6. Talcott Parsons observed that teachers give male and female students a common set of tasks and formally try to treat both sexes alike, which plays down "sex-role differentiation." See Parsons, "The School Class as a Social System: Some of Its Functions in American Society," in *Social Structure and Personality*. This theme is also discussed in Dreeban, *On What Is Learned in School*; Jackson, *Life in Classrooms*; and Tyack and Hansot, *Learning Together*.

7. See research reported in Susan S. Klein, ed., *Handbook for Achieving Sex Equity through Education*; Ray C. Rist, *The Invisible Children: School Integration in American Society*; Myra P. Sadker and David M. Sadker, *Sex Equity Handbook for Schools*; Stephen Walker and Len Barton, eds., *Gender, Class, and Education*; and Lois Weis, ed., *Class, Race, and Gender in American Education*.

8. Michael Apple, ed., *Cultural and Economic Reproduction in Education*; R. W. Connell et al., *Making the Difference*; Henry Giroux, "Theories of Reproduction and Resistance in the New Sociology of Education: A Critical Analysis"; Weis, ed., *Class, Race, and Gender in American Education*.

9. Gottman, "The World of Coordinated Play"; Hartup, "Peer Relations"; Hans Oswald, et al., "Gaps and Bridges: Interaction between Girls and Boys in Elementary School."

   In suggestive observations of rural children in Kenya, Sara Harkness and Charles M. Super found no gender separation in peer groups until around age six, when parents lessened their supervision and allowed boys and girls to roam greater distances. This increased the potential number of companions and children's autonomy to construct their own groups. See Harkness and Super, "The Cultural Context of Gender Segregation in Children's Peer Groups."

10. Ellis et al, "Age Segregation in Children's Social Interaction," and Whiting and Edwards, *Children of Different Worlds*, p. 81.

11. A speculation from P. LaFreniere, et al., "The Emergence of Same-Sex Preferences among Preschool Peers: A Developmental Ethological Perspective."

12. Further insight into the importance of context in shaping the amount of gender separation comes from observations of schoolchildren on a field trip in a children's museum (Zella Luria and Eleanor Herzog, "Sorting Gender Out in a Children's Museum"). Like schools, the museum was crowded, yet of the groups kids formed, only 20 percent were same-gender. Luria has suggested, in conversation, that this may be due to the temporary nature of the encounters; time was short, the museum setting was unfamiliar, and this was a onetime visit. The kids were not likely to be identified with or held to a pattern of action. The bureaucratic routines of schools interact with the dynamics of a dense population.

13. Evans also found that kickball, or "kicksoccer," was a game that girls

and boys often played together. A fifth-grade girl told him, "Well, kick-soccer is a lot easier to play than football; most of the girls can't throw or catch very good. Also the boys don't usually want the girls to play football or basketball" (Evans, "Gender Differences in Children's Games," p. 7).

14. Perusing photographs taken in U.S. elementary schools over the last century, Tyack and Hansot (*Learning Together*) also found that classrooms were much more gender-integrated than playgrounds.

15. Luria and Herzog, "Gender Segregation across and within Settings."

16. Maccoby and Jacklin, "Gender Segregation in Childhood."

17. For excellent discussions of patterns and pitfalls in research on sex differences, see Fausto-Sterling, *Myths of Gender*, and Carol Nagy Jacklin, "Methodological Issues in the Study of Sex-related Differences."

18. This general point is made in Michelle Z. Rosaldo, "The Use and Abuse of Anthropology: Reflections on Feminism and Cross-cultural Understanding." Also see Barrie Thorne, "Children and Gender: Constructions of Difference."

19. This line of argument might implicate greater male aggression, rooted in biology, as the ultimate cause of male dominance, but the research support for this claimed biological sex difference is extremely questionable. See Fausto-Sterling, *Myths of Gender*.

20. Nancy Chodorow, *The Reproduction of Mothering*, and Myra Dinnerstein, *The Mermaid and the Minotaur: Sexual Arrangements and Human Malaise*.

21. Miriam Johnson, *Strong Mothers, Weak Wives*, p. 115. Note that by this combined account, each gender separates from the other to avoid something. Boys separate to avoid being contaminated by girls, who threaten their sense of psychic separation, and girls separate to avoid being dominated by boys.

22. This argument is made in Whiting and Edwards, *Children of Different Worlds*; Maccoby and Jacklin, "Gender Segregation in Childhood"; Johnson, *Strong Mothers, Weak Wives*; Spencer E. Cahill, "Becoming Boys and Girls"; and Beverly I. Fagot, et al., "Gender Labeling and the Adoption of Sex-typed Behaviors."

23. Whiting and Edwards (*Children of Different Worlds*) theorize that there is an "internally regulated competence motivation to find out about the self and others by constructing knowledge about salient social categories" (p. 8). Cross-culturally, children find age and gender especially salient. But, I wondered in reading Whiting and Edwards's work, what about cultural situations, as in Northern Ireland or South Africa, where religion or race are made deeply salient in the lives of young children? In their quest for self-definition, how do children make sense of crosscutting social categories?

24. See West and Zimmerman, "Doing Gender." Working from this perspective, Cahill ("Becoming Boys and Girls") maintains that by separating

from one another, girls and boys can better display "masculine effica-ciousness" and "feminine appearance," the core features of "doing gen-der" at young ages. These ethnomethodologists argue that identity is an accomplishment of social interaction, not its cause.

This is also the line of argument that Sigurd Berentzen (*Children Constructing Their Social World: An Analysis of Gender Contrasts in Chil-dren's Interactions in a Nursery School*) uses to account for the dynam-ics of gender separation in a nursery school in Norway. Girls and boys claim and enact separate gender identities by constructing separate peer groups; they enact differences in their identities through a field of social relationships.

25. Talcott Parsons, "The Incest Taboo in Relation to Social Structure and the Socialization of the Child," in *Social Structure and Personality*, pp. 74–75 (emphasis in the original).

26. Howard S. Becker helped me grasp this point. His book of collected papers is aptly titled *Doing Things Together*, whether studying artists or marijuana users, Becker has repeatedly shown that the "how" of social interaction or the course of experience can illuminate "why," or causal, questions. See Jack Katz, "Howard S. Becker's Contributions to Sociology."

## Chapter 5. Creating a Sense of "Opposite Sides"

1. Fredrik Barth, "Introduction" to *Ethnic Groups and Boundaries*. I am grateful to Fred Erickson for suggesting the relevance of Barth's analy-sis. Sandra Wallman's writing (e.g., "The Boundaries of Race") on the process of marking race and ethnic boundaries is also suggestive. Several years after I had worked out the significance of Barth's insight for under-standing children's gender relations, I discovered a similar project in Berentzen's ethnography of a preschool in Norway, *Children Construct-ing Their Social World*.

2. Barth, "Introduction," p. 15.

3. For a taxonomy of children's games that distinguishes chasing from other forms, see Brian Sutton-Smith, "A Syntax for Play and Games."

4. Christine R. Finnan, "The Ethnography of Children's Spontaneous Play."

5. For brief descriptions of cross-gender chasing on school playgrounds, see ibid. (observations in Texas); Raphaella Best, *We've All Got Scars: What Boys and Girls Learn in Elementary School* (the Central Atlantic region); Kathryn M. Borman, "Children's Interactions in Playgrounds" (the Midwest); Corsaro, *Friendship and Peer Culture* ("cross-gender approach-avoidance" play, including chasing, in a nursery school on the West Coast); Sue Parrott, "Games Children Play: Ethnography of a Second-Grade Recess" (second-grade boys in Minnesota tell about playing

"girls-catch-the-boys"); Andy Sluckin, *Growing Up in the Playground* ("kiss-chase" in a British school); and Stephen Richert, *Boys and Girls Apart: Children's Play in Canada and Poland* ("kissing girls," a children's chasing game in Ottawa, Canada, and "kisser catchers," in the Bahamas).

6. I would like to thank Margaret Blume for sharing her fieldnotes and giving me permission to cite this example.

7. The word "cooties" may have its origins among soldiers in foxholes in World War I, who used the term for head lice (Robert L. Chapman, *New Dictionary of American Slang*). When the soldiers returned home, some playfully called their wives and other women "cooties," and "The Cooties" was the name of at least one Veterans of Foreign Wars women's auxiliary club. Since the late 1940s a toy company has marketed a children's game called Cooties, which involves rolling a dice to draw body pieces and constructing an antlike plastic creature. Iona Opie and Peter Opie (*Children's Games in Street and Playground*) have recorded versions of cootie tag from England, Spain, Madagascar, and New England. With new times come new forms of contamination; I recently heard reports of children saying to one another, "Don't touch me; I don't want your AIDS."

8. Cootie catchers are a variant of the fortune-telling devices made of folded paper that are described and illustrated in Mary Knapp and Herbert Knapp, *One Potato, Two Potato: The Secret Education of American Children*, pp. 257–259 and in Iona Opie and Peter Opie, *The Lore and Language of Schoolchildren*, pp. 341–342.

9. This pattern was also found by Sue Samuelson, a folklorist, who gathered reports about how the game has been played ("The Cooties Complex").

10. Kevin Karkau, "Sexism in Fourth Grade." Richert (*Boys and Girls Apart*) reports Canadian children talking about "girl germs" but not "boy germs."

11. Thanks to Bob Emerson for this insight.

12. College students have told me about cootie queens in the elementary schools they attended; one reported that she had been a cootie queen when she was in fourth grade, a memory fraught with shame and suffering. She speculated that the stigma was related to her being overweight, as well as new to the school.

13. Samuelson, "The Cooties Complex." A friend of mine relayed a student's description of interactions in a school in a Canadian community divided between whites and more impoverished Native Americans. If a white girl accidentally touched a "native" girl, the white girl would quickly say "superstuff" and run to touch another white girl or boy to pass on, and thereby undo, the pollution.

14. I observed this in casual conversations at Ashton and Oceanside; the pattern also emerged in the memories of college students: both men and women recalled "chasing," but men talked more generally about

"teasing girls." In extensive observations of elementary school children in West Germany, Oswald and his colleagues ("Gaps and Bridges") found a lot of mutual "bothering" between first-grade boys and girls. By fourth grade, boys bothered girls much more than the reverse; girls coped by complaining to adults and by ignoring or rebuking the botherers.

In a study of U.S. first-graders, Linda Grant ("Black Females' 'Place' in Desegregated Classrooms") found that where an initiator could be discerned, boys were responsible for 59 to 90 percent of physically aggressive encounters between boys and girls. Ruth G. Goodenough ("Small Group Culture and the Emergence of Sexist Behavior: A Comparative Study of Four Children's Groups") computed the ratio of negative to positive behavior in relations between the genders in four different kindergartens. She found a wide range, from one classroom with a relatively even balance of negative and positive behaviors to one where boys' negative behaviors to girls outweighed their positive behaviors by a ratio of thirty-one to one. In that classroom, boys repeatedly disrupted girls' play, while girls rarely disrupted the activities of boys. The girls in that classroom were generally more timid and less spontaneous than girls in the more egalitarian kindergarten.

Patricia S. Griffin ("'Gymnastics Is a Girl's Thing': Student Participation and Interaction Patterns in a Middle School Gymnastics Unit"), who observed in a coed gymnastics class at a U.S. middle school, also found a dramatic gender asymmetry. Boys, as individuals and in groups, hassled girls (by getting in their way, butting into line, giving orders, teasing, mimicking, yelling and laughing at them) much more than the reverse. The girls responded by physically moving away, acquiescing (e.g., letting boys butt into line), ignoring, and asking the boys to stop. Boys generally interacted with girls only to hassle them; girls generally interacted with boys only when they responded to being hassled.

15. In quantified observations among elementary school children in West Germany, Oswald and his colleagues ("Gaps and Bridges") also found that a few boys—four out of fourteen in a group of fifth-graders—were responsible for most of the "bothering"; they made "plaguing girls" into a kind of sport. This pattern may relate to the emergence of school "bullies," although that topic has been studied more in the context of boy-boy than of boy-girl (or girl-girl) relationships.

Dan Olweus (*Aggression in the Schools*) found that of one thousand Swedish boys, ages twelve to sixteen, 4 to 6 percent were, in the perceptions of teachers and other students, extreme bullies; another 4 to 6 percent were "whipping boys," or frequent targets of bullying. In research in Norway Olweus found that boys engaged in three times as much bullying as girls; girls' bullying tended to be more subtle, like spreading rumors. In 1983 the Norwegian government, with Olweus's help, launched a national campaign to end bullying in elementary and junior high schools. Educational materials about the bully problem were given to school staff and families, and teachers were urged to give a clear message that bullying is not acceptable, to initiate talks with victims and bullies, and to give generous praise when rules were followed. When rules were violated, teachers and parents were advised to consistently use nonhostile, noncorporal punishment. According to Olweus, this national campaign reduced bullying by as much as half (Peter Freiberg, "Bullying Gets Banned in Norway's Schools").

16. Boys succinctly express this stereotype in their equation of "tattletales, crybabies, and girls," although a girl will sometimes insult a boy by using these female-typed names.

17. Conversations with Nancy Henley illuminated this point. "Tattling" resonates with "nagging"; both belittling terms are used more to refer to females than to males, and as labels and as actual forms of verbal recourse, they may be associated with having less power.

18. Linda Grant ("Gender Roles and Statuses in School Children's Peer Interactions") found that in four of six first-grade classrooms girls tattled on boys more than the reverse. Teachers also varied widely in their rules about and responses to tattling; for example, one teacher more often reprimanded the tattler than the target, while another more often punished the target.

19. Kids recognize the scripted quality of these encounters. A third-grade girl told Jean Doyle, who interviewed students about their daily life, that boys "bother" girls and "the girls tell the teacher and she will punish them" ("Helpers, Officers, and Lunchers: Ethnography of a Third-Grade Class," p. 155). An Oceanside fifth-grade boy provided a different perspective on the same scenario: "Girls are always getting boys into trouble. They tease us and when we react, they tell on us and it's us who get into trouble."

20. Perhaps because most of the students at both Oceanside and Ashton were white and working-class, I witnessed little systematic hassling along lines of race and/or social class. Researchers in schools with larger proportions of students from different races and social classes have found those boundaries marked by teasing and bothering, with gender cutting across. Judith Lynne Hanna (*Disruptive School Behavior: Class, Race, and Culture*) observed in a recently desegregated "magnet" elementary school composed mostly of Black working-class and white middle-class students. She found recurring patterns of verbal and physical aggression that the children called "meddlin," including insults and taunts, menacing body postures, pushing, hitting, poking, and fighting. Working-class Black boys most often engaged in meddlin, and Black girls did more meddlin, especially in response to provocation, than white girls. The targets of meddlin were sometimes social equals of the aggressor but were most often the vulnerable: newcomers, children with physical handicaps or unusual dress, poor athletes, or

those afraid to stand up to provocation. Some white and more Black children responded to meddlin by reciprocating; middle-class children, Black and white, were more likely to comply with demands or to disengage by using humor, negotiation, withdrawal, or the mediation of a teacher or another child. Hanna connects this use of verbal and physical aggression to patterns of bodily self-assertion in African-American culture; she also suggests that when children lack material or academic resources, they may resort to physical means to gain power. Meddlin took place mostly among Blacks and was not specifically targeted against whites as a group, but whites were put off by it and more often saw it as aggression rather than play, a perception that contributed to racial separation.

In observations in a desegregated junior high school, Schofield (*Black and White in Conflict*) also found an association between being Black, working-class, and male, and engaging in physical hassling. Targets who were white were quicker than those who were Black to interpret the hassling as intimidation.

21. Bateson, *Steps to an Ecology of Mind*, pp. 177–193. Just as a picture frame tells a viewer to interpret what lies inside differently than the wallpaper that surrounds it, so an interactional frame sets apart a different space of meaning. In *Frame Analysis: An Essay on the Organization of Experience*, Erving Goffman extended Bateson's insight.

22. Joan P. Emerson ("Negotiating the Serious Import of Humor") analyzes tricky everyday negotiations about whether a joking comment will be taken in a humorous or serious vein.

23. For a thorough review of the vast literature on play, especially in reference to children's activities, see Schwartzman, *Transformations*. The definition of play has been extensively debated; for every list of characteristics (such as spontaneous, voluntary, unproductive), counterexamples can be found, perhaps in part, as this discussion emphasizes, because the line between "play" and "real" is inherently problematic.

24. See Nancy Henley and Cheris Kramarae, "Miscommunication, Gender, and Power."

25. Sigmund Freud, *Jokes and Their Relation to the Unconscious*, and Emerson, "Negotiating the Serious Import of Humor."

26. Susan Allen Toth, *Blooming: A Small-Town Girlhood*, pp. 29–39. The reframing of insults as a sign of liking persists in patterns of male dominance among adults; battered women sometimes try to interpret male violence as a sign of caring. See Henley and Kramarae, "Miscommunication, Gender, and Power."

27. Janet Schofield, "Complementary and Conflicting Identities: Images of Interaction in an Interracial School," p. 85.

28. A pattern of boys having access to more space than girls of the same age can also be found in research on the daily lives of kids outside school. Roger Hart (*Children's Experience of Place*) gathered information

on the space traversed by forty-seven boys and forty girls, ages five through twelve, in a town in New England. At all ages, boys traveled almost twice as far as girls; for example, among fifth- and sixth-graders, boys averaged a distance of almost half a mile, and girls around one fourth of a mile. Parents gave boys permission to roam more freely than girls and were more likely to turn an eye when a son rather than a daughter broke the rules.

In a study of 764 sixth-graders in California, Medrich and his colleagues (*The Serious Business of Growing Up*) found boys were more physically mobile than girls, with some striking individual variations; for example, girls who played team sports were more physically mobile than other girls. They also found African-Americans were more physically mobile than whites or Asian-Americans; African-American boys roamed the farthest of any gender/ethnic group. Lever ("Sex Differences in the Games Children Play") found, as have other researchers, that when they are not in school, fifth-grade boys more often play in out-of-door activities, and girls are more likely to play in and around their houses. In a comparative study of six cultures, Whiting and Edwards (*Children of Different Worlds*) found that boys more often traveled beyond the immediate neighborhood except in one culture, the Taira in Okinawa, where, at an early age, girls, as well as boys, were allowed to roam freely throughout the community.

29. Personal communication from Zella Luria.

30. Nancy Henley, *Body Politics: Power, Sex, and Nonverbal Communication*; also see Thorne et al., eds., *Language, Gender, and Society*.

31. In a classic statement, Mary Douglas argued that "pollution is a type of danger which is not likely to occur except where the lines of structure, cosmic or social, are clearly defined" (*Purity and Danger*, p. 113). Thus, depending on the context, pollution rituals may help sustain social divisions along lines of gender, race, ethnicity, social class, or age. For writings on female pollution beliefs and rituals in varied cultures, see Thomas Buckley and Alma Gottlieb, eds., *Blood Magic: The Anthropology of Menstruation*.

32. Buckley and Gottlieb, *Blood Magic*.

33. Feminist psychoanalytic theories, discussed in Chapter 4, may help explain why males may feel threatened by females and "things feminine" and thus may treat girls as polluting. Chodorow's theory (*The Reproduction of Mothering*) may also help account for a related asymmetry: to say that a boy is "like a girl" is more insulting and personally threatening than to say that a girl is "like a boy." In the repertoire of children's teases I sometimes heard the taunting charge that a given boy "is" a girl ("Ben is a girl 'cause he's sitting at the girls' table"), but I never saw kids tease a girl for "being" a boy.

34. The process I am calling "neutralization" is called "decategorization" in

Marilyn B. Brewer and Norman Miller, "Beyond the Contact Hypothesis: Theoretical Perspectives on Desegregation." In the process of decategorization, social categories like Black and white are made less salient than in "category-based contact."

35. See West and Zimmerman, "Doing Gender."

36. See Connell et al., *Making the Difference*, p. 182.

37. For a review of debates about use of the term "ritual," see Sally F. Moore and Barbara Myerhoff, eds., *Secular Ritual*.

38. Douglas, *Purity and Danger*, pp. 63–64.

39. Goffman, "The Arrangement between the Sexes," p. 321.

40. See Connell, *Gender and Power*, on the notion of "masculinities," some dominant or hegemonic, and others, like gay masculinity, more submerged.

41. Goffman, "The Arrangement between the Sexes," p. 323. Henley (*Body Politics*) earlier identified this type of cross-gender play as a reinforcement of male dominance.

    When I was in the third grade in 1949–50, our teacher had us keep journals about events at school. When I recently read my entries, which are carefully printed in pencil on wide notebook lines and illustrated with crayon drawings, I was startled to discover my matter-of-fact recording of two gender scenarios in which I was part of the objectified category of "the girls." In one entry about a class picnic, I wrote: "Some boys found watersnakes and scared the girls. After that we went home." The other is in a short report on a playground clean-up day: "Gerald teased the girls by putting earthworms down our necks, and as soon as all the weeds were out we went home."

42. Henri Tajfel, "Social Psychology of Intergroup Relations."

43. See Schwartzman, *Transformations*.

44. Clifford Geertz, "Deep Play: Notes on the Balinese Cockfight," p. 26.

## Chapter 6. Do Girls and Boys Have Different Cultures?

1. There have been several widely circulated versions of this argument: (1) Janet Lever emphasizes sex differences in the play of fifth-graders and argues that because they more often engage in team sports, males have a later advantage in the world of occupations and organizations. See Lever, "Sex Differences in the Complexity of Children's Play and Games" and "Sex Differences in the Games Children Play." Carol Gilligan uses Lever's work to support her claim that in the process of moral reasoning, girls use a voice of connection and care that is different from boys' emphasis on abstract rules. See Gilligan, *In a Different Voice: Psychological Theory and Women's Development*. (2) Daniel N. Maltz and Ruth A.

Borker ("A Cultural Approach to Male-Female Miscommunication") claim that there are different patterns of talk in all-girl and in all-boy groups, leading to miscommunication between adult women and men; Deborah Tannen's popular book, *You Just Don't Understand: Women and Men in Conversation*, elaborates this basic thesis (for criticisms, see Henley and Kramarae, "Gender, Power, and Miscommunication"). (3) Eleanor E. Maccoby argues that gender-separated groups teach different forms of prosocial and antisocial behavior ("Social Groupings in Childhood: Their Relationship to Prosocial and Antisocial Behavior in Boys and Girls").

Collaborating with Zella Luria, I have also followed this story line, arguing that groups of girls and groups of boys teach different sexual scripts, leading to tangles in the more overtly heterosexual experiences of adolescents, with girls emphasizing intimacy and romance, while boys are oriented more to active sexuality. Some of our analysis is included in this chapter, although with serious caveats. See Barrie Thorne and Zella Luria, "Sexuality and Gender in Children's Daily Worlds."

2. Tannen, *You Just Don't Understand*.

3. This generalization is supported by the studies, reviewed in Chapter 5, finding that on average, boys roam twice as far as girls. In research on children in neighborhoods Ellis et al. ("Age Segregation in Children's Social Interaction") and Medrich et al. (*The Serious Business of Growing Up*) found boys more often played outdoors and girls, indoors.

4. Lever, "Sex Differences in the Games Children Play." Similar conclusions are drawn by Mary F. Waldrop and Charles F. Halverson, "Intensive and Extensive Peer Behavior: Longitudinal and Cross-sectional Analyses"; Donna Eder and Maureen T. Hallinan, "Sex Differences in Children's Friendships"; and Schofield, *Black and White in School*.

   In *Culture against Man*, a 1960s study of adolescent culture in a high school, Jules Henry generalized: "Boys flock; girls seldom get together in groups above four. . . . Boys are dependent on masculine solidarity . . . the emphasis is on masculine unity; in girls' cliques the purpose is to shut out other girls" (p. 150). This frequently cited paragraph influenced many later researchers.

5. See reviews of research in Hartup, "Peer Relations," and in Eleanor E. Maccoby and Carol Nagy Jacklin, *The Psychology of Sex Differences*.

6. Best, *We've All Got Scars*; Schofield, *Black and White in School*; Sluckin, *Growing Up in the Playground*.

7. See Goodwin, *He-Said-She-Said*, for careful sociolinguistic documentation of this pattern among a group of boys in an African-American urban neighborhood.

8. Best, *We've All Got Scars*; also see ibid.

9. Lever, "Sex Differences in the Games Children Play" and "Sex Differences in the Complexity of Children's Play and Games."

10. See Thorne and Luria, "Sexuality and Gender in Children's Daily

Worlds." For a related analysis of bonding among adult men, enacted through forms of joking, see Peter Lyman, "The Fraternal Bond as a Joking Relationship."

11. Best, *We've All Got Scars*; Eder and Hallinan, "Sex Differences in Children's Friendships"; Lever, "Sex Differences in the Games Children Play"; Schofield, *Black and White in School*; Thorne and Luria, "Sexuality and Gender in Children's Daily Worlds"; Waldrop and Halverson, "Intensive and Extensive Peer Behavior."

12. Goodwin, *He-Said-She-Said*, and Berentzen, *Children Constructing Their Social World*.

13. Toth, *Blooming*.

14. Schofield, *Black and White in School*.

15. Lever, "Sex Differences in the Games Children Play," and Eder and Hallinan, "Sex Differences in Children's Friendships."

16. Lever, "Sex Differences in the Games Children Play"; Evans, "Gender Differences in Children's Games"; Finnan, "The Ethnography of Children's Spontaneous Play"; Schofield, *Black and White in School*.

17. Goodwin, *He-Said-She-Said*.

18. Donna Eder, "The Cycle of Popularity: Interpersonal Relations among Female Adolescents."

19. *Cat's Eye*, a novel by Margaret Atwood, vividly depicts subterranean conflict and hostility among a small group of girls.

20. Three different teachers, who may have been responding to these patterns and/or to cultural stereotypes, have told me that it's easier to discipline boys than girls; boys' arguments, they said, are more direct, and they "forgive and forget." But girls are "sneaky in their behavior"; "when girls are bad they're nasty."

21. In a study of primary school children in Australia, Davies (*Life in the Classroom and Playground*) also describes a group of boys as well as several groups of girls who maneuvered between "best friends" and "contingency friends." She notes that the availability of a contingency friend heightens one's bargaining power over a best friend. Davies does not locate the analysis within the rubric of gender difference.

22. The term and the observation about anthropology come from Sherry B. Ortner, "The Founding of the First Sherpa Nunnery and the Problem of 'Women' as an Analytic Category."

23. For example, see Carole Joffe ("As the Twig Is Bent") on the "masculine subculture" of four boys in a preschool; Vivian Gussin Paley (*Boys and Girls: Superheroes in the Doll Corner*) on "the superhero clique" in a kindergarten; and Best (*We've All Got Scars*) on "the Tent Club," a dominant male group that continued from first through second grade.

24. Everhart, *Reading, Writing, and Resistance*, and Cusick, *Inside High School*; Fine, *With the Boys*.

25. Cusick, *Inside High School*, p. 168.

26. AnnMarie Wolpe similarly observes that British ethnographies of

schooling include little about "the ordinary boy who goes through school doing minimal work, but not necessarily domineering or sexually harassing" (*Within School Walls: The Role of Discipline, Sexuality, and the Curriculum*, p. 92).

27. Goodenough, "Small Group Culture," p. 217. In comparative observations she found that four of nine kindergarten classrooms had a bonded group of disruptive and aggressive boys; relations between boys and girls were more harmonious and mutual in classes without such a group.

28. Paley, *Boys and Girls*, and Ellen Jordan, "Gender Theory and the Construction of Masculinity in the Infants School."

As another example of this process, both teachers and ethnographers have paid more attention to boys than to girls; girls have a "semi-ignored status" in traditional educational research *and* in teacher practices (see the brief discussion of sexism in teaching in Chapter 3). However, as discussed in Chapter 2, the interests of ethnographers may also counter those of teachers; for example, whereas the teacher may want an orderly classroom, the observer may want juicy material about kids' underground cultures or, as in Paul Willis's *Learning to Labour*, about school resisters.

29. Fine, *With the Boys*.

30. Connell et al., *Making the Difference*. On the conceptual pluralizing of masculinities and feminities, also see Connell, *Gender and Power*.

31. Canaan, "A Comparative Analysis of American Suburban Middle Class, Middle School, and High School Teenage Cliques." Michael Messner ("Masculinities and Athletic Careers," p. 82) quotes an African-American man from a lower-class background who recalled that in junior high "you either got identified as an athlete, a thug, or a bookworm."

In an insightful ethnography of a largely white high school in the Detroit area, Penelope Eckert traces the dynamic opposition between two categories that dominated the social life of the school. The Jocks, with a middle-class orientation, controlled school athletics and other adult-sponsored activities. The more working-class Burnouts were estranged from the school and rebelled against its authority. Girls and boys were in both categories, and, significantly, the majority of students fell in between. See Eckert, *Jocks and Burnouts: Social Categories and Identity in the High School*.

32. On the other hand, in an observational study in a British classroom of twelve- and thirteen-year-olds, Robert J. Meyenn ("School Girls' Peer Groups") found that groups and not pairs were the dominant form of social organization. He identified four distinct groups of varying sizes and with different patterns of behavior: the "PE" girls (nine members, physically mature and noisy, who "rough and tumbled" more than the boys); the "science lab girls" (four members; popular and liked by teachers); the "nice girls" (five members; unobtrusive and less physically mature); and the "quiet girls" (four girls who were socially uncertain).

Groups maneuvered to be together throughout the school day, and members gave one another help and support. Mayenn writes the girls found it "inconceivable to just have one best friend," although there were patterns of "breaking friends" internal to each group (p. 115).

33. Linda Hughes, "'But That's Not *Really* Mean': Competing in a Cooperative Mode,'" p. 684.

34. Lever, "Sex Differences in the Complexity of Children's Play and Games."

35. For a detailed analysis of arguments about rules during the playing of another turn-taking "girls'" game, see Marjorie Harness Goodwin, "The Serious Side of Jump Rope: Conversational Practices and Social Organization in the Frame of 'Play.'"

36. Luria and Herzog ("Sorting Gender Out in a Children's Museum") also found that context makes a difference in the organization of same-gender groups. On a class field trip to a children's museum, elementary school boys clustered in much smaller groups than one typically sees on school playgrounds.

37. Goodwin, *He-Said-She-Said*.

38. Ibid., and Marjorie Harness Goodwin and Charles Goodwin, "Children's Arguing."

39. For a review of literature and a description of insult exchanges among white working-class girls in a junior high cafeteria, see Donna Eder, "Serious and Playful Disputes: Variation in Conflict Talk among Female Adolescents." This point relates to the discussion in Chapter 5 of "hassling" and "meddlin" in multiracial schools, and white students being quicker than Black students to interpret the hassling as intimidation.

40. Tannen, *You Just Don't Understand*, p. 18.

41. J. A. DiPietro, "Rough and Tumble Play: A Function of Gender."

42. Jacklin, "Methodological Issues in the Study of Sex-related Differences."

43. Medrich et al., *The Serious Business of Growing Up*.

44. In a careful review of empirical research, Nancy Karweit and Stephen Hansell ("Sex Differences in Adolescent Relationships: Friendship and Status") conclude that the conventional view that boys have larger friendship groups than girls is overdrawn. Some studies find that up to age seven, boys are either situated in smaller groups than girls, or that there are no gender differences. The research literature does suggest that the *average* size of friendship groups fits the conventional depiction from age seven to adolescence, but patterns vary by setting, such as type of classroom, and by type of activity, for example, participation in team sports. Findings are mixed for junior high and high school.

45. In addition to Jacklin, "Methodological Issues in the Study of Sex-related Differences," see Maccoby and Jacklin, *The Psychology of Sex Differences*, and Fausto-Sterling, *Myths of Gender*.

46. Walkerdine, *Schoolgirl Fictions*; also see Davies, *Frogs and Snails and Feminist Tales*.

47. Gilligan, *In a Different Voice*.

48. For example, see Linda K. Kerber et al., "On *In a Different Voice: An Interdisciplinary Forum*." For a critical discussion of Gilligan's recent research on girls entering adolescence and its neglect of race, ethnicity, and social class as they interact with gender, see Judith Stacey, "On Resistance, Ambivalence, and Feminist Theory."

49. Carol Gilligan et al., eds., *Making Connections: The Relational Worlds of Adolescent Girls at Emma Willard School*.

50. Hughes, "'But That's Not *Really* Mean.'"

51. Amy Sheldon, "Conflict Talk: Sociolinguistic Challenges to Self-Assertion and How Young Girls Meet Them."

52. Julian Wood, "Groping Towards Sexism: Boys' 'Sex Talk,'" pp. 60–61.

53. For a helpful review of "reproduction" and "resistance" theories, see Dorothy C. Holland and Margaret A. Eisenhart, *Educated in Romance: Women, Achievement, and College Culture*.

54. Connell et al., *Making the Difference*, and Connell, *Gender and Power*.

55. Joan Anyon, "Intersections of Gender and Class: Accommodation and Resistance by Working-Class and Affluent Females to Contradictory Sex-Role Ideologies."

56. This point is made in Hugh C. Foot et al., eds., *Friendship and Social Relations in Children*; Hartup, "Peer Relations"; Gilligan et al., *Making Connections*; and Carol Dyhouse, *Girls Growing Up in Victorian and Edwardian England*.

57. Angela McRobbie, "Settling Accounts with Subcultures"; Willis, *Learning to Labour*.

58. Lever, "Sex Differences in the Games Children Play." A deficit approach to girls can also be found in Finnan, "The Ethnography of Children's Spontaneous Play."

59. Reviewing the evolution of the "separate spheres" metaphor in social history, Linda K. Kerber analogously observes that the notion of separate spheres "enabled historians to move the history of women out of the realm of the trivial and anecdotal and into the realm of analytic social history" ("Separate Spheres, Female Worlds, Woman's Place: The Rhetoric of Women's History," p. 37).

60. Judith Shapiro, "Gender Totemism."

61. R. W. Connell, *Which Way Is Up?: Essays on Class, Sex, and Culture*, p. 226.

62. Goodwin (*He-Said-She-Said*) resists the temptation to chalk up her findings as "children's culture," "gender cultures," and/or "African-American culture." Instead she asks how participants assemble and interpret activities through arguing, telling stories, and gossip. Starting with activities rather than an assumption of binary gender difference led her to discover both differences and commonalities between boys and girls.

63. Scott, *Gender and the Politics of History*, p. 49.

## Chapter 7. Crossing the Gender Divide

1. "Tomboy," *Oxford English Dictionary.*
2. Louisa Mae Alcott, *Little Women.* For an informative discussion of nineteenth-century tomboys in fiction and autobiography, see Anne Scott MacLeod. "The *Caddie Woodlawn* Syndrome: American Girlhood in the Nineteenth Century."
3. Carol Ryrie Brink, *Caddie Woodlawn*; Lois Lenski, *Texas Tomboy,* Jane Langton, *The Boyhood of Grace Jones.*
4. Vera Cleaver and Bill Cleaver, *Lady Ellen Grae,* and Norma Klein, *Tomboy.*
5. Louise Fitzhugh, *Harriet the Spy,* and Judy Blume, *Are You There God? It's Me, Margaret.*
6. Elizabeth Segel, "Tomboy Taming and Gender Role Socialization: The Evidence of Children's Books"; Cynthia Voigt, *Jackaroo*; Robin McKinley, *The Hero and the Crown.*
7. As Segel ("Tomboy Taming and Gender Role Socialization") has pointed out, the 1980s stories give the ending a different twist. The heroines leave behind their adventuring ways, but they move toward romantic passivity rather than the values of altruism and caring celebrated in earlier "tomboy" literature. For example, *The Hero and the Crown* concludes with Aerin marrying the king, a conclusion that resonates with the Harlequin romances now being produced for younger female readers (see Mitzi Myers, "Gender, Genres, Generations: Artist-Mothers and the Scripting of Girls' Lives").
8. On the sexism of the word "tomboy," see Casey Miller and Kate Swift, *The Handbook of Nonsexist Writing.*
9. Gender labeling is a tricky issue, not only in everyday language but also in the language of research. For example, psychologists use "masculine/ feminine/androgyny" scales to study personality. Although reworked in the last fifteen years with greater sensitivity to problems of stereotyping, these scales continue to label some behaviors as "feminine" and others as "masculine." The Bem Sex Roles Inventory gives points for "masculine" to a woman who says she is self-reliant or ambitious. Why use a gender label? Continuing to affix labels like "masculine" or "feminine" to diverse human qualities and behaviors perpetuates gender stereotyping. For fuller development of this argument, see Margrit Eichler, *The Double Standard: A Feminist Critique of Feminist Social Science,* and Bernice Lott, "A Feminist Critique of Androgyny: Toward the Elimination of Gender Attributions for Learned Behavior."
10. Janet S. Hyde and her colleagues asked undergraduate students to write autobiographies for a course on the psychology of women. Of forty-six women students, 78 percent wrote that they had been "tomboys" in childhood. In subsequent surveys, the researchers found that 51 percent of women contacted in a shopping mall, and 63 percent of

a junior high sample said they had been tomboys. See Hyde et al., "Tomboyism."

In oral histories with women who played professional sports between 1930 and 1970, Susan Cahn found that her informants often, although not always, described themselves as having been tomboys in childhood. Some remembered "tomboy" as a term of distinction and others, as merely descriptive; a few had experienced "tomboy" as a term of reproach. Cahn analyzes varied ways in which the women negotiated contradictory systems of meaning, including views of women athletes as "mannish," to create coherent and generally positive identities. See Cahn, "Coming on Strong: Gender and Sexuality in Women's Sport, 1900–1960."

11. Luisa Pesserini describes "counternarratives" told by Italian working women who, contrasting themselves with the dominant cultural model, said they had always been "rebel girls." Passerini believes that this is not always an accurate self-representation but may act as a "source of inspiration, encouragement, and excitement *in the face of* a different reality" (Pesserini, "Women's Personal Narratives: Myths, Experiences, and Emotions," p. 191).

12. Zella Luria, personal communication, 1985.

13. A 1977 *WomanSports* survey of "young women around the country" quoted an eighteen-year-old as observing that "the word 'tomboy' will soon be obsolete"; another said, "these days many of the girls don't use or understand the word 'tomboy,' but they do use 'jock'" (cited in Caryl Rivers et al., *Beyond Sugar and Spice*, pp. 97–98).

14. According to the entry under "sissy" in the *Oxford English Dictionary*, in the 1850s "siss" and "sissy," both contractions of "sister," were used in addressing girls. *Webster's Third New International Dictionary* adds two meanings: "an effeminate man or boy" and "a timid or cowardly person."

15. Peggy Miller and Linda L. Sperry ("The Socialization of Anger and Aggression") observed interactions between three white working-class mothers and their daughters, who were two and a half years old. The mothers deliberately tried to "toughen" their daughters and teach them to stand up for themselves. In addition to various teasing practices, the mothers called their daughters "sissy" to shame them for crying, fussing, or whining.

16. This point adds a layer of complexity to Cahill's argument, summarized in Chapter 3, that adult praise for "big boys" and "big girls" links gender affirmation to the positive goal of growing up. Cahill does not discuss the *female* connotations of the negative state of "being a baby" or "crybaby." See Cahill, "Language Practices and Self-Definition."

17. The meanings that cluster around the term "sissy"—girlish, childish, and gay—signal larger historical shifts in Western culture. Conceptions of gender were *not* saturated with heterosexual meanings in ancient Greece;

homosexuality was considered fully masculine. In nineteenth-century England, male homosexuality was equated with childishness more than gender deviance (Eve Kosofsky Sedgwick, "Homophobia, Misogyny, and Capital: The Example of Our Mutual Friend"). Cross-cultural research also reveals cultures that have not defined gender in terms of sexual orientation; see Walter Williams, *The Spirit and the Flesh: Sexual Diversity in American Indian Culture.*

As I discuss in Chapter 8, a hallmark of the contemporary sex/gender system of U.S. society has been the symbolic linking of sexual orientation with conceptions of masculinity and femininity. Kids draw on these symbolic meanings when they use "fag" to refer to boys who play with girls and in girls' activities. I never heard kids attribute homosexuality to girls who often played with boys and in boys' activities; when kids called girls "fag," it was not in contexts that seemed to have any relevance to gender. Homophobia may not get directed toward females until junior high.

18. In *The New Dictionary of American Slang*, Chapman lists "a male homosexual" as one of the meanings of "sissy."

19. For a thorough review of this literature, see Kenneth Zucker, "Cross-Gender–identified Children."

20. Ibid.; Richard Green, *The "Sissy Boy Syndrome" and the Development of Homosexuality.* Biologists have also used "tomboy" unreflectively; John Money and Anke Ehrhardt (*Man and Woman, Boy and Girl*) use "tomboyism" to describe the behavior of "fetally masculinized genetic females" (for a critical discussion, see Fausto-Sterling, *Myths of Gender*).

21. Allan Ellenzweig, "Cultural Bias in Action." In *Disorders of Desire: Sex and Gender in Modern American Sexology*, Janice M. Irvine places contemporary sexologists in a larger social and historical context. She criticizes writers like Green for their inattention to gender and sexual politics and to issues of culture, power, and privilege. Is it success, Irvine asks, for a boy to stop wearing a dress and to pick up a gun?

22. Green, *The "Sissy Boy Syndrome,"* p. 12.

23. Charlotte Zolotow, *William's Doll.*

24. Tomie dePaola, *Oliver Button Is a Sissy.*

25. Davies, *Frogs and Snails and Feminist Tales*, p. 50.

26. William Harris Hooks, *The Nutcracker*, and Louise Fitzhugh, *Nobody's Family Is Going to Change.*

27. Michel Foucault, *The History of Sexuality*, vol. 1.

28. Historians of sexuality have found that the term "homosexual" didn't come into use until the 1860s, and sexologists introduced the word "lesbian" in the early twentieth century (Jeffrey Weeks, *Sexuality and Its Discontents*). I am relying on the *Oxford English Dictionary* for clues to the historical appearance of "tomboy" and "sissy" as terms of identity.

29. There are varied situations of "gender passing." In the nineteenth century

a number of women dressed and lived as men, partly to acquire male privileges (John D'Emelio and Estelle Freedman, *Intimate Matters: A History of Sexuality in America*, pp. 124–125). In today's society, transsexuals and transvestites engage in various degrees of "passing" as members of the gender category other than the one to which they were originally assigned. In some traditional Native American societies, such as the Navajo and the Sioux, there was, in addition to "woman" and "man," a transitional, mixed-gender, or third gender category that individuals who were drawn to dress and activities of the other gender could join (Williams, *The Spirit and the Flesh*, and Harriet Whitehead, "The Bow and the Burden Strap: A New Look at Institutionalized Homosexuality in Native America").

30. Fine (*With the Boys*) observed that high-status Little League players had more latitude to break the frame of ongoing games and introduce playful antics, prevent fights by telling others to "knock it off," and to have girlfriends without being teased and ridiculed by their peers. With high status comes the power to define interactions on one's own terms.

31. Griffin ("'Gymnastics Is a Girls' Thing'") found that in middle-school coed PE classes, girls more often entered boys' activities in an exploratory or reluctant manner, whereas boys more often entered "girl-appropriate" activities, like gymnastics, with frivolity and hassling.

32. This asymmetry can be documented in varied ways. For example, in their survey of fifth-graders, Medrich et al. (*The Serious Business of Growing Up*) found that 18 percent of girls but only 9 percent of boys named someone of the other gender as their best friend. Girls who named a boy as their best friend were far more likely than other girls to say they played team sports.

      In an observational study in four preschools, Beverly I. Fagot found that boys who engaged in activities that children stereotyped as "for girls" (art activities, playing in the kitchen or with dolls) were much more criticized by teachers and peers than girls who engaged in activities children considered to be "for boys" (building with blocks or playing with transportation toys or in the outdoors sandbox). Of the children who frequently engaged in "cross-gender" activity, boys played alone almost three times more often than girls. See Fagot, "Consequences of Moderate Cross-Gender Behavior in Preschool Children."

33. Several researchers have found less gender separation among African-American than white children. In observations of first-grade classrooms, Grant found that Black girls had more extensive peer ties and crossed gender and race lines more readily than other children ("Black Females' 'Place' in Desegregated Classrooms"). In *Black and White in School*, a study of a racially balanced middle school, Schofield found that among sixth graders, Black students crossed gender lines twice as often as white students; however, the difference disappeared by eighth grade. Goodwin (*He-Said-She-Said*) also found that daily interactions of

African-American children in an urban neighborhood were less gender-divided than the interactions portrayed in the literature on peer relations, a literature skewed toward predominantly white school settings.

34. I have earlier reviewed literature finding that African-American girls are more likely than white girls to engage in verbal self-assertion, although there is also variation by social class. Jessie was from a working-class family, as were most of the other children in the school. See Goodwin, *He-Said-She-Said*; Grant, "Black Females' 'Place' in Desegregated Classrooms"; Schofield, *Black and White in School*; and Hanna, *Disruptive School Behavior*.

35. Skillful crossing sometimes depends on various access rituals that Corsaro ("We're Friends, Right?") identified through observations in a nursery school. These include entering the area where an episode is under way and producing appropriate behavior, verbally requesting permission to join, and using an object to gain entry to a group or activity.

36. Several kids have told me they think this is a gender difference. In elementary school playground observations, Evans found that although 21 percent of team games included girls as players, girls were almost never accepted as captains (captains choose the teams). A sixth-grade girl told him, "If the boy picks first, then he'll pick the best boy, and the girls, they pick their friends" (Evans, "Gender Differences in Children's Games," p. 7).

37. The tomboy stories of children's fiction and adult reminiscence often conclude with a painful transition when the girl's relations with boys become redefined. The girl gets marked as different, often with reference to her undeniably female body. One woman recalled that her childhood freedom came to an end when she developed breasts and her parents told her she shouldn't "run around with and touch boys anymore." Another woman remembered that when one of her male "buddies" tried to pull down her shorts, she knew their relationship had permanently changed. Such a transition seemed foreshadowed by the obstacles that heterosexual meanings posed to Jessie's full participation in groups of boys.

38. An adult woman once told me about her experiences in a situation similar to Jessie's. In fifth and sixth grade she was the only African-American student in otherwise white classrooms. Although she gained respect for her intelligence and athletic skills, she felt "neutered" in the developing gender/sexuality system; she continually got the message, "you're not really sexual; you won't be dating."

     Schofield (*Black and White in School*) found that interracial romances were rare in the middle school she studied; the few that existed nearly always involved Black boys and white girls.

39. Rosabeth Moss Kanter, *Men and Women of the Corporation*.

40. Lynne Segal, *Slow Motion: Changing Masculinities, Changing Men*, p. 16.

## Chapter 8. Lip Gloss and "Goin' with": Becoming Teens

1. Valerie Walkerdine, "Post-structuralist Theory and Everyday Practices: The Family and the School," p. 71.
2. Connell et al., *Making the Difference*.
3. J. M. Tanner, "Sequence, Tempo, and Individual Variation in Growth and Development of Boys and Girls Aged Twelve to Sixteen," p. 3.
4. Ibid., p. 8. In the history of Europe and the United States, the average age of onset of puberty has steadily declined, probably because of improved nutrition.
5. Gene I. Maeroff, "The Toughest Job in Education," p. 54.
6. Nancy Lutkehaus and Paul Roscoe, "Introduction" to *New Directions in the Study of Female Initiation*.
7. For historical perspectives, see Lois W. Banner, *In Full Flower: Aging Women, Power, and Sexuality, a History*, and Winifred Breines, *Young, White, and Miserable: Female in the Fifties*.
8. Recent writings on the anthropology, sociology, and history of the body highlight social and cultural contexts that give meaning to the physical or biological. For example, anthropologists Sylvia J. Yanagisako and Jane F. Collier question any simple biological basis for the construction of kinship: "There are no 'facts,' biological or material, that have social consequences and cultural meanings in and of themselves. Sexual intercourse, pregnancy, and parturition are cultural facts, whose form, consequences, and meanings are socially constructed in any society, as are mothering, fathering, judging, ruling, and talking with the gods" (Yanagisako and Collier, "Toward a Unified Analysis of Gender and Kinship," p. 39).

    In *Making Sex: Body and Gender from the Greeks to Freud*, Thomas W. Laqueur traces dramatic historical changes in Western conceptions of gender as they have shaped views of the body. In the Middle Ages, male and female bodies were seen as similar in structure and in function, but by the nineteenth century, as social views of gender became increasingly dichotomous, an emphasis on basic biological differences between males and females replaced this earlier view. Social changes alter the metaphors of biology.

    Emily Martin (*The Woman in the Body*) interviewed American women of varied ages and social classes about their experiences of menstruation, conception, pregnancy, and menopause. She found that middle-class women tended to accept the (negative) medical model of menstruation as failed production, a model rooted in our cultural forms of hierarchy and control. Working-class women put more trust in their own experiences of the feel, smell, and appearance of menstruation.
9. Sandra Kessler et al., "Gender Relations in Secondary Schooling," p. 44.

10. This general point is beautifully raised by Everett C. Hughes in "Cycles, Turning Points, and Careers."

11. Dreeban, *On What Is Learned in School*

12. Social class and race may affect these perceptions. Deborah Tyler provides a fascinating analysis of tensions between conceptions of childhood and conceptions about the nature of working-class female sexuality, as revealed in turn-of-the-century legislative struggles over raising the age of consent from twelve to sixteen in Australia. Middleclass male legislators were able to see physically developed middleclass girls as sexually innocent, but the bodies of working-class girls "somehow took on the physical signs of sexual maturity in ways that the bodies of middleclass girls did not" (Tyler, "The Case of Irene Tuckerman: Understanding Sexual Violence and the Protection of Women and Girls, Victoria 1890–1925," p. 54).

13. This incident was relayed to me by the girl's teacher. In a sociolinguistic study of gossip in a junior high cafeteria, Donna Eder and Janet Lynne Enke analyze conversations among a tightly knit group of eighth-grade girls, most of whom had not yet "developed sexually." They gossiped about girls who were overweight and who had large breasts, referring to them as "big fat cows." See Eder and Enke, "The Structure of Gossip: Opportunities and Constraints on Collective Expression among Adolescents."

14. This research is reviewed in Ruth T. Gross and Paula M. Duke, "The Effect of Early versus Late Physical Maturation on Adolescent Behavior," and in Anne C. Petersen, "Adolescent Development." Roberta G. Simmons and Dale A. Blyth followed 798 girls and boys from sixth through seventh grade. They found that the girls with the lowest self-esteem were those who experienced multiple changes. They reached physical puberty and dated early, and they moved to junior high school rather than staying in an elementary school that went through eighth grade. See Simmons and Blyth, *Moving into Adolescence: The Impact of Pubertal Change and School Context*.

    The pacing of development may also affect the experiences of girls and boys in later adolescence. Margaret S. Faust found that in eighth and ninth grades, girls who were late developers had less prestige, and those who matured earlier tended to fare better. Late-developing boys also tended to be at a psychological and social disadvantage. See Faust, "Developmental Maturity as a Determinant in Prestige of Adolescent Girls." One finding recurs: girls whose development is paced with the majority tend to experience the fewest problems.

15. Once at a junior high boys' soccer game, I overheard a group of white upper-middle-class parents discussing their sons. They talked about whether a specific boy had "gotten his growth" ("my son was small and then zingo, he grew") and motor coordination ("Jack is big, but not very

coordinated"). They unambivalently valued the effective deployment of height and strength, and they talked about parents who had started their boys a year late in kindergarten so they would be among the biggest in their class and "make it onto teams."

16. Canaan, "A Comparative Analysis of American Suburban Middle Class, Middle School, and High School Teenage Cliques."

17. For example, see Petersen, "Adolescent Development," and Simmons and Blyth, *Moving into Adolescence.*

18. Connell explores the themes of force, strength, and power in patterns of masculine embodiment in the essay "Men's Bodies," in *Which Way Is Up*; also see Barry Glassner, *Bodies.*

19. Haug, ed., *Female Sexualization*, p. 139.

20. Douglas, *Purity and Danger.* Paley (*Boys and Girls*) describes an event that unfolded when one of her kindergarten students, Karen, brought her Barbie doll to school. The other girls were magnetized by the Barbie's presence. Karen said her mother knew the teacher wouldn't like having the Barbie in the classroom. Paley asked why, and Karen replied, "Because it has breasts." Paley realized this was true.

21. Best describes fifth-grade girls playing "snapsies" with one another's bra straps (*We've All Got Scars*, pp. 112–113). Mary Knapp and Herbert Knapp discuss bra-snapping and other folklore used to tease girls with and without breasts (*One Potato, Two Potato*, pp. 82–86).

22. Jeanne Brooks-Gunn reports research finding that girls discussed the onset of menstruation with their mothers and close girlfriends, although they told fewer girlfriends than they expected to tell. A study of thirteen middle-class adolescent boys found that they got most of their information about topics like ejaculation from magazines and "locker room" jokes. Although they joked about ejaculation, none talked to other boys about their own experiences and feelings. See Brooks-Gunn, "The Impact of Puberty and Sexual Activity upon the Health and Education of Adolescent Girls and Boys."

23. Gary Alan Fine, "The Natural History of Preadolescent Male Friendship Groups," p. 300.

24. Thorne and Luria, "Sexuality and Gender in Children's Daily Worlds."

25. John H. Gagnon and William Simon, *Sexual Conduct*; also see John Gagnon, "The Creation of the Sexual in Early Adolescence."

26. Thanks to Joyce Canaan for this insight.

27. This raises an interesting topic: how different kids pick up on, interpret, utilize, or resist the commercialized teen culture so much in evidence in the media and marketplace and geared to younger and younger ages. Students of British youth culture have explored these themes with some attention to social class and gender variation; for example, see Angela McRobbie and Mica Nava, eds., *Gender and Generation.*

28. A large-scale survey of twelve- to seventeen-year-olds revealed that level of sexual maturation did *not* correlate with dating; age was a better

predictor. See Sanford M. Dornbusch et al., "Sexual Development, Age, and Dating: A Comparison of Biological and Social Influences upon One Set of Behaviors."

29. Other ethnographers have also observed variation in the adoption of teen culture. Wulff (*Twelve Girls*) describes a group of Black and white girls, ages thirteen to sixteen, in London and their vacillation between the conduct of teenagers and that of children. In a study of twelve- and thirteen-year-old girls in a British school, Meyenn ("School Girls' Peer Groups") found that the girls in some groups had boyfriends and wore makeup, jewelry, and "modern dress"; girls in other groups were not interested in boys or in "fashion."

   Symbolic variation becomes entrenched in the clique structure that appears to be omnipresent in junior high and middle schools. Canaan found that members of the top or "cool" group in an East Coast middle school were "more complete teenagers." Their conduct—dating, drinking, going to parties, taking drugs—was more like that of high schoolers. (See Canaan, "A Comparative Analysis of American Suburban Middle Class, Middle School, and High School Teenage Cliques.") In a complementary observational study in a Detroit suburb, Eckert (*Jocks and Burnouts*) noted that entrance into junior high marked the formal transition to teenage status. The Burnouts, who dated, partied, and smoked, were seen as cool because they had departed the most from childhood forms. They continued to claim adult prerogatives and gradually became estranged from official school culture; others saw them as trying to grow up too fast. The Jocks, who emerged a little later, embraced a different sort of teen culture, more involved in the corporate life of the school and less claiming of full adult status. They fit the adult middle-class view of what teenagers should be like.

30. Max Gluckman, ed., *Essays on the Ritual of Social Relations*.

31. Toth, *Blooming*, p. 58. Davies (*Life in the Classroom and Playground*) observed that older elementary school children in Australia took up romantic relationships, and let them lapse, with little emotional investment; they had much deeper ties with those of the same gender. The reverse, she observes, is true of many adults.

32. Willard Waller, "The Rating and Dating Complex," and Pepper Schwartz and Janet Lever, "Fear and Loathing at a College Mixer." For an insightful analysis of "attractiveness" as a commodity in the "sexual auction" world of college students, see Holland and Eisenhart, *Educated in Romance*.

33. Gagnon, "The Creation of the Sexual in Early Adolescence," p. 238.

34. Ruth Benedict, "Continuities and Discontinuities in Cultural Conditioning."

35. Stevi Jackson, *Childhood and Sexuality*. Eisenhart and Holland ("Learning Gender from Peers") observed that elementary school staff, who were invested in the structural division between adults and children, went

out of their way to see students as asexual, downplaying the romantic and sexual interests that were quite evident in the peer groups of
fourth- and fifth-graders.

36. Whitehead, "The Bow and the Burden Strap"; also see Williams, *The Spirit and the Flesh*.

37. Foucault, *The History of Sexuality*, vol. 1, and Weeks, *Sexuality and Its Discontents*.

38. Adrienne Rich, "Compulsory Heterosexuality and Lesbian Existence."

39. See research reviewed in Gilligan et al., eds., *Making Connections*; and Simmons and Blyth, *Moving into Adolescence*.

   A 1990 survey of three thousand children, sponsored by the American Association of University Women, found that from fourth to tenth
grade the percentage of girls who said they were "happy the way I am"
dropped from 60 to 29 percent; for boys, the figure dropped from 67 to
46 percent. Black girls retained more self-confidence than white girls,
perhaps, the researchers concluded from other responses, because of support from families and communities rather than the school system. See
Suzanne Daley, "Girls' Self-esteem Is Lost on Way to Adolescence, New
Study Finds."

40. See Schofield, *Black and White in School*; Canaan, "A Comparative Analysis of American Suburban Middle Class, Middle School, and High School Teenage Cliques"; and Holland and Eisenhart, *Educated in Romance*.

41. For a fascinating discussion of the processes by which "sexualized female bodies" are produced, see Haug, *Female Sexualization*.

42. Anyon, "Intersections of Gender and Class"; Angela McRobbie, "Working-Class Girls and the Culture of Femininity"; Wolpe, *Within School Walls*.

43. Joyce Canaan, "Why a 'Slut' Is a 'Slut': Cautionary Tales of Middle-Class Teenage Girls," and Susan Lees, *Losing Out: Sexuality and Adolescent Girls*.

44. Rosalind Petchesky, *Abortion and Women's Choice*, p. 224. For another insightful discussion of the paradoxical sexual discourses bombarded at girls, see Michelle Fine, "Sexuality, Schooling, and Adolescent Females: The Missing Discourse of Desire."

45. Mica Nava, "Youth Service Provision, Social Order, and the Question of Girls" p. 15.

## Chapter 9. Lessons for Adults

1. This step in my thinking was facilitated by Sandra Harding (*The Science Question in Feminism*) and Scott (*Gender and the Politics of History*), who each distinguish individual or personal gender, gender as social structure, and gender as symbolism or culture.

2. Sandra Wallman ("Epistemologies of Sex") calls this "the peculiar episte-mology of sex." Also see Shapiro, "Gender Totemism," and Yanakgisako and Collier, "Toward a Unified Analysis of Gender and Kinship."

3. In a letter from Susan B. Anthony to Elizabeth Cady Stanton, quoted in Theodore Stanton and Harriet Stanton Blatch, eds., *Elizabeth Cady Stanton as Revealed in Her Letters, Diary and Reminiscences*, vol. 2, pp. 64–66.

4. Concrete suggestions for nonsexist elementary school education can be found in Susan S. Klein, ed., *Handbook for Achieving Sex Equity through Education*; Sadker and Sadker, *Sex Equity Handbook for Schools*; and Marcia Guttentag and Helen Bray, *Undoing Sex Stereotypes: Research and Resources for Educators*; and in the American Association of Univer-sity Women Educational Foundation and the Wellesley College Center for Research on Women, *How Schools Shortchange Girls*. For sugges-tions on nonsexist childrearing, see Letty Cottin Pogrebin, *Growing Up Free*.

5. Wilkinson and Marrett, ed., *Gender Influences in Classroom Interac-tion*; Klein, ed., *Handbook for Achieving Sex Equity through Education*; and Goodenough, "Small Group Culture and the Emergence of Sexist Behavior."

6. This incident raises a topic that needs more extensive research: how teach-ers and staff influence one another's gender practices. Feminist teachers report collegial experiences ranging from acceptance to hostility. See Sara Delamont, *Sex Roles and the School*; R. W. Connell, *Teachers' Work*; and Kathleen Weiler, *Women Teaching for Change: Gender, Class, and Power*.

7. Drawing on research in schools in England, Walkerdine (*Schoolgirl Fic-tions*) describes this process, She also observed that teachers tended to adulate boys more than girls, "reading" boys as independent, intelligent, and rational as well as, and through displays of, "naughty." In contrast, she found that teachers downplayed the good performance of girls by calling them "hardworking," "boring," and "not brilliant."

8. In *Women Teaching for Change*, Weiler provides a detailed account of the backgrounds, experiences, and daily practices of feminist teach-ers in public high schools, including the contradictions they face, for example, as white middle-class women teaching Black working-class boys. Also see Connell, *Teachers' Work*, and Delamont, *Sex Roles and the School*.

9. Patricia S. Griffin compares the techniques of three teachers of physical education in the same middle school. Two used practices that assumed that boys and girls are groups with separate and nonoverlapping inter-ests, talents, and physical characteristics. For example, these teachers had all girls use nerf or rubber footballs, while all boys used regular footballs, and they instituted a rule that "a girl must touch the ball before a shot on goal is taken." Some girls, in fact, were bigger and played better than

some boys. The third teacher, who had attended a gender equity workshop, used inclusive language (e.g., changing "defenseman" to "defense person"), grouped students by ability or randomly rather than by gender, deliberately chose both girls and boys for leadership positions, and interrupted sexist student interactions. See Griffin, "Teachers' Perceptions of and Responses to Sex Equity Problems in a Middle School Physical Education Program."

10. I have heard of no contemporary examples of staff explicitly sorting students by race, religion, or social class in U.S. public schools, although grouping by performance builds on and may reinforce the dynamics of race and class divisions and inequality (see Oakes, *Keeping Track*). Sorting students on the basis of age seems more defensible, because of the loose association with capability, but cross-age mixing may have beneficial consequences, including, as argued in Chapter 4, the encouragement of gender integration.

11. Lisa Serbin et al., "Shaping Cooperative Cross-Sex Play." Eleanor E. Maccoby takes this experiment as evidence that children's gender segregation is "surprisingly resistant to modification by adult intervention" ("Gender as a Social Category," p. 756). In contrast, I am struck by the dramatic results after a short period of intervention and wonder what the consequences might be if efforts to reinforce cross-gender interaction were more sustained and widespread. Lisa Serbin also remains relatively optimistic, concluding that if teachers wish to do so, they can increase cooperative play between boys and girls. Serbin also found that teachers can reduce the amount of gender stereotyping in children's choice of activities by avoiding gender-typed labels and instructions, by demonstrating toys to everyone, and by encouraging both girls and boys to try out all activities. See Serbin, "The Hidden Curriculum: Academic Consequences of Teacher Expectations."

12. Barbara Porro, "The Nonsexist Classroom: A Process Approach," p. 94.

13. Karkau, "Sexism in the Fourth Grade."

14. Elliot Aronson et al., *The Jigsaw Classroom*, and Lockheed with Klein, "Sex Equity in Classroom Organization and Climate." Also see Robert E. Slavin, "Cooperative Learning"; Tajfel, "Social Psychology of Intergroup Relations"; and Brewer and Miller, "Beyond the Contact Hypothesis." Most of the research on intergroup relations focuses on improving race relations; some studies focus on gender relations; few systematically explore connections between race and gender.

15. In the kindergarten, second-grade, and fourth-fifth–grade classrooms where I observed, the African-American, Filipino, Chicano, and Latino students were in a token position, and, with the exception of the two recent immigrants from Mexico in Miss Bailey's class, they were fairly well integrated into the groups formed by kids and adults.

16. Marlaine S. Lockheed, "Women, Girls, and Computers: A First Look at the Evidence."

17. Porro, "The Nonsexist Classroom."
18. Personal communication from Zella Luria. Various college students, remembering back to fourth, fifth, and sixth grades, have told me about playground activities where boys and girls mixed in relatively even numbers. In addition to kickball, handball, and foursquare, these included group games like capture-the-flag, fox-and-hound (which involved making trails on the snow), Red Rover, and upset-the-fruit-basket (played like musical chairs). Indoor games like seven-up and dominoes are also often mixed-gender terrains.
19. A point made by Richert in *Boys and Girls Apart*.
20. Schofield, *Black and White in School*. In *Disruptive School Behavior*, Hanna provides concrete suggestions for helping children learn about different multicultural styles and about the nature of prejudice and racism.
21. Porro, "The Nonsexist Classroom," p. 97, and Karkau, "Sexism in the Fourth Grade."
22. Best, *We've All Got Scars*.
23. Ellen Jordan observed that teachers in an Australian "infants school" (encompassing kindergarten, first, and second grades) expected students to move quietly and keep their voices low; they defined body contact, quick movement, and impatient expressions of anger as "naughty." The majority of students called up for being "naughty" were boys. See Jordan, "Gender Theory and the Construction of Masculinity in the Infants School."
24. Hanna (*Disruptive School Behavior*) provides useful information and suggestions for teachers working in schools mixed by social class, race, and ethnicity (African-American and white).
25. Paley, *Boys and Girls*, and Goodenough, "Small Group Culture," p. 423.
26. Fine, *With the Boys*, and Willis, *Learning to Labour*.
27. As Jordan notes, this cycle foreshadows the gender-defined school resistance of the older working-class "lads" Paul Willis writes about in *Learning to Labour*. R. W. Connell has written about schools as "masculinity-making devices." In a process linking class and gender, some masculinities, like "cool guys" in an Australian secondary school setting, are formed by "battering against the schools' authority structure" and others ("swots and wimps") by doing well in school ("Cool Guys, Swots, and Wimps: The Interplay of Masculinity and Education," p. 300).
28. Jordan, "Gender Theory and the Construction of Masculinity in the Infants School," p. 11.
29. Connell, *Gender and Power*.
30. For analyses of the shaping of adolescent girls' desires through the marketing of romance, see McRobbie and Nava, eds., *Gender and Generation*, and Walkerdine, *Schoolgirl Fictions*.
31. Holland and Eisenhart, *Educated in Romance*, p. 109.

32. Jane Roland Martin, "The Ideal of the Educated Person"; also see Barbara Houston, "Gender Freedom and the Subtleties of Sexist Education."

33. In *Sisters and Wives: The Past and Future of Sexual Equality*, Karen Sacks, an anthropologist, reports comparative research in Africa finding that in societies where women and men are relatively more equal, the public status of women is framed in terms of women as sisters rather than wives. "Wife and sister have similar contrastive meanings in a variety of patrilineal societies with reference to a woman's relations to productive means, to other adults, to power, and to their own sexuality. I do not think I do much violence to the data by interpreting sister in situations of corporate patrilineages to mean one who is an owner, a decision maker among others of the corporation, and a person who controls her own sexuality. By contrast, a wife is a subordinate in much the way Engels asserted for the family based on private property" (p. 110).

Obviously, relationships between brothers and sisters are sometimes riddled with rivalry and dominance; I am idealizing the model.

34. Research on the labor of girls compared with boys indicates, however, that even in middle childhood, girls may do more routinized, unpaid household work. Whiting and Edwards found that in four of six cultures, including a New England town, girls worked more than boys; "in baldest terms: girls work while boys play" (*Children of Different Worlds*, p. 117). In a study of 764 sixth-graders in Oakland, California, Medrich and his colleagues (*The Serious Business of Growing Up*) found that girls did twice as much domestic work as boys.

## Afterword

1. Centers for Disease Control and Prevention (CDC), "1991–2019 High School Youth Risk Behavior Survey Data," accessed December 16, 2022, http://yrbs-explorer.services.cdc.gov/; and J. L. Herman, A. R. Flores, and K. K. O'Neill, *How Many Adults and Youth Identify as Transgender in the United States?* (Los Angeles: Williams Institute, UCLA School of Law, 2022).

2. Tey Meadow, *Trans Kids* (Berkeley: University of California Press, 2018).

3. Travers, *The Trans Generation* (New York: New York University Press, 2018).

# References

Alanen, Leena. "Rethinking Childhood." *Acta Sociologica* 31 (1988): 53–67.

Alcott, Louisa May. *Little Women*. [1871]. New York: World Publishing, 1946.

Ambert, Anne-Marie. "Sociology of Sociology: The Place of Children in North American Sociology." In *Sociological Studies of Child Development*, vol. 1, ed. Patricia A. Adler and Peter Adler, 11–31. Greenwich, Conn.: JAI Press, 1986.

American Association of University Women Educational Foundation and the Wellesley College Center for Research on Women, *How Schools Shortchange Girls*. Washington, D.C.: AAUW Educational Foundation, 1992.

Anyon, Joan. "Intersections of Gender and Class: Accommodation and Resistance by Working-Class and Affluent Females to Contradictory Sex-Role Ideologies." In *Gender, Class, and Education*, ed. Stephen Walker and Len Barton, 1–19. Sussex, England: Falmer Press, 1983.

Apple, Michael, ed. *Cultural and Economic Reproduction in Education*. Boston: Routledge and Kegan Paul, 1982.

Ariès, Philippe. *Centuries of Childhood*. New York: Vintage, 1962.

Aronson, Elliot, Nancy Blaney, Cookie Stephen, Jev Sikes, and Matthew Snapp. *The Jigsaw Classroom*. Beverly Hills: Sage, 1978.

Atwood, Margaret. *Cat's Eye*. New York: Bantam, 1989.

Banner, Lois W. *In Full Flower: Aging Women, Power, and Sexuality, a History*. New York: Knopf, 1992.

Barth, Fredrik. "Introduction." In *Ethnic Groups and Boundaries*, ed. Fredrik Barth, 9–38. Boston: Little, Brown, 1969.

Bateson, Gregory. *Steps to an Ecology of Mind*. New York: Ballantine, 1972.

Becker, Howard S. *Doing Things Together: Selected Papers*. Evanston: Northwestern University Press, 1986.

Benedict, Ruth. "Continuities and Discontinuities in Cultural Conditioning." *Psychiatry* 1 (1938): 161–167.

Berentzen, Sigurd. *Children Constructing Their Social World: An Analysis of Gender Contrasts in Children's Interactions in a Nursery School*. Bergen, Norway: Department of Social Anthropology, University of Bergen, 1984.

Best, Raphaella. *We've All Got Scars: What Boys and Girls Learn in Elementary School*. Bloomington: Indiana University Press, 1983.

Blume, Judy. *Are You There God? It's Me, Margaret*. New York: Dell, 1970.

———. *Then Again, Maybe I Won't*. New York: Dell, 1971.

Borman, Kathryn M. "Children's Interactions in Playgrounds." *Theory Into Practice* 18 (1979): 251–257.

Bossert, Steven T. *Tasks and Social Relationships in Classrooms*. New York: Cambridge University Press, 1979.

Breines, Winifred. *Young, White, and Miserable: Female in the Fifties*. Boston: Beacon Press, 1992.

Brewer, Marilynn B. "Ethnocentrism and Its Role in Interpersonal Trust." In *Scientific Inquiry and the Social Sciences*, ed. M. B. Brewer and B. E. Collins, 345–360. San Francisco: Jossey-Bass, 1981.

Brewer, Marilynn B., and Norman Miller. "Beyond the Contact Hypothesis: Theoretical Perspectives on Desegregation." In *Groups in Contact*, ed. Norman Miller and Marilynn B. Brewer, 281–302. New York: Academic Press, 1984.

Brink, Carol Ryrie. *Caddie Woodlawn*. New York: Macmillan, 1952.

Brittan, Arthur, and Mary Maynard. *Sexism, Racism, and Oppression*. New York: Blackwell, 1984.

Brooks-Gunn, Jeanne. "The Impact of Puberty and Sexual Activity upon the Health and Education of Adolescent Girls and Boys." *Peabody Journal of Education* 64 (1987): 88–112.

Brophy, Jere E., and Thomas L. Good. *Teacher-Student Relations*. New York: Holt, 1974.

Buckley, Thomas, and Alma Gottlieb, eds. *Blood Magic: The Anthropology of Menstruation*. Berkeley: University of California Press, 1988.

Butler, Judith. *Gender Trouble: Feminism and the Subversion of Identity*. New York: Routledge, 1990.

Cahill, Spencer E. "Becoming Boys and Girls." Ph.D. dissertation, University of California, Santa Barbara, 1982.

———. "Language Practices and Self-Definition: The Case of Gender Identity Acquisition." *Sociological Quarterly* 27 (1987): 295–311.

Cahn, Susan. "Coming On Strong: Gender and Sexuality in Women's Sport,

1900–1960." Ph.D. dissertation, University of Minnesota, Minneapolis, 1990.

Canaan, Joyce. "A Comparative Analysis of American Suburban Middle Class, Middle School, and High School Teenage Cliques." In *Interpretive Ethnography of Education*, ed. George Spindler and Louise Spindler, 385–406. Hillsdale, N.J.: Lawrence Erlbaum, 1987.

———. "Why a 'Slut' Is a 'Slut': Cautionary Tales of Middle-Class Teenage Girls." In *Symbolizing America*, ed. Varenne Hervé, 184–208. Lincoln: University of Nebraska Press, 1986.

Chapman, Robert L. *New Dictionary of American Slang.* New York: Harper and Row, 1986.

Chodorow, Nancy. *The Reproduction of Mothering.* Berkeley: University of California Press, 1978.

Cleaver, Vera, and Bill Cleaver. *Lady Ellen Grae.* New York: Lippincott, 1968.

Clifford, James, and George E. Marcus, eds. *Writing Culture: The Poetics and Politics of Ethnography.* Berkeley: University of California Press, 1986.

Cobb, Edith. *The Ecology of Imagination in Childhood.* New York: Columbia University Press, 1977.

Collins, Patricia Hill. *Black Feminist Thought.* Boston: Unwin Hyman, 1990.

Cone, Cynthia A., and Berta E. Perez. "Peer Groups and the Organization of Classroom Space." *Human Organization* 45 (1986): 80–88.

Connell, R. W. "Cool Guys, Swots, and Wimps: The Interplay of Masculinity and Education." *Oxford Review of Education* 15 (1989): 291–303.

———. *Gender and Power.* Stanford, Calif.: Stanford University Press, 1987.

———. *Teachers' Work.* Boston: Allen and Unwin, 1985.

———. *Which Way Is Up?: Essays on Class, Sex, and Culture.* Boston: Allen and Unwin, 1983.

Connell, R. W., Dean J. Ashenden, Sandra Kessler, and Gary W. Dowsett. *Making the Difference: Schools, Families, and Social Division.* Boston: Allen and Unwin, 1982.

Corsaro, William A. *Friendship and Peer Culture in the Early Years.* Norwood, N.J.: Ablex Publishing, 1985.

———. "'We're Friends, Right?' Children's Use of Access Rituals in a Nursery School." *Language in Society* 8 (1979): 315–336.

Csikszentmihalyi, Mihaly, and Stith Bennett. "An Exploratory Model of Play." *American Anthropologist* 73 (1971): 45–58.

Cusick, Philip A. *Inside High School.* New York: Holt, Rinehart and Winston, 1973.

Daley, Suzanne. "Girls' Self-Esteem Is Lost on Way to Adolescence, New Study Finds." *New York Times*, January 9, 1991, pp. B1 and B6.

Davies, Bronwyn. *Frogs and Snails and Feminist Tales: Preschool Children and Gender.* Boston: Allen and Unwin, 1989.

———. *Life in the Classroom and Playground: The Accounts of Primary School Children.* Boston: Routledge and Kegan Paul, 1982.

Deaux, Kay, and Brenda Major. "Putting Gender into Context: An Interactive

Model of Gender-related Behavior." *Psychological Review* 94 (1987): 369–389.

Delamont, Sara. *Sex Roles and the School*. 2 ed. New York: Routledge, 1990.

D'Emelio, John, and Estelle B. Freedman. *Intimate Matters: A History of Sexuality in America*. New York: Harper and Row, 1988.

dePaola, Tomie. *Oliver Button Is a Sissy*. Orlando, Fla.: Harcourt Brace Jovanovich, 1979.

Dinnerstein, Dorothy. *The Mermaid and the Minotaur: Sexual Arrangements and Human Malaise*. New York: Harper and Row, 1977.

DiPietro, J. A. "Rough and Tumble Play: A Function of Gender." *Developmental Psychology* 17 (1981): 50–58.

Dornbusch, Sanford M., J. Merrill Carlsmith, Ruth T. Gross, John A. Martin, Dennis Jennings, Anne Rosenberg, and Paula Duke. "Sexual Development, Age, and Dating: A Comparison of Biological and Social Influences upon One Set of Behaviors." *Child Development* 52 (1981): 179–185.

Douglas, Mary. *Purity and Danger*. New York: Praeger, 1966.

Doyle, Jean. "Helpers, Officers, and Lunchers: Ethnography of a Third-Grade Class." In *The Cultural Experience*, ed. James P. Spradley and David W. McCurdy, 147–156. Chicago: Science Research Associates, 1972.

Dreeban, Robert. *On What Is Learned in School*. Reading, Mass.: Addison-Wesley, 1968.

Dyhouse, Carol. *Girls Growing Up in Victorian and Edwardian England*. Boston: Routledge and Kegan Paul, 1981.

Eckert, Penelope. *Jocks and Burnouts: Social Categories and Identity in the High School*. New York: Teachers College Press, 1989.

Eder, Donna. "The Cycle of Popularity: Interpersonal Relations among Female Adolescents." *Sociology of Education* 58 (1985): 154–165.

———. "Serious and Playful Disputes: Variation in Conflict Talk among Female Adolescents." In *Conflict Talk*, ed. Allen D. Grimshaw, 67–84. New York: Cambridge University Press, 1990.

Eder, Donna, and Janet Lynne Enke. "The Structure of Gossip: Opportunities and Constraints on Collective Expression among Adolescents." *American Sociological Review* 56 (1991): 494–508.

Eder, Donna, and Maureen T. Hallinan. "Sex Differences in Children's Friendships." *American Sociological Review* 43 (1978): 237–250.

Eichler, Margrit. *The Double Standard: A Feminist Critique of Feminist Social Science*. New York: St. Martin's Press, 1980.

Eisenhart, Margaret A., and Dorothy C. Holland. "Learning Gender from Peers: The Role of Peer Groups in the Cultural Transmission of Gender." *Human Organization* 42 (1983): 321–332.

Ellenzweig, Allan. "Cultural Bias in Action." Letter to the *New York Times*, January 2, 1987.

Ellis, Shari, Barbara Rogoff, and Cindy C. Cromer. "Age Segregation in Children's Social Interaction." *Developmental Psychology* 17 (1981): 399–407.

Emerson, Joan P. "Negotiating the Serious Import of Humor." *Sociometry* 32 (1969): 169–181.

Evans, John. "Gender Differences in Children's Games: A Look at the Team Selection Process." *Canadian Association for Health, Physical Education, and Recreation Journal* 52 (1986): 4–9.

Everhart, Robert B. *Reading, Writing, and Resistance.* Boston: Routledge & Kegan Paul, 1983.

Fagot, Beverly I. "Consequences of Moderate Cross-Gender Behavior in Preschool Children," *Child Development* 49 (1977): 902–907.

Fagot, Beverly I., Mary D. Leinbach, and Richard Hogan. "Gender Labeling and the Adoption of Sex-typed Behaviors." *Developmental Psychology* 22 (1986): 440–443.

Faust, Margaret S. "Developmental Maturity as a Determinant in Prestige of Adolescent Girls." *Child Development* 31 (1960): 173–184.

Fausto-Sterling, Anne. *Myths of Gender: Biological Theories about Women and Men.* New York: Basic Books, 1985.

Fine, Gary Alan. "The Natural History of Preadolescent Male Friendship Groups." In *Friendship and Social Relations in Children*, ed. Hugh C. Foot and Anthony J. Chapman, 293–320. New York: Wiley, 1980.

———*With the Boys: Little League Baseball and Preadolescent Culture.* Chicago: University of Chicago Press, 1987.

Fine, Gary Alan, and Barry Glassner. "Participant Observation with Children: Promise and Problems." *Urban Life* 8 (19879): 153–174.

Fine, Gary Alan, and Kent L. Sandstrom. *Knowing Children: Participant Observation with Minors.* Newbury Park, Calif.: Sage Publications, 1988.

Fine, Michelle. "Sexuality, Schooling, and Adolescent Females: The Missing Discourse of Desire." *Harvard Educational Review* 58 (1988): 29–53.

Finnan, Christine R. "The Ethnography of Children's Spontaneous Play." In *Doing the Ethnography of Schooling*, ed. George Spindler, 358–380. New York: Holt, Rinehart and Winston, 1982.

Fitzhugh, Louise. *Harriet the Spy.* New York: Harper and Row, 1964.

———*Nobody's Family Is Going to Change.* New York: Farrar, Straus, Giroux, 1967.

Flax, Jane. "Postmodernism and Gender Relations in Feminist Theory." *Signs* 12 (1987): 621–643.

Foot, Hugh C., Anthony J. Chapman, and Jean R. Smith, eds. *Friendship and Social Relations in Children.* New York: Wiley, 1980.

Foucault, Michel. *The History of Sexuality.* New York: Vintage, 1980.

Freiberg, Peter. "Bullying Gets Banned in Norway's Schools." *APA (American Psychological Association) Monitor*, October 1990, p. 30.

Freud, Sigmund. *Jokes and Their Relation to the Unconscious.* [1905]. New York: Norton, 1963.

Gagnon, John H. "The Creation of the Sexual in Early Adolescence." In *Twelve to Sixteen*, ed. Jerome Kagan and Robert Coles, 231–257. New York: Norton, 1972.

Gagnon, John H., and William Simon. *Sexual Conduct.* Chicago: Aldine, 1973.

Geertz, Clifford. "Deep Play: Notes on the Balinese Cockfight." *Daedalus* 101 (1972): 1–37.

Giddens, Anthony. *Central Problems in Social Theory*. Berkeley: University of California Press, 1979.

Gilligan, Carol. *In a Different Voice: Psychological Theory and Women's Development*. Cambridge, Mass.: Harvard University Press, 1982.

Gilligan, Carol, Nona P. Lyons, and Trudy J. Hanmer, eds. *Making Connections: The Relational Worlds of Adolescent Girls at Emma Willard School*. Troy, N.Y.: Emma Willard School, 1989.

Giroux, Henry. "Theories of Reproduction and Resistance in the New Sociology of Education: A Critical Analysis." *Harvard Educational Review* 53 (1987): 257–293.

Glassner, Barry. *Bodies*. New York: Putnam, 1988.

———. "Kid Society." *Urban Education* 11 (1976): 5–21.

Gluckman, Max, ed. *Essays on the Ritual of Social Relations*. Manchester, England: Manchester University Press, 1962.

Goffman, Erving. "The Arrangement between the Sexes." *Theory and Society* 4 (1977): 301–336.

———. *Asylums*. Garden City, N.Y.: Anchor Books, Doubleday, 1961.

———. *Frame Analysis: An Essay on the Organization of Experience*. New York: Harper and Row, 1974.

Goode, David A. "Kids, Culture, and Innocents." *Human Studies* 9 (1986): 83–106.

Goodenough, Ruth G. "Small Group Culture and the Emergence of Sexist Behavior: A Comparative Study of Four Children's Groups." In *Interpretive Ethnography of Communication*, ed. George Spindler and Louise Spindler, 409–445. Hillsdale, N.J.: Lawrence Erlbaum, 1987.

Goodwin, Marjorie Harness. *He-Said-She-Said: Talk as Social Organization among Black Children*. Bloomington: Indiana University Press, 1991.

———. "The Serious Side of Jump Rope: Conversational Practices and Social Organization in the Frame of 'Play.'" *Journal of American Folklore* 98 (1985): 315–330.

Goodwin, Marjorie Harness, and Charles Goodwin. "Children's Arguing." In *Language, Gender, and Sex in Comparative Perspective*, ed. Susan Philips, Susan Steele, and Christine Tanz, 200–248. New York: Cambridge University Press, 1987.

Gottman, John. "The World of Coordinated Play: Same- and Cross-Sex Friendship in Young Children." In *Conversations of Friends: Speculations on Affective Development*, ed. John M. Gottman and Jeffrey G. Parker, 139–191. New York: Cambridge University Press, 1986.

Grant, Linda. "Black Females' 'Place' in Desegregated Classrooms." *Sociology of Education* 57 (1984): 98–110.

———. "Gender Roles and Statuses in School Children's Peer Interactions." *Western Sociological Review* 14 (1984): 58–76.

Green, Richard. *The "Sissy Boy Syndrome" and the Development of Homosexuality*. New Haven, Conn.: Yale University Press, 1987.

Griffin, Patricia S. "'Gymnastics Is a Girls' Thing': Student Participation and Interaction Patterns in a Middle School Gymnastics Unit." In

*Teaching in Physical Education*, ed. T. J. Templin and J. Olson, 71–85. Champaign, Ill.: Human Kinetics Publishers, 1983.

———"Teachers' Perceptions of and Responses to Sex Equity Problems in a Middle School Physical Education Program." *Research Quarterly for Exercise and Sport* 56 (1985): 103–110.

Gross, Ruth T., and Paula M. Duke. "The Effect of Early versus Late Physical Maturation on Adolescent Behavior." *Symposium on Adolescent Medicine* 27 (1986): 71–77.

Guttentag, Marcia, and Helen Bray. *Undoing Sex Stereotypes: Research and Resources for Educators.* New York: McGraw-Hill, 1976.

Hallinan, Maureen. "Structural Effects of Children's Friendships and Cliques." *Social Psychology Quarterly* 42 (1979): 54–77.

Hallinan, Maureen, and Nancy B. Tuma. "Classroom Effects on Change in Children's Friendships." *Sociology of Education* 51 (1978): 270–282.

Hanna, Judith Lynne. *Disruptive School Behavior: Class, Race, and Culture.* New York: Holmes and Meier, 1988.

Harding, Sandra. *The Science Question in Feminism.* Ithaca: Cornell University Press, 1986.

Harkness, Sara, and Charles M. Super. "The Cultural Context of Gender Segregation in Children's Peer Groups." *Child Development* 56 (1985): 219–224.

Harré, Rom. "The Step to Social Constructionism." In *Children of Social Worlds*, ed. Martin Richards and Paul Light, 287–296. Cambridge, Mass.: Harvard University Press, 1986.

Hart, Roger. *Children's Experience of Place.* New York: Irvington, 1979.

Hartup, Willard W. "Peer Relations." In *Handbook of Child Psychology, vol. 4: Socialization, Personality and Social Development*, 4th ed., ed. Paul H. Mussen and E. Mavis Heatherington, 103–196. New York: Wiley, 1983.

Haug, Frigga, ed. *Female Sexualization: A Collective Work of Memory.* London: Verso, 1987.

Henley, Nancy. *Body Politics: Power, Sex, and Nonverbal Communication.* Englewood, N.J.: Prentice-Hall, 1977.

Henley, Nancy, and Cheris Kramarae. "Gender, Power, and Miscommunication." In *"Miscommunication" and Problematic Talk*, ed. Nikolas Coupland, Howard Giles, and John M. Wiemann, 18–43. Newbury Park, Calif.: Sage Publications, 1991.

Henry, Jules. *Culture against Man.* New York: Vintage, 1963.

Holland, Dorothy C., and Margaret A. Eisenhart. *Educated in Romance: Women, Achievement, and College Culture.* Chicago: University of Chicago Press, 1990.

Hooks, William Harris. *The Nutcracker.* New York: Frederick Warne, 1977.

Houston, Barbara. "Gender Freedom and the Subtleties of Sexist Education." *Educational Theory* 35 (1985): 359–369.

Hughes, Everett C. "Cycles, Turning Points, and Careers." In *The Sociological Eye*, 124–131. Chicago: Aldine, 1971.

Hughes, Linda. "'But That's Not *Really* Mean': Competing in a Cooperative Mode." *Sex Roles* 19 (1988): 669–687.

Hunt, Jennifer C., *Psychoanalytic Aspects of Fieldwork*. Newbury Park, Calif.: Sage, 1989.

Hyde, Janet S., Benjamin G. Rosenberg, and Jo Ann Behrman. "Tomboyism." *Psychology of Women Quarterly* 2 (1977): 73–75.

Irvine, Janice M. *Disorders of Desire: Sex and Gender in Modern American Sexology*. Philadelphia: Temple University Press, 1990.

Jacklin, Carol Nagy. "Methodological Issues in the Study of Sex-related Differences." *Developmental Review* 1 (1981): 226–273.

Jackson, Philip W. *Life in Classrooms*. New York: Holt, Rinehart and Winston, 1968.

Jackson, Stevi. *Childhood and Sexuality*. Oxford: Blackwell, 1982.

Jenks, Chris. "Introduction: Constituting the Child." In *The Sociology of Childhood*, ed. Chris Jenks, 9–24. London: Batsford Academic, 1982.

Joffe, Carole. "As the Twig Is Bent." In *And Jill Came Tumbling After*, ed. Judith Stacey, Susan Bereaud, and Joan Daniels, 79–90. New York: Dell, 1974.

Johnson, Miriam. *Strong Mothers, Weak Wives*. Berkeley: University of California Press, 1988.

John-Steiner, Vera. *Notebooks of the Mind: Explorations of Thinking*. New York: Harper and Row, 1985.

Jordan, Ellen. "Gender Theory and the Construction of Masculinity in the Infants School." Unpublished paper, Department of Sociology, University of Newcastle, Australia, 1990.

Kanter, Rosabeth Moss. *Men and Women of the Corporation*. New York: Basic Books, 1977.

Karkau, Kevin. "Sexism in the Fourth Grade." Pittsburgh: KNOW, 1973. (Reprinted in *Undoing Sex Stereotypes*. See Guttentag, Marcia, and Helen Bray.)

Karweit, Nancy, and Stephen Hansell. "Sex Differences in Adolescent Relationships: Friendship and Status." In *Friends in School*, ed. Joyce Levy Epstein and Nancy Karweit, 115–130. New York: Academic Press, 1983.

Katriel, Tamar. "'*Bexibudim!*': Ritualized Sharing among Israeli Children." *Language and Society* 16 (1987): 305–320.

Katz, Jack. "Howard S. Becker's Contributions to Sociology." Presentation at the annual meetings of the Midwestern Sociological Association, St. Louis, Missouri, 1989.

Kerber, Linda K. "Separate Spheres, Female Worlds, Woman's Place: The Rhetoric of Women's History." *Journal of American History* 75 (June–September, 1988): 9–39.

Kerber, Linda K., Catherine G. Greeno, Eleanor Maccoby, Zella Luria, Carol B. Stack, and Carol Gilligan. "On *In a Different Voice*: An Interdisciplinary Forum." *Signs* 11 (1986): 304–333.

Kessen, William. "The American Child and Other Cultural Inventions." *American Psychologist* 34 (1979): 815–820.

Kessler, Sandra, Dean J. Ashenden, R. W. Connell, and Gary W. Dowsett. "Gender Relations in Secondary Schooling." *Sociology of Education* 58 (1985): 34–48.

Kessler, Suzanne J., and Wendy McKenna. *Gender: An Ethnomethodological Approach.* New York: Wiley, 1978.

Klein, Norma. *Tomboy.* New York: Fair Winds Press, 1978.

Klein, Susan S., ed. *Handbook for Achieving Sex Equity through Education.* Baltimore: Johns Hopkins University Press, 1985.

Knapp, Mary, and Herbert Knapp. *One Potato, Two Potato: The Secret Education of American Children.* New York: Norton, 1976.

Krieger, Susan. *Social Science and the Self: Personal Essays on an Art Form.* New Brunswick, N.J.: Rutgers University Press, 1991.

LaFreniere, P., F. F. Strayer, and R. Gauthier. "The Emergence of Same-Sex Preferences among Preschool Peers: A Developmental Ethological Perspective." *Child Development* 55 (1984): 1958–1965.

Langton, Jane. *The Boyhood of Grace Jones.* Harper and Row, 1972.

Laqueur, Thomas W. *Making Sex: Body and Gender from the Greeks to Freud.* Cambridge, Mass.: Harvard University Press, 1990.

Lees, Susan. *Losing Out: Sexuality and Adolescent Girls.* London: Hutchinson, 1986.

Lenski, Lois. *Texas Tomboy.* New York: Lippincott, 1950.

Leonard, Diana. "Persons in Their Own Right: Children and Sociology in the UK." In *Childhood, Youth, and Social Change: A Comparative Perspective,* ed. Lynne Chisholm, Peter Büchner, Heinz-Herman Krüger, and Phillip Brown, 58–70. New York: Falmer Press, 1990.

Lever, Janet. "Sex Differences in the Complexity of Children's Play and Games." *American Sociological Review* 43 (1978): 471–483.

———"Sex Differences in the Games Children Play." *Social Problems* 23 (1976): 478–487.

Lockheed, Marlaine S. "Some Determinants and Consequences of Sex Segregation in the Classroom." In *Gender Influences in Classroom Interaction,* 167–184. (See Wilkinson, Louise Cherry, and Cora B. Marrett.)

———. "Women, Girls, and Computers: A First Look at the Evidence." *Sex Roles* 13 (1985): 115–122.

Lockheed, Marlaine S., and Abigail M. Harris. "Cross-Sex Collaborative Learning in Elementary Classrooms." *American Educational Research Journal* 21 (1984): 275–294.

Lockheed, Marlaine S., with Susan S. Klein. "Sex Equity in Classroom Organization and Climate." In *Handbook for Achieving Sex Equity through Education,* 189–217. (See Klein, Susan S.)

Lott, Bernice. "A Feminist Critique of Androgyny: Toward the Elimination of Gender Attributions for Learned Behavior." In *Gender and Nonverbal*

*Behavior*, ed. Clara Mayo and Nancy M. Henley, 171–180. New York: Springer-Verlag, 1981.

Luria, Zella, and Eleanor W. Herzog. "Gender Segregation across and within Settings." Paper presented at annual meeting of the Society for Research on Child Development, Toronto, Canada, 1985.

———. "Sorting Gender Out in a Children's Museum." *Gender & Society* 5 (1991): 224–232.

Lutkehaus, Nancy, and Paul Roscoe. "Introduction." In *New Directions in the Study of Female Initiation*, ed. Nancy Lutkehaus and Paul Roscoe (forthcoming).

Lyman, Peter. "The Fraternal Bond as a Joking Relationship." In *Changing Men*, ed. Michael Kimmel, 148–163. Beverly Hills, Calif.: Sage, 1988.

Maccoby, Eleanor E. "Gender as a Social Category." *Developmental Psychology* 24 (1988): 755–765.

———. "Social Groupings in Childhood: Their Relationship to Prosocial and Antisocial Behavior in Boys and Girls." In *Development of Antisocial and Prosocial Behavior*, ed. Dan Olweus, Jack Block, and Marian Radke-Yarrow, 263–284. San Diego: Academic Press, 1985.

Maccoby, Eleanor E., and Carol Nagy Jacklin. "Gender Segregation in Childhood." In *Advances in Child Development and Behavior*, vol. 20, ed. E. H. Reese, 239–287. New York: Academic Press, 1987.

———. *The Psychology of Sex Differences*. Stanford, Calif.: Stanford University Press, 1974.

MacKay, Robert W. "Conceptions of Children and Models of Socialization." In *Childhood and Socialization*, ed. Hans Peter Dreitzel, 27–43. New York: Macmillan, 1973.

McKinley, Robin. *The Hero and the Crown*. New York: Greenwillow, 1985.

MacLeod, Anne Scott. "The *Caddie Woodlawn* Syndrome: American Girlhood in the Nineteenth Century." In *A Century of Childhood: 1820–1920*, ed. Mary Lynn Stevens, 97–119. Rochester, N.Y.: Margaret Woodbury Strong Museum, 1984.

McRobbie, Angela. "Settling Accounts with Subcultures." *Screen Education* 34 (1980): 37–49.

———. "Working-Class Girls and the Culture of Femininity." In *Women Take Issue*, ed. Women's Studies Group, Centre for Contemporary Cultural Studies, 96–108. London: Hutchinson, 1978.

McRobbie, Angela, and Mica Nava, eds. *Gender and Generation*. London: Macmillan, 1984.

Maeroff, Gene I. "The Toughest Job in Education." *New York Times Education Section*, April 13, 1986, pp. 54–57.

Maltz, Daniel N., and Ruth A. Borker. "A Cultural Approach to Male-Female Miscommunication." In *Language and Social Identity*, ed. John A. Gumperz, 195–216. New York: Cambridge University Press, 1983.

Mandell, Nancy. "The Least-Adult Role in Studying Children." *Journal of Contemporary Ethnography* 16 (1988): 433–467.

Martin, Emily. *The Woman in the Body*. Boston: Beacon Press, 1987.

Martin, Jane Roland. "The Ideal of the Educated Person." *Educational Theory* 37 (1987): 97–109.

Mascia-Lees, Frances E., Patricia Sharpe, and Colleen Ballerino Cohen. "The Postmodernist Turn in Anthropology: Cautions from a Feminist Perspective." *Signs* 15 (1989): 7–33.

Medrich, Elliott A., Judith Roizen, Victor Rubin, and Stuart Buckley. *The Serious Business of Growing Up: A Study of Children's Lives Outside School*. Berkeley: University of California Press, 1982.

Messner, Michael. "Masculinities and Athletic Careers." *Gender & Society* 3 (1989): 71–88.

Meyenn, Robert J. "School Girls' Peer Groups." In *Pupil Strategies*, ed. Peter Wood, 108–142. London: Croom Helm, 1980.

Miller, Alice. *The Drama of the Gifted Child*. New York: Basic Books, 1983.

Miller, Casey, and Kate Swift. *The Handbook of Nonsexist Writing*. New York: Lippincott and Crowell, 1980.

Miller, Peggy, and Linda L. Sperry. "The Socialization of Anger and Aggression." *Merrill-Palmer Quarterly* 33 (1987): 1–37.

Mishler, Elliot. "Wou' You Trade Cookies with the Popcorn? Talk of Trades among Six-Year-Olds." In *Language, Culture, and Society*, ed. O. Garnica and M. King, 221–236. Oxford: Pergamon, 1979.

Money, John, and Anke Ehrhardt. *Man and Woman, Boy and Girl*. Baltimore: Johns Hopkins University Press, 1972.

Moore, Sally F. and Barbara Myerhoff, eds. *Secular Ritual*. Amsterdam: Van Gorcum, Assen, 1977.

Myers, Mitzi. "Gender, Genres, Generations: Artist-Mothers and the Scripting of Girls' Lives." *NWSA Journal 2* (1990): 273–281.

Nava, Mica. "Youth Service Provision, Social Order, and the Question of Girls." In *Gender and Generation*, 1–30. (See McRobbie, Angela, and Mica Nava.)

Oakes, Jeannie. *Keeping Track: How Schools Structure Inequality*. New Haven: Yale University Press, 1985.

Olweus, Dan. *Aggression in the Schools*. New York: Wiley, 1978.

Opie, Iona, and Peter Opie. *Children's Games in Street and Playground*. Oxford: Clarendon Press, 1969.

———. *The Lore and Language of Schoolchildren*. New York: Oxford University Press, 1959.

Ortner, Sherry B. "The Founding of the First Sherpa Nunnery and the Problem of 'Women' as an Analytic Category." In *Feminist Re-visions*, ed. Vivian Patraka and Louise Tilly, 98–134. Ann Arbor: University of Michigan Women's Studies Program, 1984.

Oswald, Hans, Lothar Krappman, Irene Chowdhuri, and Maria von Salisch. "Gaps and Bridges: Interactions between Girls and Boys in Elementary School." In *Sociological Studies of Child Development*, vol. 2, ed. Peter Adler and Patricia Adler, 205–223. Greenwich, Conn.: JAI Press, 1987.

*Oxford English Dictionary.* Entries for "boy," "child," "girl," "play," "sissy," "tomboy." New York: Oxford University Press, 1971.

Paley, Vivian Gussin. "On Listening to What the Children Say." *Harvard Educational Review* 56 (1986): 122–131.

———. *Boys and Girls: Superheroes in the Doll Corner.* Chicago: University of Chicago Press, 1984.

Parrott, Sue. "Games Children Play: Ethnography of a Second-Grade Recess." In *The Cultural Experience,* ed. James P. Spradley and David W. McCurdy, 206–219. Chicago: Science Research Associates, 1979.

Parsons, Talcott. *Social Structure and Personality.* Glencoe, Ill.: Free Press, 1964.

Passuth, Patricia M. "Age Hierarchies within Children's Groups." In *Sociological Studies of Child Development,* vol. 2, ed. Peter Adler and Patricia Adler, 185–203. Greenwich, Conn.: JAI Press, 1987.

Pessereni, Luisa. "Women's Personal Narratives: Myths, Experiences, and Emotions." In *Interpreting Women's Lives,* ed. Personal Narratives Group, 189–197. Bloomington: Indiana University Press, 1989.

Petchesky, Rosalind. *Abortion and Women's Choice.* New York: Longman, 1984.

Petersen, Anne C. "Adolescent Development." *Annual Review of Psychology* 39 (1988): 583–607.

Pogrebin, Letty Cottin. *Growing Up Free.* New York: McGraw-Hill, 1980.

Porro, Barbara. "The Nonsexist Classroom: A Process Approach." In *Sex Stereotypes and Reading,* ed. E. Marcia Sheridan, 91–101. Newark, Del.: International Reading Association, 1982.

Purrington, Beverly T. "Effects of Children on Their Parents: Parents' Perceptions." Ph.D. dissertation, Michigan State University, East Lansing, 1980.

Rich, Adrienne. "Compulsory Heterosexuality and Lesbian Existence." *Signs* 5 (1980): 198–210.

———. *Of Woman Born: Motherhood as Experience and Institution.* New York: Bantam.

Richert, Stephen. *Boys and Girls Apart: Children's Play in Canada and Poland.* Ottawa, Canada: Carleton University Press, 1990.

Rist, Ray C. *The Invisible Children: School Integration in American Society.* Cambridge, Mass.: Harvard University Press, 1978.

Rivers, Caryl, Rosalind Barnett, and Grace Baruch. *Beyond Sugar and Spice.* New York: Ballantine, 1979.

Rosaldo, Michelle Z. "The Use and Abuse of Anthropology: Reflections on Feminism and Cross-cultural Understanding." *Signs* 5 (1980): 389–417.

Sacks, Karen. *Sisters and Wives: The Past and Future of Sexual Equality.* Westport, Conn.: Greenwood Press, 1979.

Sadker, Myra P., and David M. Sadker. *Sex Equity Handbook for Schools.* New York: Longman, 1982.

Samuelson, Sue. "The Cooties Complex." *Western Folklore* 39 (1980): 198–210.

Schachtel, Ernest G. *Metamorphosis.* New York: Basic Books, 1959.

Schildkrout, Enid. "Age and Gender in Hausa Society: Socio-Economic Roles of Children in Urban Kano." In *Sex and Age as Principles of Social Differentiation,* ed. Jean La Fontaine, 109–137. New York: Academic Press, 1975.

Schofield, Janet W. *Black and White in School.* New York: Praeger, 1982.

———. "Complementary and Conflicting Identities: Images of Interaction in an Interracial School." In *The Development of Children's Friendships,* ed. Steven R. Asher and John M. Gottman, 53–90. New York: Cambridge University Press, 1981.

Schwartz, Pepper, and Janet Lever. "Fear and Loathing at a College Mixer." *Urban Life* 4 (1976): 413–431.

Schwartzman, Helen B. *Transformations: The Anthropology of Children's Play.* New York: Plenum, 1978.

Scott, Joan Wallach. *Gender and the Politics of History.* New York: Columbia University Press, 1988.

Sedgwick, Eve Kosofsky. "Homophobia, Misogyny, and Capital: The Example of Our Mutual Friend." *Raritan Review* 2 (no. 3, 1983): 126–151.

Segal, Lynne. *Slow Motion: Changing Masculinities, Changing Men.* New Brunswick, N.J.: Rutgers University Press, 1990.

Segel, Elizabeth. "Tomboy Taming and Gender Role Socialization: The Evidence of Children's Books." Unpublished paper, 1988.

Serbin, Lisa. "The Hidden Curriculum: Academic Consequences of Teacher Expectations." In *Sex Differentiation and Schooling,* ed. Michael Marland, 41–48. London: Heinemann, 1983.

Serbin, Lisa, I. J. Tonick, and Sally H. Sternglanz. "Shaping Cooperative Cross-Sex Play." *Child Development* 48 (1977): 924–929.

Shapiro, Judith. "Gender Totemism." In *Dialectics and Gender: Anthropological Approaches,* ed. Richard R. Randolph, David M. Schneider, and May N. Diaz, 1–19. Boulder: Westview, 1988.

Sheldon, Amy. "Conflict Talk: Sociolinguistic Challenges to Self-Assertion and How Young Girls Meet Them." *Merrill-Palmer Quarterly* 38 (1992): 95–117.

Simmons, Roberta G., and Dale A. Blyth. *Moving into Adolescence: The Impact of Pubertal Change and School Context.* New York: Aldine de Gruyer, 1987.

Slavin, Robert E. "Cooperative Learning." *Review of Educational Research* 50 (1980): 315–342.

Sluckin, Andy. *Growing Up in the Playground.* London: Routledge and Kegan Paul, 1981.

Smith, Dorothy E. *The Everyday World as Problematic.* Boston: Northeastern University Press, 1987.

Snow, Edward. "The Play of Sexes in Bruegel's *Children's Games.*" *Raritan: A Quarterly Review* 6 (summer 1985): 43–66.

Speier, Matthew. "The Adult Ideological Viewpoint in Studies of Childhood."

In *Rethinking Childhood*, ed. Arlene Skolnick, 168–186. Boston: Little, Brown, 1976.

Spelman, Elizabeth V. *Inessential Woman: Problems of Exclusion in Feminist Thought*. Boston: Beacon Press, 1988.

Stacey, Judith. "On Resistance, Ambivalence, and Feminist Theory." *Michigan Quarterly Review* 29 (1990): 537–546.

Stanton, Theodore and Harriet Stanton Blatch, eds. *Elizabeth Cady Stanton as Revealed in Her Letters, Diary and Reminiscences*. Vol. 2. New York: Harper and Bros., 1922.

Suransky, Valerie Polakow. *The Erosion of Childhood*. Chicago: University of Chicago Press,

Sutton-Smith, Brian. "A Performance Theory of Peer Relations." In *The Social Life of Children in a Changing Society*, ed., Kathryn Borman, 65–77. Hillsdale, N.J.: Lawrence Erlbaum, 1982.

———. "A Syntax for Play and Games." In *Child's Play*, ed. R. E. Herron and Brian Sutton Smith, 298–307. New York: Wiley, 1971.

Sutton-Smith, Brian, and B. G. Rosenberg. "Sixty Years of Historical Change in the Game Preferences of American Children." *Journal of American Folklore* 74 (1961): 17–46.

Tajfel, Henri. "Social Psychology of Intergroup Relations." *Annual Review of Psychology* 33 (1982): 1–39.

Tannen, Deborah. *You Just Don't Understand: Women and Men in Conversation*. New York: Morrow, 1990.

Tanner, J. M. "Sequence, Tempo, and Individual Variation in Growth and Development of Boys and Girls Aged Twelve to Sixteen." *Daedalus* 4 (1971): 907–930.

Thorne, Barrie. "Children and Gender: Constructions of Difference." In *Theoretical Perspectives on Sexual Difference*, ed. Deborah Rhode, 100–113. New Haven: Yale University Press, 1990.

———. "Political Activist as Participant Observer: Conflicts of Commitment in a Study of the Draft Resistance Movement of the 1960s." *Symbolic Interaction* 2 (1978): 73–88.

———. "Re-visioning Women and Social Change: Where Are the Children?" *Gender & Society* 1 (1987): 85–109.

Thorne, Barrie, Cheris Kramarae, and Nancy Henley, eds. *Language, Gender, and Society*. New York: Newbury House, 1983.

Thorne, Barrie, and Zella Luria. "Sexuality and Gender in Children's Daily Worlds." *Social Problems* 33 (1986): 176–190.

Toth, Susan Allen. *Blooming: A Small-Town Girlhood*. Boston: Little, Brown, 1978.

Tyack, David, and Elizabeth Hansot. *Learning Together: A History of Coeducation in American Schools*. New Haven: Yale University Press, 1990.

Tyler, Deborah. "The Case of Irene Tuckerman: Understanding Sexual Violence and the Protection of Women and Girls, Victoria 1890–1925." *History of Education Review* 15 (1986): 52–67.

Voigt, Cynthia. *Jackaroo*. New York: Macmillan, 1985.

Waksler, Frances Chaput. "Studying Children: Phenomenological Insights." *Human Studies* 9 (1986): 71–82.

Waldrop, Mary F., and Charles F. Halverson. "Intensive and Extensive Peer Behavior: Longitudinal and Cross-sectional Analyses." *Child Development* 46 (1975): 19–26.

Walker, Stephen, and Len Barton, eds. *Gender, Class, and Education*. New York: Falmer, 1983.

Walkerdine, Valerie. "Post-structuralist Theory and Everyday Practices: The Family and the School." In *Feminist Social Psychology*, ed. Sue Wilkinson, 57–76. Philadelphia: Open University Press, 1986.

———. *Schoolgirl Fictions*. New York: Verso, 1990.

Waller, Willard. "The Rating and Dating Complex." *American Sociological Review* 2 (1937): 727–734.

Wallman, Sandra. "The Boundaries of 'Race': Processes of Ethnicity in England." *Man* 13 (1978): 200–217.

———. "Epistemologies of Sex." In *Female Hierarchies*, ed. Lionel Tiger and Heather T. Fowler, 21–59. Chicago: Aldine, 1978.

*Webster's Third New International Dictionary*. Entries for "play," "sissy," "tomboy." Springfield, Mass.: G. C. Merriam, 1976.

Weeks, Jeffrey. *Sexuality and Its Discontents*. Boston: Routledge and Kegan Paul, 1985.

Weiler, Kathleen. *Women Teaching for Change: Gender, Class, and Power*. South Hadley, Mass.: Bergin and Garvey, 1988.

Weis, Lois, ed. *Class, Race, and Gender in American Education*. Albany: State University of New York Press, 1988.

West, Candace, and Zimmerman, Don H. "Doing Gender." *Gender & Society* 1 (1987): 125–151.

Whitehead, Harriet. "The Bow and the Burden Strap: A New Look at Institutionalized Homosexuality in Native America." In *Sexual Meanings*, ed. Sherry B. Ortner and Harriet Whitehead, 80–115. New York: Cambridge University Press, 1981.

Whiting, Beatrice B., and Carolyn P. Edwards. *Children of Different Worlds*. Cambridge, Mass.: Harvard University Press, 1988.

Wilkinson, Louise Cherry, and Cora B. Marrett, eds. *Gender Influences in Classroom Interaction*. New York: Academic Press, 1985.

Williams, Walter. *The Spirit and the Flesh: Sexual Diversity in American Indian Culture*. Boston: Beacon Press, 1986.

Willis, Paul. *Learning to Labour*. New York: Columbia University Press, 1977.

Wolpe, AnnMarie. *Within School Walls: The Role of Discipline, Sexuality, and the Curriculum*. London: Routledge, 1988.

Wood, Julian. "Groping Towards Sexism: Boys' 'Sex Talk.'" In *Gender and Generation*, 54–84. (See McRobbie, Angela, and Mica Nava.)

Wordsworth, William. *The Prelude: Or Growth of a Poet's Mind*. [1850]. Oxford: Clarendon, 1926.

Wulff, Helena. *Twelve Girls: Growing Up, Ethnicity, and Excitement in a South London Microculture.* Stockholm: University of Stockholm, 1988.

Yanagisako, Sylvia J., and Jane F. Collier. "Toward a Unified Analysis of Gender and Kinship." In *Gender and Kinship: Toward a Unified Analysis,* ed. Jane F. Collier and Sylvia J. Yanagisako, 14–50. Stanford, Calif.: Stanford University Press, 1987.

Zelizer, Viviana A. *Pricing the Priceless Child: The Changing Social Value of Children.* New York: Basic Books, 1985.

Zolotow, Charlotte. *William's Doll.* New York: Harper and Row, 1972.

Zucker, Kenneth. "Cross-Gender-Identified Children." In *Gender Dysphoria: Development, Research, Management,* ed. B. W. Steiner, 75–172. New York: Plenum, 1985.

# Index

access strategies, 45, 54, 121, 123, 126, 128, 165–166, 189n19

activities: access to, 165–166; collective, 4; cross-gender, 44, 46, 54, 55; disruption of, 76–77, 78, 83; gender-typing of, 44, 55, 119, 124, 130, 159, 166, 188n18, 208n32; playground, 1, 15, 44–45, 54, 65, 67–78, 90, 121, 125–126, 166, 188n18, 217n18 (*see also* chasing; cooties; games; sports, team); self-structured, 31

adolescence: cultural meanings of, 137–138, 213n29; disjunctures in, 147–148, 212n28, 213n29; physical changes in, 136–137, 141, 211n14; problems of girls in, 155, 170, 214n39; sexual meanings, 154–156; transition to, 113, 135–156, 170, 209n37, 211n14. *See also* bodies

adult-child dichotomy, 27

adults: cross-gender relations, 82; and early developing girls, 139; ideological viewpoint, 3; influence on children, 4; power over children, 3, 12, 16–20, 27, 31, 55–56, 154, 156, 159, 163, 172; "tattling" to, 77–78; vulnerability in, 12

African Americans, 7, 9, 33, 51, 73, 97, 102, 104, 127–128, 165, 186n5, 196n20, 208n33, 209n34

age: categories, 27, 136–138, 141, 147, 154, 155; factor in chasing, 70–72; grouping by, 31, 32, 42; in relation to gender, 85, 159, 184n15, 211n12; separation, 32, 50; structures, 155. *See also* gender: in relation to age

aggression, 78, 79, 80–81, 100, 192n19, 195n14, 196n20; boys against girls, 93; in chasing, 80; among girls, 106; in play, 5, 66; and "tattling," 77; types of, 80

alliances, 101, 201n21; cross-gender, 47; shifting, 94, 97, 98, 101; use of objects in, 21

androgyny, 169

Anthony, Susan B., 157, 159

Anyon, Joan, 106

Aronson, Eliot, 165

authority: challenges to, 92; evading, 16–20, 56; maintaining, 22–23

Barth, Fredrik, 64, 65, 193n1

Bateson, Gregory, 35–36, 79, 187n10, 197n21

Best, Raphaella, 92, 167

"Big Man" bias, 97–99

Blume, Judy, 142, 143

Blume, Margaret, 71, 144

bodies: breasts, 71, 72, 139, 141, 142–143, 211nn12–13, 212n20; changing, 135; height, 139, 140–141; images of, 155; meanings ascribed to, 138, 154, 210n8; menstruation, 75, 141, 142, 144–147, 212n22; physicality of children, 14–16, 92, 136; variation in, 136, 137; violations of, 80; wet dreams, 141, 143. See also adolescence

bonding: children in opposition to adults, 9; female, 94, 101, 171; group, 99–100; male, 59, 93, 97, 98, 99–100, 168–169, 202n27

borderwork, 64–88, 132, 162, 195n14; aggression in, 80–81; ambiguity in, 79, 81; conflict in, 78–80, 85; and crossing gender boundaries, 121; invasions, 76; and power, 82; sexual themes, 81–82. See also boundaries: gender; chasing

boundaries: crossing, 37; gender, 5, 23, 35–36, 37, 54, 64–66, 68, 80, 84, 111, 119–134, 193n1, 198n34 (see also crossing gender boundaries); generational, 154; group, 61; in play, 79

"boys-against-the-girls," 4, 66–68, 85

Cahill, Spencer, 35, 192n24

Canaan, Joyce, 100, 184n14, 202n31

"catch-and-kiss," 68, 71, 85, 151

chasing, 68–70, 76, 79; aggression in, 80; cross-gender, 64, 66, 67–73, 79, 80, 85, 109, 161, 194n14; girls' provocation of, 78; same-gender, 80; sexual meaning of, 68–69, 71; variations by age, 70–72; verbal hostility in, 70. See also borderwork

Chicanos, 9, 33, 51, 74, 83, 98, 165

child development, as concept, 3–4, 13, 16, 61, 157, 182n8

childhood: as gender-separated world, 89; memories of, 7, 23–27, 186n18

children: adult identification with, 12; challenging gender structure, 4; control by adults, 3, 12, 16–20, 27, 154, 156, 159, 163, 172; coping with lack of power, 21; defined as asexual, 141; and gender, 1–10; imagination in, 14–16; influence of adults on, 4; learning from, 11–27; neighborhood relations and, 46, 49–50, 124, 190n4; oppositional culture of, 20, 185n14; passive socialization of, 5, 13; perspectives of, 12, 20, 163; physicality in, 14–16, 71–72, 92, 94, 136; private worlds of, 19; protected status of, 172; sexism in research on, 107; sexualization of, 116, 141, 154; social divisions of, 13; sociology of, 4, 7, 157, 182n5; stereotyping of, 12, 77, 154

Chodorow, Nancy, 59, 198n33

cliques, 47, 99, 100–101, 202n31, 213n29

Cobb, Edith, 16, 185n10

competition, 93, 105–106

Connell, R. W., 85, 100, 106, 108, 136, 184n14

contests: cross-gender, 66–68; playground, 93

control: of children by adults, 12; in schools, 20, 27, 29; social, 17, 34

cooperation, 105–106, 162–167
cooties, 12–13, 71, 73–76, 79, 83, 85, 164, 194nn7–8. *See also* borderwork
cosmetic culture, 148–151, 156
cross-dressing, 117
crossing gender boundaries, 119–134, 150; asymmetry, 125; earnest vs. disruptive, 121–123; earnest vs. playing at, 208n31; heterosexual meanings, 132–133; vs. passing, 121, 207n29; persistence in, 130, 131, 132; successful, 129–132; variation by location and activity, 124–125
culture: beliefs, 4, 75; boys', 108; cosmetic, 148–151, 156; girls', 101, 102, 108; popular, 170; and representations of gender, 119–120; and sexuality, 75; significance of breasts in, 141; teen, 52, 73, 135, 147–154; youth, 99
Cusick, Philip, 99, 185n14

dating, 151–154
Davies, Bronwyn, 118–119, 185n14, 201n21, 213n30
depression, 155
determinism, biological, 2
devaluation of girls, 74–76, 83, 99, 107, 108, 116, 118, 120, 168–169, 171. *See also* male dominance
development: boys', 138–140; child, 3, 13, 16, 61, 157, 182n8; cognitive, 139; as concept, 7; early, 138–140, 211n13; gender, 3; girls', 138–139; individual stages of, 13; physical, 71, 72
differences: class, 33; gender, 2; in group formation, 32; in performance, 32
different cultures model, 89–110, 199n1; criticism of, 90–91, 95–109; described, 89–95
Dinnerstein, Myra, 59

DiPietro, Janet, 104
discourses, 5, 103, 105, 119, 120, 158
dominance, male, 2, 58–59, 75, 77, 81, 82, 86, 108, 134, 140, 156, 168–169, 170, 172, 192n19, 197n26; in classrooms, 38; girls' resistance to, 58, 59, 83, 133, 159, 171. *See also* devaluation of girls
Douglas, Mary, 85, 141, 198n31, 212n20

Eder, Donna, 95
education, nonsexist, 2, 159–167, 169, 170, 215n4
Edwards, Carolyn, 52, 190n1, 192n23, 198n28
Eisenhart, Margaret, 170, 187n8
Ellis, Shari, 50, 52, 190n4, 200n3
empathy, 26
ethnicity, 96; and gender, 9–10; group, 65; grouping by, 33; marginalization and, 102; separation by, 33
ethnography, 6–10; biases in, 98, 102, 202n28. *See also* fieldwork
Evans, John, 188n17
Everhart, Robert, 99

families, 29; cross-gender interaction in, 36; and group membership, 60; individualism in, 32; interaction in, 90
fantasy, 98; in chasing, 70; shared, 68
femininity: construction of, 138; as cultural ideal, 140, 156; emphasized, 100, 170; exaggerated, 107, 156; heterosexualized, 169–171; imposed, 112; multiple forms of, 85, 100, 106–107, 153–155, 170; sexual styles, 154; stereotyped, 113, 114; symbolic notions of, 106
feminism: postmodernist theory, 5; psychoanalytic theory, 59
feminist movement, 2, 107
feminist theory, 5, 59, 157, 183n9

fieldwork: bias in, 96; with children, 12, 185n12; and emotions, 25; ethics in, 18, 19, 185n11; and memory, 23–27; and the "other," 12; roles, 14, 16, 22–23, 25, 27; strategies, 6–8, 13, 15, 17, 26

Fine, Gary Alan, 99, 100, 143, 168, 184n14, 185n12, 208n30

Finnan, Christine, 68

Foucault, Michel, 120

Freud, Sigmund, 60, 81

friendship, 94, 101, 131–132, 165; African-American, 104; children's perceptions of, 46; cross-gender, 46–47, 50, 53–54, 164, 172, 189n25, 190n2; gender differences in, 203n44; gender separation and integration in, 21, 46, 50; same-gender, 37, 46–47, 170; underground, 54, 124; unstable, 94. See also alliances

Gagnon, John, 144

games: gender-divided, 67; group formation of, 54–55; pollution, 74; racial themes in, 67; turn-taking, 93, 94, 101, 124, 188n17

Geertz, Clifford, 87

gender: antagonism, 23, 65, 67, 76, 80, 87, 116, 161, 162, 167; boundaries, 5, 23, 35–36, 37, 54, 64–66, 68, 80, 84, 111, 119–134, 193n1, 198n34; categories, 8, 34, 35, 59–60, 66, 84–85, 158; changing relations of, 7; and children, 1–10; classification, 59–61, 192n23; as contextual, 108, 159, 160; cultural representations of, 119–120; derogatory meanings of, 67; development, 3; deviance, 3, 103, 111, 115, 116, 117, 120, 130, 207n17; dichotomies, 4, 35, 59, 64, 65, 86–87, 88, 89, 96, 104, 111, 158, 161; differences, 2, 57–58, 86, 96, 103–105, 108, 109, 111, 158; divisions, 4; dominance, 83;

equality, 171–173; and ethnicity, 9–10; geography of, 1, 42–44; hegemonic view of, 86; "hidden curricula" of, 51; identity, 4, 34, 35–36, 57, 59, 60, 66, 84–85, 113, 120, 158; individual, 35–36, 57, 84–85, 158, 214n1; inequality, 51, 74; labeling, 57; meanings, 4, 158; and moral reasoning, 105; neutralization, 84, 198n34; as opposition, 4, 86, 108, 127, 133–134, 158; organization, 35–36, 60, 61, 64, 108, 159, 214n1; play, 8; and race, 9–10; relations, 5, 29; in relation to age, 85, 159, 184n15, 211n12; in relation to race, 34, 85, 102, 159, 184n15, 196n20, 198n28, 209n34; in relation to sexuality, 184n15, 207n17; in relation to social class, 34, 85, 102, 159, 184n15, 185n17, 209n34; ritualization of, 85, 87; and sexuality, 9, 135; significance of, 158; similarities, 57–58, 86, 103–105, 109; and social class, 9; as social construction, 2, 3, 4, 82, 157; as social relation, 4, 158–159; sociology of, 7; stereotyping, 2, 51, 77, 85, 86, 96, 99, 105, 107, 114, 115, 118, 120, 164, 166–167, 205n9, 216n11; structures, 155; symbolism, 35–36, 60, 64, 66, 103, 105, 120, 155, 158, 214n1; in terms of address, 34; tokenism, 133; variable salience of, 29, 35–36, 61, 64, 83, 84, 85, 87, 132, 159, 187n10, 191n12. See also femininity; gender separation and integration; gender-typing; masculinity

"genderism," 85

gender separation and integration, 36, 163–167, 187n6; and behavioral compatibility, 57–59; classroom, 36–39, 46; cross-cultural patterns of, 189n1, 191n9;

feminist psychoanalytic theories of, 59; in friendship, 46–47, 50; and gender classification, 59–61, 192n23; in lunchrooms, 42–44, 161; in neighborhoods, 49–50; on playgrounds, 45, 46, 161, 217n18; in relation to adult practices, 55, 216n11; in relation to age, 51–52; in relation to crowding, 52–53; research on, 45–47; on school lines, 39–42; in schools, 51

gender-typing: of activities, 44, 55, 119, 124, 130, 159, 166, 188n18, 208n32; of objects, 21, 119, 124, 130, 159, 166, 188n18, 208n32

Giddens, Anthony, 181n4

Gilligan, Carol, 105, 199n1, 204n48

"girls-against-the-boys," 66, 67, 68, 85, 86, 87

Goffman, Erving, 36, 85

"goin' with," 132, 135, 147, 151–154. See also heterosexuality

Goodenough, Ruth, 99, 160, 168, 195n14, 202n27

Goodwin, Marjorie Harness, 95, 102, 190n4

Gottman, John, 190n2

Green, Richard, 117, 118, 207n20

groups: access strategies, 45, 54, 121, 123, 126, 128, 165–166, 189n19; adult intervention in, 55–56; boundaries of, 61; boys', 91–93, 97–101; child-structured, 32; crossing, 23; ethnic, 65; formation of, 14, 29, 31–34, 36–39, 40–47, 54, 55, 131, 160–162, 163, 216n10; in games, 54–55; gender-based, 8; girls', 94–95, 101–103, 202n32; interaction of, 65; loyalty to, 60; marginalization of, 90; membership in, 86; opposing, 64; rival, 158; same-gender, 4, 5, 23, 42, 43, 55–56, 60

Hallinan, Maureen, 47

Harris, Abigail, 46

Haug, Frigga, 141

Henley, Nancy, 83, 196n17

Herzog, Eleanor, 46, 56, 191n12

heterosexuality, 5, 50, 52, 61, 66, 81, 82, 86, 128, 132–133, 134, 144, 147, 151–154, 169–171, 172, 209n38, 213n30; as institution, 155, 170

hierarchy: among boys, 74–75, 92, 95, 168–169; among girls, 102, 106; marking, 21; social, 26, 140; and somatic type, 140. See also male dominance

Holland, Dorothy, 170, 187n8

homophobia, 116, 118, 133–134, 154, 169, 207n17

homosexuality, 117, 154, 207n17, 207n28

Hughes, Linda, 101, 102, 105

humor, 79; hostility in, 81; targeted, 81

Hunt, Jennifer, 26

identity: categories, 65; deviant, 117; gender, 4, 34, 35–36, 57, 59, 60, 66, 84–85, 113, 120, 158; individual, 35–36, 87; sexual, 120; social, 83; stigmatized, 120

insults, 102, 116, 203n39

interaction: cross-gender, 36; determinants of, 86; family, 90; gender-typed, 2, 26; group, 65; hierarchical, 102; male dominance in, 58; mixed-gender, 58, 162–167; same-gender, 47; teacher intervention in, 55–56

invasions, 73, 76–77, 79, 80, 81, 83, 84, 93, 109, 121, 161. See also borderwork

isolation, 24

Jacklin, Carol, 57, 58, 59, 61, 104

Johnson, Miriam, 59, 61

John-Steiner, Vera, 16, 185n10

Jordan, Ellen, 99, 169

Karkau, Kevin, 164, 165, 167
Kessler, Sandra, 138
kids. *See* children
kissing, as weapon, 71

labeling, 27, 35, 114, 115, 117, 120, 130,
    133–134, 156, 164
language use: "boys and girls," 8,
    163, 187n8; "children vs. kids,"
    8, 183n14; collaborative, 102;
    gendered, 76; "peer group," 9;
    of social sciences, 17; "tattling,"
    77–78, 196n17; teacher practices,
    34
Latinos, 9, 33, 74, 98
*Learning to Labour* (Willis), 99
Lever, Janet, 92, 93, 94, 102, 107,
    188n17, 198n28, 199n1
Lockheed, Marlaine, 46, 165
Luria, Zella, 46, 56, 83, 93, 114, 143,
    191n12, 200n1

Maccoby, Eleanor, 57, 58, 59, 61,
    200n1, 216n11
*Making the Difference* (Connell), 100
male dominance, 2, 58–59, 75, 81, 82,
    86, 108, 134, 140, 156, 168–169,
    170, 172, 192n19, 197n26; in
    classrooms, 38; girls' resistance
    to, 58, 59, 77, 83, 133, 159, 171. *See
    also* devaluation of girls
Martin, Jane, 171
masculinity, 106; aggressive, 167–169;
    construction of, 138; dominant
    notions of, 120; hegemonic, 86,
    100, 117; multiple forms of, 85,
    98, 99–100, 106–107, 153–155,
    168–169, 217n27; prevailing
    image of, 100; sexual styles of,
    154
McRobbie, Angela, 107
Medrich, Elliott, 104, 198n28, 200n3
memory: childhood, 7, 23–27,
    186n18; as obstacle, 7; as
    resource, 7, 26

menstruation, 75, 141, 142, 144–147,
    212n22
metacommunication, 79
Miller, Alice, 12

Nava, Mica, 156
neighborhoods, 29; children's social
    relations in, 46, 49–50, 124,
    190n4; cross-gender interaction in,
    36, 52–53, 90; gender separation
    and integration in, 49–50, 51
nonsexist education, 4, 159–167, 169,
    170, 215n4

Oakes, Jeannie, 186n4

Paley, Vivian, 11, 99, 168–169
Parsons, Talcott, 60, 61, 191n6
Petchesky, Rosalind, 156
physical development. *See* bodies
play, 63–64; as activity, 4; aggression
    in, 66; boundaries in, 79; cross-
    gender, 86, 164, 166; as frame of
    meaning, 5, 15, 75, 79, 87, 166,
    197n21, 197n23; gender-typed,
    2, 5, 8, 44; as performance, 5;
    of possibilities, 5; ritualized, 87;
    same-age, 52; same-gender, 52; vs.
    work, 5, 183n12
playground: activities, 1, 15, 44–45,
    54, 65, 67–78, 90, 121, 125–126,
    166, 188n18, 217n18 (*see also*
    chasing; cooties; games; invasions;
    sports, team); arrangements, 1;
    boys' control of, 83; contests, 93;
    ethnicity on, 33; gender separation
    and integration on, 2, 33, 44–45,
    46, 49, 161, 217n18; movement on,
    14, 15; safety zones, 68, 69, 70;
    same-gender groupings, 4
pollution, 66, 141; and gender
    separation, 83; rituals, 73–76, 83,
    198n31; as source of power, 83, 84
popularity, 24, 25
pornography, 143

Porro, Barbara, 164, 166, 167
power, 6; between adults and
    children, 3, 12, 16–20, 27,
    55–56, 154, 156, 159, 163, 172; and
    borderwork, 82; issues of, 82–84;
    pollution as source of, 83; and
    race, 74–75; relationships, 83; and
    sexual meanings, 156; and social
    class, 74. See also hierarchy; male
    dominance
pregnancy, 156
provocation, 68, 71, 80

race: divisions, 165; and gender,
    9–10; grouping by, 33; "hidden
    curricula" of, 51; inequalities
    of, 74, 75, 162; marginalization
    and, 83, 102; and power, 75–75;
    relations, 72, 82, 128, 162–167,
    190n4, 196n20, 209n38; in
    relation to gender, 184n15,
    196n20, 209n34; separation by,
    33, 187n5; stereotyping, 166, 167;
    tokenism, 128
racism, 80, 82, 131, 167; dynamics
    of, 169
rape, 156
relationality, 105, 108
relations: adult cross-gender, 82;
    cross-gender, 151; gender, 5, 29;
    intergroup, 86, 165, 216n14; race,
    72, 82, 128, 162–167, 190n4,
    196n20, 209n38
relationships: boy/girl, 3; power in, 3,
    83; same-gender, 163
religion, grouping by, 32
"resistance" theory, 106
Rich, Adrienne, 12, 155

Schachtel, Ernest, 16, 185n10
Schofield, Janet, 47, 82, 92, 167,
    184n14, 186n5, 189n25, 197n20,
    208n33
schools: and age-grading, 51, 138;
    collective regulation of students,
    31; control in, 20, 27, 29; as
    crowded environments, 29, 51,
    52–53, 82–83, 124, 186n1; gender
    separation and integration in,
    51; groups in, 30–36; physical
    structure of, 27; power of
    adults in, 55; routines in, 29–36;
    seating arrangements in, 30–31,
    37–39; sexism in, 51; as "total
    institutions," 20, 21; underground
    economy in, 20–23, 136, 185n15
Scott, Joan, 109, 183n10
seating: classroom, 30–31, 37–39, 75,
    165, 188n12; lunchroom, 42–44, 75
Segal, Lynne, 134
Segel, Elizabeth, 112
self-discovery, 60
self-esteem, 155, 170
sex: biological, 2, 60, 137, 192n19;
    education, 144–147; segregation,
    36, 49, 52 (see also gender
    separation and integration);
    self-categorization by, 60; talk,
    143–144
sex-gender systems, 135, 154, 155
sexism, 168; dynamics of, 169; in
    research on children, 107; in
    schools, 51; and teacher practices,
    160–162; in tomboy imagery, 113.
    See also stereotyping: gender
sexual: abuse, 154; activity, 143;
    deviance, 120; dimorphism, 137;
    double standard, 156; harassment,
    81, 156; identity, 120; idioms, 23;
    maturation, 136; meanings, 81;
    reproduction, 144
sexuality, 100; and culture, 75;
    female, 141; and gender, 9; and
    menstruation, 75, 141, 142,
    144–147, 212n22; messages about,
    5; in play, 5; in relation to gender,
    184n15, 207n17; reproductive,
    75; structures of, 155; taboos
    against, 154; and "tattling," 78; in
    troupes, 73; wet dreams, 141, 143

sexualization: of children, 116, 141, 154; of girls, 75, 147, 155, 211n12

Sheldon, Amy, 106

Simon, William, 144

"sissy," 158, 168–169; as identity, 120; in literature, 118–119; medicalization of, 117–118; as narrative of childhood, 117; in popular culture, 111, 118–119; as term, 115–117, 120, 206n15, 206n17; use of label, 120

Sluckin, Andy, 92

Snow, Edward, 91

social: bias, 51; categories, 35–36, 87; change, 61, 115, 159–162; class, 9, 32, 33, 74, 75, 96, 102, 159, 184n15, 209n34; control, 17, 34, 120; distance, 18, 22, 27, 75, 86; divisions, 13, 76; exclusion, 21, 24, 25; hierarchy, 26, 140; identification, 35; identity, 83; inclusion, 21, 24; inequality, 51; isolation, 25–26; marginality, 41; networks among girls, 94; organization, 64; ostracism, 117; position, 21, 24, 25, 26, 27, 74, 95, 97, 101, 123, 208n30; practices, 3; reproduction, 106; status, 153

socialization: as concept, 2, 3, 7, 13, 16, 107, 157, 181nn3–4, 182n5, 183n8; passive, 5, 13

sociology: of children, 4, 7, 157, 182n5; of gender, 7

space, boys' control of, 82–83, 92, 197n28, 200n3

Speier, Matthew, 3, 13

sports, team, 93, 94, 97, 104, 123–124, 125, 127, 134, 188n17, 199n1

stereotyping, 2, 163; of children, 12, 77, 154; in different cultures model, 91; gender, 51, 77, 85, 86, 96, 99, 105, 107, 114, 115, 118, 120, 164, 166, 167, 205n9, 216n11; of "other," 60; by race, 166, 167

submission, ritual, 93

Tajfel, Henri, 86

Tannen, Deborah, 89, 103, 200n1

Tanner, James, 137

"tattling," 77–78, 80, 196n17

teacher practices, 162; collective regulation of students, 31; with different genders, 39; differential treatment of students, 51, 160, 188n13, 202n28, 215n7; of language use, 34; maintenance of social distance, 22; and sexism, 160–162; universalistic treatment of students, 22, 51, 55, 191n6

teasing, 76, 85, 130, 139, 151, 163, 168–169, 212n21; avoidance of, 53; about body changes, 136, 142; in cross-gender situations, 53; dynamics of, 53–54, 81; effects of, 54; fear of, 50, 153; heterosexual, 50, 52, 53; lessening the risk of, 55–56; and pollution beliefs, 75

theories: feminist, 7, 157; feminist psychoanalytic, 59; postmodern feminist, 5, 183n9; psychoanalytic, 198n33; resistance, 106, 107; social reproduction, 106, 107

Title IX, 6, 16, 41, 160

"tomboy," 158; as identity, 120; in literature, 112–113; medicalization of, 117, 207n20; as narrative of childhood, 113–114, 205n10; in popular culture, 111, 205n7; as term, 113, 206n13; use of label, 114, 120, 130

Toth, Susan Allen, 81, 94, 153, 197n26

touch. See children: physicality in

tracking, academic, 51

troupes, 72–73, 90, 101, 148; interracial, 72; sexuality in, 73, 156

Tyack, David, 187n6

tyranny of averages, 58

vulnerability: in adolescence, 155; in adults, 12; in dating,

153–154; among friends, 94; and
pollution, 83

Walkerdine, Valerie, 105, 136, 215n7
Waller, Willard, 153
Wallman, Sandra, 187n10
West, Candace, 5

Whiting, Beatrice, 52, 190n1, 192n23,
198n28
Willis, Paul, 99, 107, 168, 202n28
witnessing, 53, 54, 162
Wood, Julian, 106

Zimmerman, Don, 5

## About the Author

BARRIE THORNE is a professor of sociology and women's studies emerita at the University of California at Berkeley. She is a former vice president of the American Sociological Association and served for ten years as the U.S. editor of the journal *Childhood*. In 2022, she received the American Sociological Association's Jessie Bernard Award for lifelong achievement in opening sociology to the role of women in society. Her many books include *Feminist Sociology* and *Rethinking the Family*.

## About the Introduction Authors

RAEWYN CONNELL is professor emerita of sociology at the University of Sydney and the author of fifteen books, including *Making the Difference*, *Gender and Power*, and *Masculinities*.

MICHAEL A. MESSNER is a professor emeritus of sociology at the University of Southern California in Los Angeles. He is the author or editor of many books, including *Some Men: Feminist Allies and the Movement to End Violence against Women*, *King of the Wild Suburb: A Memoir of Fathers, Sons and Guns*, and *No Slam Dunk: Gender, Sport and the Unevenness of Social Change* (Rutgers University Press).

## About the Afterword Author

C. J. PASCOE is an associate professor of sociology at the University of Oregon, where she teaches courses on sexuality, education, social psychology, and inequality. She is the author of *Nice Is Not Enough: Inequality and the Limits of Kindness at American High*.